BETTE DAVIS

★

LARGER THAN LIFE

Richard Schickel and George Perry

RUNNING PRESS
PHILADELPHIA · LONDON

Introduction © 2009 by Lorac Productions Inc
All text for parts one to five © 2009 by George Perry

First published in the United States in 2009 by Running Press Book Publishers
All rights reserved under the Pan-American and International Copyright Conventions

Printed in Thailand by Imago

This book may not be reproduced in whole or in part, in any form or by any means, electronic or mechanical, including photocopying, recording, or by any information storage and retrieval system now known or hereafter invented, without written permission from the publisher.

9   8   7   6   5   4   3   2   1
Digit on the right indicates the number of this printing

Library of Congress Control Number: 2009927636

ISBN 978-0-7624-3688-0

Created and produced by
PALAZZO EDITIONS LTD
2 Wood Street
Bath, BA1 2JQ
www.palazzoeditions.com

Publisher: Colin Webb
Art director: Bernard Higton
Cover art and design: Frank Sipala
Managing editor: Sonya Newland

Running Press Book Publishers
2300 Chestnut Street
Philadelphia, PA 19103-4371

Visit us on the web!
www.runningpress.com

CONTENTS

Introduction

by Richard Schickel

PEOPLE continue to say two things about Bette Davis: that she was not beautiful, not at least in the conventional movie star way, and that, as an actress, she was often too neurotic, too hysterical, to retain our loyalty in an age where female suffering on screen is no longer a major cinematic topic and tends to be presented less fulsomely.

These critics might have a point, though I think they are ignoring the conventions and constraints within which Davis was obliged to operate in her day. They also ignore her sheer gutsiness, her determination to assert her uniqueness in a world that was always more than a little dubious about women who refused to accept their fates with no more than a sniffle and a whimper. In any case, more than any of her female peers, who have dwindled to the status of unexamined premises or are completely forgotten, she remains, a hundred years after her birth, a presence, someone to conjure with.

For me, there is a more subjective element in this discussion. How was it, I wonder, that in my earliest days as a moviegoer—sometime in the early 1940s—I was drawn to her? It doesn't make sense. Yes, I loved the movies from the first moment I saw one—but not more than I loved football, baseball, comic books, radio serials, and hanging out with the guys. Nor was my primary movie addiction to the kind of pictures she appeared in. In general, my allegiance was to war movies, with particular emphasis on those that explored the underground resistance to Nazism in Europe. Also, westerns, historical epics (especially when they starred Errol Flynn), and, of course, anything starring Rita Hayworth or Abbott and Costello. There is no reason to suppose, given these explicably boyish tastes, that I would be fascinated by a pop-eyed woman given to playing iron-maiden Southern belles, variously threatened (if not downright doomed) heiresses, and the occasional unredeemable bitch. But so it was. And so it remains.

Above: Bette Davis, young and hopeful, in *The Rich Are Always With Us.*

Opposite: Davis photographed by George Hurrell in 1940.

Glamorously lit, the sleek portraiture of 1930s Hollywood.

I sometimes like to think that my affection for Bette Davis is an early example of instinctive critical perspicacity, but it probably wasn't. She was, I think, so simply and obviously unique that a child could somehow cotton on to her—as if she were some sort of slightly weird maiden aunt haunting the attic of one's mind. There were male stars who, for very different reasons, had a similar hold on me (I think of James Cagney and Cary Grant among others) but there was no woman on the screen who was quite like her. I think now that what I was perceiving—underneath the scheming and the hysteria—was a thwarted masculine will, a desire to claim for herself what male stars possessed as a birthright, which was autonomy, the right to do as they pleased whatever the surrounding society thought—especially when they were playing, as they so often did, good-bad guys, rebels with a cause the rest of the world had to be wooed to. You can see why a little boy, himself fairly desperately in search of his own autonomy, might take an interest in someone like Davis—even if he was far from able to articulate that need.

OK, her cause was generally herself. She was not often attached—as the male stars were—to some generally idealistic and uplifting sentiment or ideology. But then, neither was I. Mostly she was trying to free herself from romantic constraint. Or she was learning to accept, without damage to her integrity, some fate that, in the end, she could not elude, but which she could learn to live with. So, somehow, across all the gaps of age, gender, status that separated us, I forged my odd little bond with her. I could not, of course, pitch a public fit the way her characters did, but underneath the taciturnity dictated by time and place to lads like me, I was seething right along with her. And I was utterly willing to pay the price for my restlessness if somehow I was presented with the opportunity.

As to her looks, in those years prior to her final incarnation as a camp harridan, I thought she was quite an attractive woman, obviously no great beauty, though her ferocious energy, her trim figure and well-calculated costuming and coiffeurs, and her sublime self-confidence rendered her so. Later in life, she complained that her breasts (or "bulbs" as Jack Warner was wont to call them) lacked starlet perkiness. But so what? As the critic Molly Haskell has observed, she could convincingly impersonate beauty—"act" it, if you will—even though one almost never had a sexual thought or fantasy about her. Indeed, I think it very largely true that great beauty is a bar to being taken seriously as an actor or actress—the ironic defect that handsome people of both sexes often struggle hardest and longest against in their fight for serious critical recognition.

As for acting, she defied all our current conventional wisdom about self-presentation on the screen. We came to hold in the latter half of the twentieth century that naturalism, often including hints of the player's autobiography, was the correct path to admiration, particularly in the movies. Ben Kingsley recently put that thought very neatly: "The camera abhors acting. What it likes is behavior." But that was not Davis's way. And that was OK with her first audiences; when she first came to fame, a certain boldness of attack, a brash and theatrical seizing of our attention, was more than acceptable to audiences and critics.

Davis was possibly the most highly stylized leading actress in the history of movie stardom. It began with the brisk way she clipped her words, and the singular pauses she took between syllables. Nobody took command of the language quite the way she did, bending it to her inner rhythms, rather than submitting to its tyranny. Then there were the abrupt gestures that accompanied her speeches—it was as if she were brushing aside the gnats of insincerity and indecision that so often distract ordinary mortals. The impatient twitch of her shoulders, the dismissive arabesques she described with her omnipresent cigarette (in her contemporary roles), the driving (or driven) impatience of her pace through often lugubrious plots, always implied something less

than gladness in the face of foolishness—even on occasion her own. She suggested that she could bear tragedy, if that's where fate was leading her, more readily than she could stand dither or inconsequence.

In other words, "staginess" was not, in her case, regarded as a defect—quite the contrary. It was, instead, the earnest of her seriousness and her devotion—as she saw it—to her art. "High-spirited"—popular fiction's genteel synonym for neurotic—she more often than not entered the closed world that most movies are. "High-spirited" she left it, usually unhappily, despite the occasional, and generally unconvincing, efforts of the writers and the studio to give her audience some semblance of hope (or nobility) to cling to as they emerged from most of the movies she

The portrait camera emphasized Davis's high cheek bones and translucent skin.

made in her great decade (from the late Thirties to the late Forties) when she was the undeniable queen of the Warner Bros. lot.

This was, I believe, a remarkable act of self-assertion and one that could not have been made or sustained without a high degree of talent. And willfulness. In the course of one of her many battles for better roles, better pictures, with Jack Warner, production chief of the family business, she wrote, "I ... am ambitious to become known as a great actress," and she never wavered from pursuit of that goal—not even, I think, at the end of her career when her parts in generally cheesy pictures were so often ludicrous.

Grotesque as Baby Jane: Davis was never afraid of looking hideous.

Look at her in something like *Whatever Happened to Baby Jane?*, which is not at all a bad picture, just a really weird one. She is playing behind a fright mask of dead white makeup punctuated by glaring lipstick, but there is nothing masked in her performance. She's alert to every nuance of monstrousness in her character, every possibility of cracked grandeur, and there's not an actor in the picture who can stand up to her ferocious attack—especially her costar (and victim) Joan Crawford, who's supposed to collect our sympathy, but only nominally does. Somehow—against all odds—it keeps sliding to the nut job, the former headliner whose movie career was blighted by the stardom her sister achieved through her patient sufferings in 1930s women's pictures. There's real pathos beneath her monstrousness, though Davis never once explains or sues for our sympathy. She's just triumphantly, heedlessly there—in our astonished faces. The regrets came later, when she finally saw the film at the Cannes festival, where the director, Robert Aldrich, reported her sobbing at his side: "I just look awful," she wept. "Do I really look that awful?"

I think this curious, wildly successful enterprise is the most obviously emblematic movie of her career, the one in which her hell-for-leather approach to acting was most deliriously visible, though it was not really any different in commitment, in passion, from her slightly more conventional offerings.

But we are getting ahead of our story, in which there is a certain logic and inevitability. In her many autobiographical musings, in books and interviews, she liked to stress her New England roots, the "flintiness" she absorbed from the region's rocky soil and hard-shelled natives, which stiffened her spine and put iron in her soul. There's something in that, but not as much as she liked to think. There is more taciturnity, a much deeper reserve, in the Yankee temperament than there ever was in Davis. I suspect that her spirit was more profoundly afflicted by a much more common show-biz complaint.

I'm talking here about her broken home. From Mary Pickford onward, the absence of a father or mother is uncommonly common in driving actors toward public display. Death, divorce, desertion—it doesn't seem to matter what separates child from parent. What matters is that an unattainable love is denied him or her and that this can condition an often desperate need for approval. It generally begins with instantly gratifying applause, which is soon enough followed by fawning entourages, a press eager to do pieces about the sobriety with which they pursue their art—Hamlet, Hedda Gabler, whoever—their displays of temperament, often directed at surrogate father figures (like a studio boss), also follow. So too do addictions—to drink, to drugs, to a certain carelessness in their sexual adventurings.

In Davis's case, the parental absentee was her father, Harlow. By every account he was a chilly and withholding man, a reasonably successful lawyer who pursued an extra-marital affair for some years, then left his family in 1918, when his oldest daughter was ten. There is evidence that Harlow and Bette stayed more in touch than she later let on, and that he took considerable pride in her achievements. There is evidence as well that her extraordinarily close relationship with her devouring mother was not as heartwarming as she pretended it was. But no matter. The absence was there—never slaked by her several marriages to non-entities—and the attempts to heal it began in her early teens, when, in Boston, she happened to see Blanche Yurka in a touring production of *The Wild Duck*.

It rendered her permanently stage struck, and she devoutly pursued instruction and the practice of her craft in all the usual places—schools, stock and touring companies—including a stint with Yurka's troupe, but not with Eva Le Gallienne's company. She was a famously dedicated theater-saint of the time, but Davis was overtaken by the giggles during her interview with the great lady. In this period she and her sister were often separated from their mother, who was seeking jobs to supplement her alimony, and it has been estimated that Davis and her sibling moved something like eighty times in their teens, before the former attained New York and roles both on and off Broadway. By 1929 she had won a contract at Universal studios.

Young, but plain when the part demanded it.

She was so lacking in star quality that the studio functionary dispatched to meet her train failed to spot her and the studio boss, Carl Laemmle, essentially dismissed her for lack of sex appeal. She got a few small parts in Universal pictures and on loan-outs to long-forgotten independent outfits. In 1931 the studio dropped her contract. She was preparing to leave Los Angeles when fate, in the rather curious form of George Arliss, took a hand in her career.

Arliss was a middle-aged, horse-faced British actor specializing in historical characters—Disraeli was probably the most famous of them—and wise old guys in contemporary dramas, which he played on stage and in some silent pictures. Roughneck Warner Bros., looking for a touch of class, signed him to repeat these successes in the early days of talking pictures and he became perhaps the most unlikely star of that era—foxy grandpa to the nation. He knew Davis—he had been her teacher in one of the acting schools she attended—and as she was packing to leave Hollywood, he called to offer her a part in his 1932 production of *The Man Who Played God,* which was for her a career-saving opportunity—and, it must be said, the palimpsest for many roles to come.

In the film, Arliss plays a concert pianist, deafened by a bomb explosion at one of his recitals. She plays his protégé—smartly dressed, energetic and inappropriately in love with him. He is, at first, suicidally depressed by the loss of his career, but he becomes a kind of benign busybody, intervening anonymously in troubled lives—playing God as it were, while she is weaned away from her infatuation. Arliss himself was something of an overplayer, given to large gestures and fine talk, though there was an appealing sweetness to him as well. Their manners matched quite seamlessly and Davis shone in his company. According to Charlotte Chandler, one of her biographers, she carried Arliss's photograph in a locket for the rest of her life, correctly believing, as the writer put it, that he had saved her life by saving her career, "which was her life."

Warner Bros. signed her to a term contract, and almost instantly began misusing her in a string of minor roles in program pictures—*The Dark Horse, Parachute Jumper, Ex-Lady,* et al. There were exceptions, of course—a Southern melodrama called *The Cabin in the Cotton* (in which she uttered a memorably absurdist line "I'd like to kiss you, but

Tended between takes on the set of *Jezebel* (1938).

I just washed my hair"); *Three on a Match,* a story of a trio of young working women, in which the most intense and riveting acting is done by the long-forgotten Ann Dvorak, playing a drug-addled woman heading toward suicide; and a snappy little James Cagney movie called *Jimmy the Gent.* It was as Cagney always said, "factory work" (between 1932 and 1934 Davis did sixteen movies at the studio), though it could be argued that in these years she was doing about as well as anyone on the lot when it came to appearing in movies of some quality.

You probably would not have wanted to make that argument to her face just then. For Warner Bros.—Arliss aside—was a hardnosed studio in those years. With Darryl Zanuck in charge of production, its glorious specialty was lowlife realism—gangster films, to be sure, but equally, slices of working-stiff life in Depression Era America—chain-gang fugitives, homeless kids on the road, newspaper guys wisecracking their way to the big story. Even the great Busby Berkeley musicals tended to focus narratively on chorus girls clinging to the hope that their show wouldn't close before they drew their first paychecks. At least once it was hinted that prostitution might be their only alternative should the sheriff shut them down.

In other words, the place was not a natural fit for Davis. The film historian Jeanine Basinger has suggested that glossy MGM, where slick "women's pictures" were a house specialty, might have been a better place for her—except that she did not quite have the glamour (or the accommodationist spirit) Louis B. Mayer required of his stars. What saved Davis was a loan-out—to RKO for *Of Human Bondage,* an adaptation of the Somerset Maugham novel about a crippled upper-class artist-doctor's obsession with Mildred, a grasping, ignorant, and slatternly waitress. Leslie Howard played the male lead in a rather genteel manner with Davis as the cruel slut.

From today's perspective the picture seems rather pokey and self-conscious, but at the time it was a revelation. One magazine went so far as to call Davis's work "probably the best performance ever recorded on the screen by a U.S. actress," which may be something of an exaggeration. But still … Davis is divinely mean and self-serving. She fully deserved an Academy Award, but did not even receive a nomination. The myth is that Jack Warner, upon seeing *Of Human Bondage,* immediately perceived the error of his ways and began giving Davis the roles she deserved. But her filmography does not bear out this idea. Back at Warner's she quickly made six pictures, of which only one, *Bordertown* (opposite Paul Muni), offered her any real opportunity—she has a great mad scene in a courtroom—until *Dangerous* came her way.

It was tosh, but upscale tosh. She's a great actress—her character, it has been said, was based on Jeanne Eagels, the brilliant and legendarily self-destructive stage actress—who is rendered unemployable because she jinxes every production in which she appears. When we meet her she's drunkenly wandering skid row, where a slumming architect (Franchot Tone) who's always admired her from afar, undertakes to rescue her. Soon they're sharing his perfectly appointed country retreat and falling in love. He agrees to back her (ultimately successful) Broadway comeback, not knowing that she's already married to a good-natured weakling. Eventually, driving with her husband, she decides to wreck the car—hoping to kill him, or herself, or conceivably both of them, thus, one way or another, resolving her romantic dilemma. That would have been too much for the studio, the audience, and the newly emboldened movie censors. They both live, and she abandons Tone for her husband—whose dynamism is not at all improved by his escape from death. One does not imagine a marriage for the ages.

Still, Davis got to display her full emotional range, from self-pity to self-aggrandizement, and this time won the Oscar. She was not alone in

Waiting for her cue: Davis on set.

thinking it a consolation prize—a make-good for the *Bondage* snub—but Warner Bros. responded by casting her in *The Petrified Forest*, its prestigious adaptation of Robert Sherwood's much-admired drama about a wandering, world-weary poet (Leslie Howard again) encountering a mad-dog killer (Humphrey Bogart, making his first serious mark on the movies) in the Southwestern café where Davis is a waitress. It's a slow, glum, fake-poetic movie that is an agony to watch. People thought well of it at the time, however. Now that movies could talk there was a feeling among their more sternly aspiring devotees that their talk should be high-flown and high-minded (as it often was on the stage)—an opinion I suspect that Davis (among other actors of the time) shared; she was never completely comfortable in lighter fare.

This is a point she proved with the picture that brought her to the breaking point with Warner Bros.—*Satan Met a Lady*. It was the second of the three attempts by the studio to successfully adapt Dashiell Hamett's *The Maltese Falcon* to the screen. This time, the feckless idea was to turn it into a cross-talking romantic-detective story, something along the lines of the then hugely popular *The Thin Man* series. What a mess it was! The reliably smarmy Warren William was miscast as Sam Spade (herein known as Ted Shane), and the plot bore only the most nominal relation to the novel, with Davis never finding a plausible character to play.

By now, even critics as dim as the *New York Times*'s Bosley Crowther were calling for the studio to mount a reclamation project, to which Jack Warner replied that in her next picture Davis would play a female lumberjack. Jack tried to placate her by telling her he was about to option a great new novel for her, *Gone with the Wind*. She told the boss she imagined that would be "a dilly" and fled the jurisdiction. She had a two-picture deal in England, where she believed she would be beyond the reach of Warner, his contract, and his lawyers. Not so. The English courts ruled against her and back she went to Burbank—to a changing studio and to changing times, both of which would suit her much better.

Zanuck had left the studio in 1933, after one fight too many with Jack Warner. He was succeeded by Hal B. Wallis, who was by the mid-Thirties firmly in charge of the studio's output. A one-time publicist, he was a smooth, soft-spoken, highly intelligent man, more than the equal of Zanuck, Thalberg, or any of the better-known heads of production in his era. He had a superb eye for efficiency and detail, was a

Perc Westmore adjusts makeup for *The Little Foxes.*

firm handler of the many fractious talents on what was surely the most rebellious (and left-wing) group of actors, directors, and writers ever gathered on a single Hollywood lot. He remained willing to make socially conscientious movies of the kind with which Warner Bros. had long been identified (*Black Legion*—about murderous, hooded nativists—and *They Won't Forget*—about Southern lynch law). But whether they were more to his taste or because he sensed a shift in audience taste as the nation began recovering from the depths of the Depression, Warner Bros. began in the late Thirties to specialize in three types of films it had largely avoided in the Zanuck years. They were dashing historical spectacles, sober biopics about great figures of the past whose lives had lessons to teach to citizens of a modern world, and romantic tragedies and near-tragedies in which women—really just one woman at Warner Bros.—risked their lives (or at the very least their happiness) on the dictates of their hearts.

Whatever their genre, these pictures were richer and darker in their production values, shot on longer and more expensive schedules than had previously been the case at Warner Bros. To a certain degree their content was dictated by the talent at hand. Insouciant Errol Flynn was the great new find—handsome, athletic, at once twinkling and touched with a certain romantic rue, he was, from the moment he burst on the scene as a last-minute replacement for the much less bold (and toned) Robert Donat in *Captain Blood* (1935), the great swashbuckler of his era and, until Bogart finally burst through in the early Forties, the only romantically charged male

star on the studio's roster. Still, there was Paul Muni and Edward G. Robinson to do the heavy lifting in the more earnest and talkative biopics. And then there was Davis.

When she returned to the studio in 1937, they put her in *Marked Woman*, which had the look of a standard Warner Bros. offering—a "ripped from the headlines" story based on New York District Attorney Thomas E. Dewey's prosecution of the "Murder Inc." mobsters. She played the hooker who informs the DA of the gangsters' activities and—hence the title—she is scarred on the face for her betrayal. But the movie is well-written, lively in its melodrama, a modest cut above most of the work she had previously done.

A late 1930s studio portrait. Davis, in common with stars of her generation, smoked. And smoked.

Commissary lunch with William Wyler, the director of *Jezebel*.

It is true that she's more uppercrust in manner than the other "escorts" she works with, and it's worth remarking that in the vast majority of her films in her great days Davis was well-born and well-off. It was something demanded by their primarily female and middle-class audiences; they wanted to be reminded that money could not buy escape from misery.

So bravely she confronted whatever fate the plot dealt her—death, madness, romantic anguish, even occasionally a slightly ambiguous happiness. But the main thing about the movies she made in her great period at Warner Bros. is that she is never permanently beaten down. She may be victimized, but she never plays the victim. Most of the movies she appeared in, once she hit her stride, fall into the oxymoronic category of "tragedies with happy endings"—a description offered by the American novelist William Dean Howells to his friend Edith Wharton, as we learn in Julian Barnes's profound and witty contemplation of death, *Nothing To Be Frightened Of*. This mode is wonderfully cinematic, wonderfully American. Even if she was ostensibly crushed (or dead) at the end of the picture, she—and we—*learned something valuable* from that conclusion.

As it happens, *Marked Woman* concludes conventionally—with the bad guys vanquished and Davis and the crusading prosecutor (Humphrey Bogart) in love. But within a year she was in *Jezebel*. It permanently debarred her from playing Scarlett in *Gone with the Wind*, a disappointment that rankled in Davis for decades. She's a careless New Orleans belle, the kind of girl who defiantly wears a red dress to a white dress ball and suffers ostracism as a result. But when yellow fever rages through the town she returns to nurse her rejected fiancé (Henry Fonda). The last we see of her she is accompanying him to the island where those most afflicted are sent to die—a fate we sense she will share.

I like *Jezebel* much more than I do *GWTW,* that glacially paced faux epic, which remains, for me, a triumph of publicity over filmmaking. *Jezebel* was directed by William Wyler at his customary patient, not to say maddening, pace, which appealed to Davis (at last someone was taking her seriously). It was photographed by Ernest Haller in the deepest, most beautifully burnished tones of the gray scale. And it runs a brisk 100 minutes, which means that there are no wasted moments or emotions in it. Above all, it gave Davis her second Academy Award and poised her for her great years.

After *Jezebel* in 1938 through *Beyond the Forest* in 1949 she made twenty-four pictures, of which by my estimate at least half remain eminently, deliciously watchable today. I suppose that's because the social conventions that Davis's characters so often violated—love affairs disapproved of by society, pregnancies unblessed by marriage, or just sheer outspokenness, the failure of the female to keep her behavior chaste, her opinions to herself—seem no big deal to us. The drama in most of her films in those days utterly depended on an ostensibly inviolable social code, which it was her business to violate.

For the record, the pictures of this period that I like the best are: *Dark Victory* (bitchy heiress finds humanity as she confronts death); *The Old Maid* (woman bears child out of wedlock, surren-

ders it to her sister, becomes keeper of an orphanage, watches helplessly as her child visits contempt on someone she thinks is an irrelevant and spunkless maiden aunt); *All This, and Heaven Too* (nanny falls into hopeless love with the children's aristocratic father who is married to a cold, cruel monster); *The Letter* (need one say more than: "With all my heart I still love the man I killed"); *In This Our Life* (totally selfish Southern belle accidentally kills mother and child in auto accident, attempts to shift blame to young black man—and the first film to mention, however

Wyler, seated right, directs Davis in *Jezebel.*

The sophisticated studio look, portrait still, *Dark Victory.*

Claude Rains's rich, sober, Jewish banker—this is one of the rare movies of its time that openly refers to anti-Semitism—then loses her looks to illness even as he loses his eyesight to Nazi cruelty, preparing for an O. Henry ending that does not entirely vitiate the film's attempt to say something socially significant); *Beyond the Forest* (Davis reverts to her slatternly *Of Human Bondage* ways as a woman willing to murder to escape her "What a dump" smalltown life in King Vidor's overheated drama, which gives Davis a chance to let herself rip, yet somehow maintain our gape-mouthed respect for what may be her most feverish performance).

The last is not, though, an out-of-control performance. That's something I don't believe I ever saw her give. No more than I ever saw her give a lackadaisical one, even in the silliest material. Art, particularly the actor's art, depends on achieving a delicate balance between an instinctive understanding of the character you are playing and a rather close calculation of how little or how much you should do to convey that understanding in performance. Do too little and you risk a fatal subjectivity, work that does not permit the audience to achieve any sort of identification with your character. Do too much and you are heading for a hamminess that has the same effect on them—not to mention inducing the impulse to giggle.

When we think of Davis now, we think of an actress who painted with a broad brush, and one who was constantly flirting with hysteria. Even when she was a mouse, as she was, say, at the beginning of *Now, Voyager,* or pretty much

gingerly, modern American racism); *Now, Voyager* (affecting comically bushy eyebrows and ratty clothes in her early appearances as a dowager's much put-upon daughter, she allows love, psychiatry, and an ocean voyage to transform her into a beautiful and romantically alive woman); *Old Acquaintance* (She's a serious novelist, her best friend—Miriam Hopkins—is a bestselling one and a ditz brain, with Davis making a great romantic sacrifice to maintain her integrity and our admiration); *Mr. Skeffington* (careless and devoted to flirtation, she marries throughout *The Old Maid*, she was a mouse that roared—or at least passionately festered—entrapped in ideas of correct behavior that she did not endorse and was frantic to escape. There is, for example, something almost steely in her good novelist's need to write truthfully in *Old Acquaintance* and in her indifference to her old friend's cheerful embrace of trashy best-seller-dom. Indeed, what's funny in Miriam Hopkins's performance is that she doesn't seem to notice the difference between them. Hey, we're both writers aren't we? I may, in fact, be the better writer, since I'm richer and more famous than you are. To which Davis responds with a shrug and a look of amused contempt.

Or consider her governess in *All This, and Heaven Too*. You cannot miss her growing love for the Duc de Preslan, who is after all played by

Charles Boyer and Davis in *All This, and Heaven Too.*

Charles Boyer, the reigning international heart-throb of the time, who always hinted at a certain weakness of character on screen (which, para-doxically, made him more attractive to certain women who imagined they might just be the ones who could insert a little steel in his spine). But Davis is having none of that. She keeps suppress-ing her feelings for him in favor of her duty to his children, whom she loves uncomplicatedly. In short, her needs, her desires, must be sublimated to the dutiful New England values that Davis herself endorsed. (It might incidentally be noted that her savior in this film is, yes, a minister who hails from New England.)

Davis's movies in this period are pre-mod-ernist in tone. Even when they are not set in the past, they often take place in large, gloomy, oppressive mansions, and the issues they explore often have to do with class—what constitutes correct or respectable behavior for a woman of a

Davis makes her dowdy entrance in *Now, Voyager.*

Even allegedly candid shots were carefully posed and lit.

certain breeding. The values she must eventually rebel against, or be crushed by, are traditional and largely unexamined ones. A case could be made that the Davis screen character was, in these days, a sort of instinctive modernist, not fully understanding the forces arrayed against her; there is at least as much suppressed emotion in Davis's work as there is expressed emotion in it. What she couldn't directly state fed those abrupt gestures of hers and the curious rhythms of her speech. What she was obliged to leave unsaid—even though she was never at a loss for words—was, I think, a large part of her glory.

Her on-screen manner fed her latter-day status as a camp icon. Before it was absorbed by the larger cultural community, camp was largely a product of the homosexual community, seeing something deliriously subversive in the dangerous exaggerations of emotion (think of Judy Garland appearing to tremble on the brink of collapse during performance) or merely of intense stylization (a Busby Berkeley musical extravaganza) which the straight, square world saw as no more than amusing entertainment. Camp is not ironic in that it is far less sly in its appeal. It boldly flaunts the conventions of performance and it is at its most potent when the performer or the movie or stage director appears to be utterly unaware of his or her campness. For self-conscious camp never works. Like all the truly telling performance conventions it has to be a projection of something authentic, something completely instinctive, in the performer.

Which still leaves us with the question of why Davis's on-screen sexuality always stopped at flirtatiousness. Or at the manipulative and controlling. Or with conversations that hinted at desire, but never ended in physical expressions of it. This was not for lack of intense sexual feelings (and activities) in her life off-screen. Late in life she confessed—or perhaps made up—the idea that she became aware of her powerful sexual impulses when she was six years old and could hardly wait to grow up so she could act upon them. On the other hand, she elsewhere confessed that she remained a virgin until she was twenty-six, which might account for some of her feverishness. Yet the grand passions that supposedly motivated so many of her on-screen choices we pretty much have to take on faith. The heavy censorship that was imposed on the movies just before her career took off can explain some of her chaste behavior, but not all of it. Cast your mind back and it is difficult to summon up, say, a hot exchange of kisses, or glances, between Davis and her male costars. Even in something like *Now, Voyager,* which is all about a young woman coming into her own sexuality, she and Paul Henreid are the souls of discretion—yes, there's a famous scene where he lights two cigarettes and passes one to her. But that's a very symbolic passage.

Perhaps, one thinks, this lack of visible romantic charge in her movies stems from the fact that she did not herself think she was beautiful, so that she always played women whose attractiveness derived from qualities that had little to do with appearance. It may also have something to do with her age—or lack of same. She had come to the movies as a twenty-one-year-old and she remained in her twenties and

Relaxing under the powerful lights of the photographer.

thirties throughout the period we are discussing. Yet her ambitions were those of an older woman and, come to think of it, in many of her roles she appeared to be—or aged into—women who were older than she actually was. This sort of thing goes on quite a bit in opera, where the great divas tend to play roles older than their chronological ages. And who can doubt that Davis was of their company—perhaps the grandest diva the movies have ever known.

But, true to her type, she was ever an insecure diva. This was doubtless a factor in her unwillingness to play opposite strong leading men. She preferred to work with polite, well-spoken men of the Anglo-Irish brigade who would not challenge her dominance—George Brent, Herbert Marshall, Brian Aherne, Leslie Howard. She and Errol Flynn didn't take to one another and their two appearances together are distant and awkward. She and Cagney twice exchanged brisk badinage, but no one believed there was any authentic sexual charge between them, and that was also true of her appearances with the likes of Henry Fonda and Humphrey Bogart. Among the men she worked with more than once she did have an affair with the least interesting of them—George Brent—and had an unrequited love for—of all people—Claude Rains.

She had great professional respect for him—Rains really was a great actor, possibly the greatest character actor of his time. He was also quite tiny—about Davis's size—which explains why he never became a star on a sexually heroic scale. He was, as well, elegant, courtly, witty, and, by all accounts, sexually avaricious. His dressing room must have been as "busy as Gimbels at Christmas," Davis said to his daughter, who recently collaborated on a biography of him. He was also, like Davis, a heavy drinker—"If only he would have let me get him drunk," she said—but, alas for her, one who did not mix his business with his pleasures. Being a subtle man, he knew how to draw out the best in her without alarming her. Too gifted to be one of Bette's lapdogs, he was also not one of Hollywood's showier breeds—a mastiff or a greyhound—to be avoided by her at all costs.

What was true of actors was also true of directors. The best of them, William Wyler, she tried to tame by having an affair with him. She did the same with the more easygoing Vincent Sherman, who was the best of the Warner Bros. contract directors—below the level of Raoul Walsh and Michael Curtiz, that is. When Sherman's production of *Mr. Skeffington,* starring Davis and Rains, fell behind schedule, Jack Warner asked the congenitally sardonic Epstein brothers, who were writing about half of Warner's best pictures in those days, why, and one of them replied, "because Bette Davis is a slow director." There was more truth than fiction in the remark. Always improving the lighting or suggesting better camera angles, she mostly did not work with men intent on putting a personal stamp on their pictures. Put simply, the typical Bette Davis film was usually an exercise in solipsism. She is nearly always the only interesting creature on the screen and on the set—"she who must be obeyed," as H. Rider Haggard's most famous line has it.

But the *zeitgeist* turned against her in the immediate postwar years. During World War II women began entering the workplace in large numbers, as they would continue to do for the rest of the twentieth century and beyond. This had a liberating effect on them. So did increasing sexual freedom. So did the rising divorce rate. The need to suffer in well-upholstered silence began to seem almost quaint. And the arrival of Joan Crawford at Warner Bros. symbolized that change. In films like *Mildred Pierce* and *The Damned Don't Cry,* she was closer in spirit to the modern woman than Davis was in this period—

much more of a careerist in her roles than Davis typically was.

The possible exception to that rule is *Beyond the Forest,* in which she avidly pursues Brian Keith's rich guy. It was, I think, a terrific picture, the best of what critic Andrew Sarris called King Vidor's "delirious modern period." It features, among many slightly arcane references, a Hellmouth sequence that would do credit to a Medieval Mystery Play and a Night Town piece that James Joyce might appreciate. (Vidor, as Sarris also suggests, was, particularly in the sound era, always a better director of astonishing sequences than he was of entire films.) In any event, *Beyond the Forest* is a brilliant portrait of a grasping, heedless woman at the end of her tether and, like *Of Human Bondage,* a hint that lower-class suffering was a realm Davis might profitably have explored more often.

Not that she was done. How could she be? She was, in 1950, only forty-two years old. And, perhaps, due for a bit of luck. Which arrived in the form of some bad luck for Claudette Colbert, who was set for Joseph L. Mankiewicz's *All About Eve* when she injured her back and was forced to withdraw. Davis replaced her on short notice and was a revelation in the film. She was younger by a few years than Colbert, but somehow she looked much older. Slightly thickened, puffy in the face, she seemed to be flirting with age fifty. She was imperious, of course, but riven with insecurities about her relationship with her younger director-lover, about the new role she was rehearsing, about—eventually—Eve Harrington, Ann Baxter's scheming young actress who has moved into her life and is bent upon taking it over. The

Bette Davis plays pool, *Beyond the Forest.*

movie now seems to me a little too coy and self-conscious, particularly in its arch (and sometimes pretentious) dialogue. But it's well played by everyone, and the thing that makes Davis's a great performance is her vulnerability. She had played that quality before, of course, but not with the open demonstration of the hurt beneath her brusque and queenly manner. When, in the scene in the stalled car with Celeste Holm, she surfaces her insecurities, her womanly need for the warmth of a sympathetic man, she is touching in a way that, in her previous, more melodramatic sufferings, she had never quite been—not excluding her Oscar-winning performance as another put-upon actress in *Dangerous.* The thought also occurred that showbiz diva was a territory she might have explored more often.

Davis and husband-to-be Gary Merrill in *All About Eve*.

That thought recurred two years later in *The Star,* which remains one of her more overlooked films. All right, it's one of those anti-Hollywood fairy tales that Hollywood itself from time to time embraces. But it is also a strong portrait of an ego frazzling under pressure and, shot on locations all over Los Angeles, it is, under Stuart Heisler's no-nonsense direction, effectively realistic. It didn't do much business, but Davis's performance is exemplary. She's puzzled by her unhappy fate, also angry and self-pitying at times. But there's a brave reality in her work, doubtless informed by the fact that the parallels between her own life and Margaret's were starting to coincide.

And, in truth, *Baby Jane* aside, there wasn't much left for her—except a lengthy career, which embraced her second attempt at Queen Elizabeth I (*The Virgin Queen*), a doughty librarian beset by book burners (*Storm Center*), a game attempt at playing a Bronx housewife (*The Catered Affair*), in which she couldn't help but seem to be self-consciously slumming, Apple Annie in Frank Capra's last film, a dismal remake of his *Lady for a Day* of 1934. She had started doing television as early as 1956 and was not above playing in episodic TV programs like *Gunsmoke*. Nor was she above appearing in modest horror movies, trading on her *Baby Jane* hit.

I lost touch with her movies and her television appearances in the Seventies and Eighties, though I did get a little bit in touch with her. One time I was visiting the director Robert Rossen at his weekend house in Connecticut. She was staying with friends down the road and dropped by for a drink. She was, as Vincent Sherman later observed, completely without actressy qualities when she wasn't actually acting. She and Rossen pleasantly reminisced about their days at Warner Bros. (he had co-written *Marked Woman*) and pretty soon I forgot who she was, so convincingly did she play a nice suburban lady filling an idle Sunday hour. A few years later, I interviewed her for a PBS television show I was writing. Her demand for a hairdresser, who charged $1,000 for his services, somewhat rattled the chronically frugal public broadcasters, but she gave good value as she again recalled her studio days. On this occasion, she turned out to be just what I had hoped she would be—intelligent, self-assured, eager to be correctly understood.

In the years thereafter, she added bravery to that list of virtues. Her movies in the Seventies and Eighties tended to be carelessly horrific, though she did some better, or at least more plausible, work on television. But so far as one can tell, she never patronized her roles. She gave her all to them, as if it were still 1940 and she was still queen of the Warner lot. In her last decade, however, she was assailed with illness (breast cancer) and became almost bizarrely thin and shrunken as she went about collecting awards and appearing on the talk shows, telling ever-more outrageous tales of her past, surrendering the dignity to which her great roles entitled her, to the harridanish image which was the only one the younger audiences knew. One never knew if she needed the money or just needed to stay in the game—even if that meant assuming the role of our designated grotesque.

In 1987 she received one of the Kennedy Center Honors and I was asked to write a little appreciation of her for the program book, which I did. Something like a year later, my phone rang and an assistant's voice informed me that a Miss Davis was calling. I wondered who that might be—I didn't know any Miss Davises. But then a version of that remarkable voice, quavery but unmistakable, was addressing me. She had apparently just caught up with my program note. She wondered if we had ever met. I mentioned our two previous encounters. She expressed flattering wonder that a virtual stranger had so well caught what she considered her essence. I made modest sounds. We chatted a bit, then she said, "We ought to have a date." I said I would be more than pleased. And then she was gone. Within a year she was dead—in Paris, having been to Spain where she picked up one last meaningless award.

We never had that date. Which was all right with me. I really would not have known what to say—one last George Brent politely quailing before the force of her ego. I naturally wonder what people will make of her as the years continue to roll on. The kind of movies she made are so foreign to us now, and those of us who "took all that nonsense seriously" (as Robert Warshow once put it) are now fewer and fewer in number, and soon to be completely erased from the conversation. The world is smitten by newer forms of nonsense. Still, one has to think that the potent emotional reality Bette Davis found beneath the cinematic conventions of her day will continue to resonate with a discerning minority. I hope so. I don't want to give her up. And I don't want the rest of the world to do so, either.

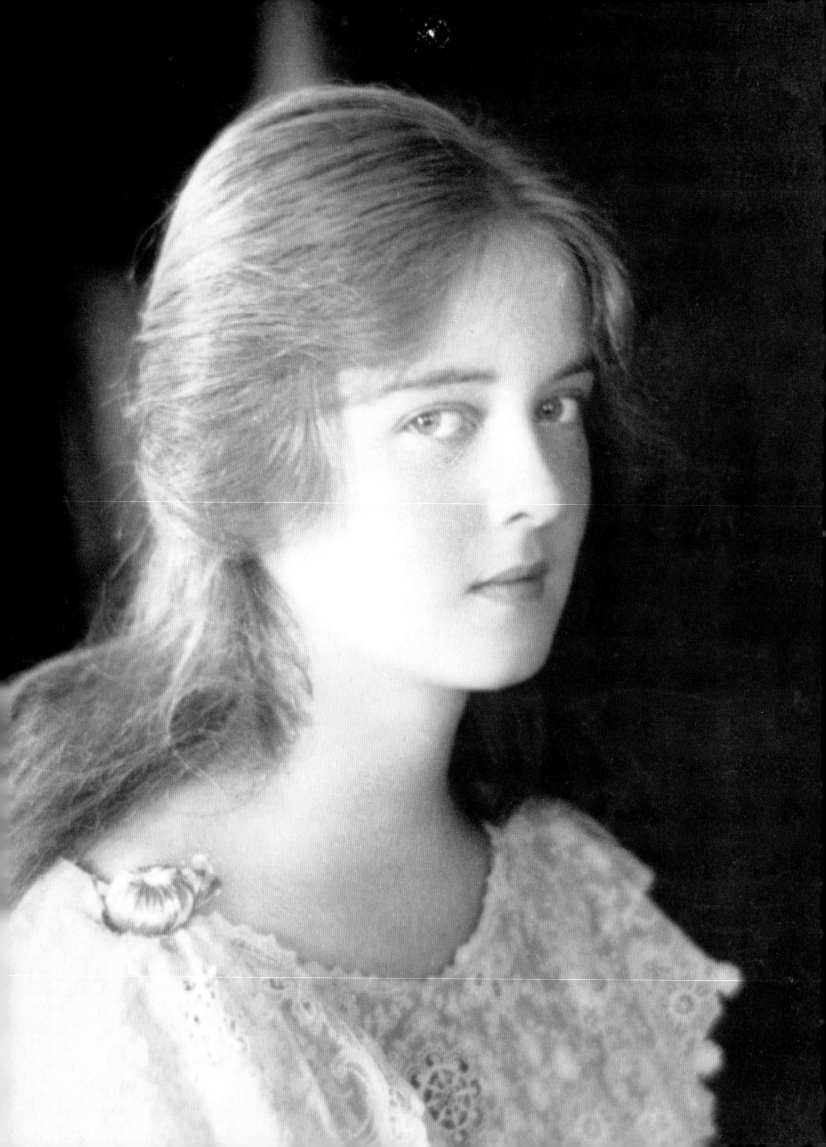

PART 1
A STAR IS BORN
1908–30

by George Perry

Ruthie Davis with her newborn daughter, 1908.

Opposite: Betty, soon to be Bette, at 16 at grammar-school graduation.

START as you mean to carry on is a motto, one of many, that could well have applied to Bette Davis. It was apt from the moment she was born on April 5, 1908, in an upstairs room of her grandparents' home on Chester Street, in Lowell, north of Boston, Massachusetts. Allegedly her birth took place in the midst of a vigorous New England spring storm, with the lightning flashing, the thunder rolling and crashing. It was the sort of night that would now require air passengers to be firmly buckled up. In those hardier times it would still have been advisable to stay indoors, protected from the driving rain and wayward tree branches. "I happened between a clap of thunder and a streak of lightning. It almost hit the house and destroyed a tree out front," Davis wrote in her autobiographical account, *The Lonely Life*. It was unquestionably an unruly night, as Shakespeare would have put it, and it somehow served as a dramatic leitmotif for her entry into the world. It is only to be expected that her later account of the circumstances, gleaned from her mother's constantly reiterated description, would have exaggerated the details, since as a newborn she could hardly have remembered them herself, but the circumstances were indelibly etched into the family's folklore.

At the time of her birth Davis's parents had been married a mere nine months and one day, by a hairsbreadth just long enough to stifle gossip. Yet the child's arrival was not welcomed, as the couple had not yet acquired their own home, and Davis's father, a Phi Beta graduate of Bates College, had enrolled at Harvard Law School. Both her parents were of sound Yankee stock with seventeenth-century antecedents, her father's from Welsh Puritans and her mother's from Huguenot immigrants. Harlow Morell Davis later became a New England patents attorney of a starchy demeanor, a cold fish not given to sentimentality or anything resembling a display of emotion, unlike her mother, Ruthie, who was of a much more volatile disposition and did not believe in concealing her feelings. The incompatibility of parental temperaments ensured the

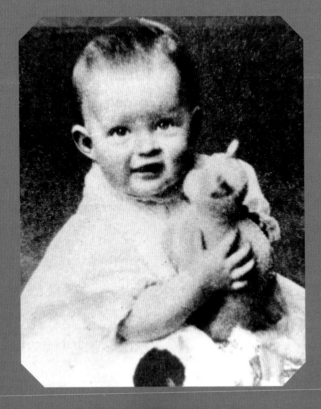

Bette Davis before she was one year old.

A lively three-year-old.

Riding with her father Harlow at age three.

Betty, 14, and her younger sister, Bobby.

failure of their marriage, although it did produce two children, Ruth Elizabeth, or Betty, being the elder by two years. Her sister Barbara Harriet, or Bobby, who was born on October 25, 1909, after a move to Winchester, Massachusetts, ten miles west of Boston, trailed in her glory from childhood and ever more.

The early years were uneasy. Harlow was still studying and money was tight. His austere personality did not help, putting a strain on the fragile marriage. In later life Bette Davis said that she could not recall a single moment of affection between her parents. After Bobby's birth and Harlow's Harvard graduation, he was appointed patents attorney to the United Shoe Machinery Corporation of Boston, initiating a well-paid career in which he rose through the ranks to a position of power and influence. The family fortunes changed substantially: a new house, a smart car, good dresses for the children, summer vacations on the Maine coast, all the trappings were there for a successful middle-class careerist to enjoy. Yet he was hostile and indifferent to his daughters, cold and uncaring toward his wife, who made the best of things by forming a close liaison with Bette. It was a double-edged relationship. "If I could never win my father," she wrote in *A Lonely Life,* "I completely conquered Ruthie. I became an absolute despot at the age of two.... I sensed her weaknesses early and I pounced on them. The tantrum got me what I wanted."

Thus the occasionally headstrong self-possession and relentless drive that characterized her in later life was formed, a necessary childhood technique of survival and triumph over circumstance.

She made light of the difficulties of her childhood, although havoc was wreaked on the health of her mother and sister. After Bobby's birth, Ruthie underwent a spell in a sanatorium, undoubtedly suffering from severe stress. She never referred to it afterward, but the inference is that she was clinically depressed. Bobby fought mental illness and nervous breakdowns for much of her life, and her failure to win her father's approval was probably a contributing factor.

When Bette was seven years old Ruthie embarked on a vacation to St. Petersburg, Florida, with the girls. Before taking the train from Boston they went to have dinner at the Copley Plaza Hotel, where their father was to see them off. Davis remembered the string orchestra and the hot rolls served on silver, and noted that her

Betty at 12, with 10-year-old Bobby in 1920.

Bette, on the beach lifesaving, 1928.

On return, they moved to Newton, another Boston suburb, and Ruthie soon found that the $200 monthly alimony check did not stretch very far. She would have to find a job. She applied for a position as governess to three boys living in New York City. The girls were packed off to Crestalban, a small, Spartan boarding school in the Berkshires, which had been found by their grand-mother while she was perusing the ads in *Atlantic Monthly*. For the next three years, the girls lived a largely outdoor life in this rural outpost, without electricity, high in the hills between the Hoosac and Housatonic rivers. They would even sleep on the porch and undergo naked snow baths during the long winter. Pigs and chickens, horses and cows shared the enclave, and as well as academic studies, the children were taught sewing, cooking, and other housework. Meals were robust and at lunch the rule was that only French be spoken. It was a healthy existence, calculated to test the hardiness and stamina of the Yankee character.

Just before her third Crestalban Christmas an accident imperiled Davis. Playing the school's Santa Claus, she ventured too close to the tree, which was festooned with real candles. One caught the sleeve of her costume, and in her efforts to put it out, the flames leapt to her false beard. In response to her screams she was quickly wrapped in a rug. When it was removed she kept her eyes closed, fantasizing that she had been blinded.

parents seemed unusually taciturn, even for them. At the station her father kissed Ruthie goodbye, an unusual gesture. As the train pulled out the children waved at the steam-girt, lonely figure watching their departure. When they arrived in Florida Ruthie told the children that they would not be living with him any more. Bobby was more affected than Bette, and cried copiously. Her better-adjusted sister, with aston-ishing composure for a seven-year-old, began re-planning her life without father, but she later said, "I still cry when I hear a string orchestra."

"Of course I replaced my father. I became my own father and everyone else's."

The reactions of others gave her a *frisson* of power. The next morning she was packed off to New York, covered in blisters that had become impregnated with ash and cinders from the train, and had to be immediately rushed to hospital for treatment. Her mother was told that the only way to prevent scarring for life was to apply grease night and day for at least two weeks. In spite of the discomfort, lack of sleep, and the pain of healing burns, Ruthie kept it up—and saved what was to become one of the world's most famous faces. Davis's skin would remain fragile and susceptible to sunburn, but it would also have an unusual translucent quality that gave her a particular appeal.

Ruthie decided to pull the girls out of Crestalban and have them live with her in New York. After a number of less-than-skilled posts she had enrolled in a photography course, and got a job as a photo developer. The family lived in a shabby one-bedroom walkup apartment on 144th Street and Broadway, and the girls were enrolled in P.S. 186, which, with its 3,000 students, fifty to a classroom, was a startling contrast to the sparsely populated Crestalban. It was a new life, but Davis soon began to relish it, enjoying the multicultural ethnicity of school, learning the joys of downhill rollerskating, and crunching mouthwatering shaved ice bought from an Italian umbrella stand. Ruthie made nocturnal entertainment by turning off the lights, raising the shades, and watching the neighbors across the court conduct their lives. Davis even became a Girl Scout, and her natural bossiness soon saw her raised to the status of patrol leader, her sleeves studded with innumerable merit badges.

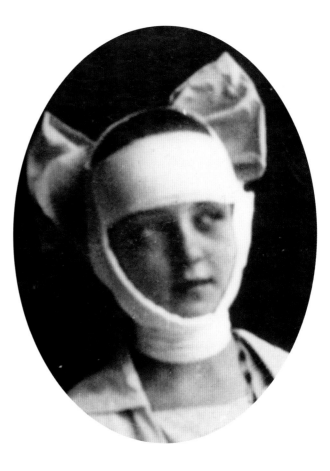

A friend, one Myrtis Gethner, had been reading Balzac's *La Cousine Bette,* and suggested that Ruth Elizabeth, always familiarly known as Betty, should consider changing the spelling, so she did, although she did not adopt the French pronunciation "Bet." The decision has provoked confusion ever since, with some commentators insisting on saying "Bet" Davis, unaware that in this instance it is a solecism. Her father, discovering the new name in a letter, pronounced it a passing fancy, a challenge that ensured it would stick.

Ruthie eked out enough money to send the girls to a Maine summer camp in 1922, where they enjoyed the outdoors, canoeing on the Kezar lakes. There was a move to East Orange, New Jersey, close to where she had found a job as a photo developer, but osteomyelitis of the jaw, the result of a bacterial infection, blighted her career

Bandaged after her Christmas-tree accident in 1919.

Bette and younger sister Bobby, 1928.

and forced move after move from one boarding house to another. Enrolled at East Orange High School, Davis made few friends, but became increasingly depressed by the lack of a home of her own, the consequences of which were frequent bouts of rage and manipulative tantrums. Eventually, Ruthie took herself and the girls back to Massachusetts, to the Boston suburb of Newton, close to her sister. For a while Davis attended Newton High School, where she became better adjusted, while her mother earned money as a portrait photographer. Davis attended high-school dances, but although she was a popular student, she was awkward with boys and totally lacked sexual experience, as though the atavistic clasp of her Puritan forebears reined her in.

In 1924 her unsettled adolescence was jolted yet again when Ruthie placed the girls in another private boarding school, the Northfield Seminary for Young Ladies. They lasted one semester, finding the atmosphere too overtly religious and the food appalling. The following January they were installed in the coed Cushing Academy at Ashburnham, Massachusetts, Ruthie's own *alma mater*. Young Bette was surprised and humiliated in her early days there to discover that she was expected to wait table in mitigation of part of the fees. After her initial apprehension she discovered that, far from looking down on her, the other girls were appreciative, and it was an effective way to make friends. Soon she was one of the most popular students. Cushing had a liberal tradition and allowed Davis's ambition, drive, assertiveness, and energy to have its head. She acted in school plays, was eloquent in debates, became a sorority president, and was even voted the prettiest girl in her class. She also met Harmon Oscar Nelson, "Ham," a young singer, musician, and composer whose student jazz band provided the music for a drama-club production, and as they became an "item" her classmate presented her with a real ham joint.

During the summer of 1925 Ruthie, Bette, and Bobby ("the Three Musketeers," as Ruthie called them) went to Mariarden, a theater school at Peterboro, New Hampshire. Ruthie opened a photographic studio in the town, and Davis attracted the attention of Jean Cradduck, a British woman who had spent many years in India and taught dance under the name of Roshanara. She did a deal with Ruthie, in which she engaged Bobby's services at the piano in exchange for giving Bette dance tuition. From her Davis learned about subtle movement, and how to

Bette in a school play, 1924.

convey emotion through bodily attitudes. She was delighted to find that Roshanara regarded her as a natural. That summer Davis gave her first dramatic performances in front of a paying audience, as one of the dancing fairies in *A Midsummer Night's Dream*, and as a moth in a white silk gown with wings attached to handheld balsam sticks. The theater director, Frank Conroy, who saw her perform, told Ruthie that it would be a crime to keep her off the stage.

Davis returned to Cushing for her senior year and appeared in more school productions, but she found her remaining time less memorable because Ham had left for Massachusetts Agricultural College. Ruthie toiled away in photography to pay the dues. She was now almost totally devoted to Davis, to the detriment of her other daughter, Bobby, who was increasingly left to fend for herself.

Ruthie wanted Bette to have serious stage training. An attempt to get into Eva Le Gallienne's drama school failed through nervousness and a poorly chosen test piece. Ruthie, now living in Norwalk, Connecticut, personally stormed the John Murray Anderson Drama School in New York, and steamrollered the directors into listening to Bette, who gave such an impassioned, impressive reading that they were persuaded to take her on in spite of Ruthie not having the $500 tuition fee. They agreed to accept the money in deferred installments. Ruthie immediately quit her job in Norwalk and found another at a school in New Jersey. Bobby was sent back to Ruthie's sister in Newton, and Bette was set up in a grim rooming house adjacent to the drama school.

No attempt was made to dress up acting as a glamorous profession. It was instilled in the students that they could expect a tough life, filled

Ruthie with her movie-star daughter, circa 1940.

with long periods of idleness interspersed with exacting toil, and that only a handful of them would ever be able to earn a respectable income. As a technique to weed out unpromising talents it worked, and there were many dropouts. The school was renowned for realism and among its alumni, although not Davis's contemporaries, were Paul Muni, Katharine Hepburn, Joan Blondell, and Lucille Ball. The most influential of her teachers was the dance instructor, Martha Graham, who Davis found extended the theories of Roshanara into transcendentalism, regarding the body as the essence of expression. Graham argued that acting was a fusion of voice and bodily movement that flowed as one. Davis learned her essential technique from Graham, and was forever scornful of those in the business who relied entirely on their vocal abilities to establish a stage presence. Even in closeups in her film career Davis would make sure that her

posture was aligned to whatever mood she was conveying. The school also got her to work on her high-pitched Boston accent, purging the open vowels and giving her the lowered, clipped tones that became her trademark.

Davis played the lead role in the school's end-of-term play, *The Fair Mrs. Fair*, directed by James Light. On the strength of it she was awarded a scholarship, and Light also offered her a professional job in his production of *The Earth Between*. It seemed too good an opportunity to miss, so she dropped out of the school. Then the play was postponed for a year, and Davis found herself without a job or a scholarship. An appeal to Frank Conroy in Mariarden put her name before George Cukor, who had a stock company in Rochester, upstate New York, and he hired her to play a chorus girl in the backstage melodrama *Broadway*. Ruthie urged Davis to learn the part of the female lead, Pearl, just because she had a hunch. During the third performance Ruth Lerner, the actress in the role, twisted her ankle, and Cukor asked Davis to learn the lines. He was surprised when she said she already knew them, and was even more surprised to find that, thanks to her Martha Graham training, she was able to fall down stairs entirely convincingly. Although the play only ran for a week Davis was widely praised, and she was asked to return to the company for the following fall. That left a long gap, though, and Davis soon discovered how difficult it was for actors to find work. Somebody offered her a job in summer stock at the Cape Playhouse in Dennis, Massachusetts, and Ruthie rented a house on Cape Cod. It turned out that

MARTHA GRAHAM

Martha Graham in *Salem Shore*, 1924.

Almost everything about the dancer and choreographer Martha Graham (1894–1991) was phenomenal, including her longevity—she died at the age of ninety-six. Her influence on American modern dance was extraordinary and unrivaled. Born in Allegheny, Pennsylvania, and living in California from the age of fourteen, she was unable to win parental approval and only began to dance seriously in her late teens. After her Manhattan debut in 1926 she brought a revolutionary approach to the art. She believed in the fusion of body and mind to coordinate and control movement, bringing intense dramatic expression to her work. For Graham, dance and acting were one, and her productions were animated, poetic, and unfettered by the classical formality of conventional ballet. "To act is to dance," she would tell her students,

including the young Bette Davis. From Graham, Davis learned how to move and to express herself using her whole body. Davis had the rare ability among actors of being able to convey a full range of human emotions even with her back to the audience, a skill that was one of her lifelong legacies from Martha Graham.

Bette Davis in 1928, fulfilling the dictum of her muse: "To act is to dance."

she had been hired by somebody without the authority to do so, and when she reported to the Playhouse she was told firmly that the company was full. Feeling sorry for her, though, they said Davis could work as an usherette. The leading women were no doubt aware that a potential *ingénue* in the front of the house was keeping an anxious eye on their health. One night Davis and Ruthie entertained a handsome young actor in the company to a steamed-clam supper but, being from Nebraska, he failed to relish the seafood, and her hopes of romance were dashed. His name was Henry Fonda.

Laura Hope Crews, a theatrical grande dame, felt that the resident *ingénue* was not up to playing Dinah in A. A. Milne's *Mr. Pym Passes By,* and was prepared to consider Bette Davis if she could learn a little-known English song, the sheet music for which was missing. Ruthie trudged round music stores, and after many hours stumbled on a church organist who not only knew the song but was prepared to rehearse it with Davis into the small hours. She won the part. Although Crews was an exacting disciplinarian, taking exception to Davis's excessive gestures and finding fault with her diction, she was pleased that the critics found favor with the performance. Davis returned to Cukor's company and found herself in a new production every week, submerging herself in her art.

It was in Rochester that Davis first encountered Miriam Hopkins, six years her senior and very much the company queen bee, who shamelessly stole scenes from her fellow cast members. Davis was still sexually naïve and failed to recognize overtures from Hopkins, who was bisexual. Soon afterward Hopkins was making vocal complaints about Davis's acting to anyone who would listen. It was not long before she was summarily fired, the official grounds being that she was too aloof and not a good team player who socialized with colleagues. Hopkins had undoubtedly influenced the decision.

James Light still wanted her for *The Earth Between,* a play about a Nebraska farmer, his daughter, and incest. It opened at the Provincetown Playhouse in Greenwich Village on March 5, 1929. Although off-Broadway, the Playhouse had made its name for controversial productions and had been a starting point for many talented playwrights and performers. It was Davis's New York debut, and the first and only time that the *New York Times* commented on her "soft, unassertive style." In the audience was Blanche Yurka, a renowned Broadway figure, who offered Davis the role of Hedwig in Ibsen's *The Wild Duck,* which was about to go on tour. An inopportune assault of measles nearly caused her to miss out, but somehow she made it. The play's theme of paternal rebuff had a particular resonance for Davis. Shortly before, on the opening night at Provincetown, her father had sent her a bouquet. It was the last contact she ever had with him.

Davis had become engaged to Charles Ainsley, a young man from a good Boston family, but he called it off shortly before the opening of *The Wild Duck,* allowing her to submerge herself in acting and to relish the fact that so many of her old friends and schoolmates were out front to watch her. So impressed by her portrayal of

Hedwig was Yurka that she unhesitatingly allowed her a solo bow.

When the run of *The Wild Duck,* which had alternated with *The Lady and the Sea,* in which Davis played one of the young sisters, had ended she went back to Cape Cod, not as an usherette this time, but as a full member of the company. In October 1929, just as Wall Street was falling into turmoil, she was signed to appear in *Broken Dishes,* a comedy in which she played Donald Meek's daughter. It opened at the Ritz on West 48th Street on November 5, 1929, transferring in January to the Theatre Masque on West 45th, and closing in April after 178 performances. She was good enough to warrant a salary of $150 a week, sufficient to propel her into the upper league of Broadway players. *Broken Dishes* moved to Boston, and after a summer hiatus (more time on the Cape), it played in Baltimore and Washington. Davis was then invited to appear in *Solid South* with Richard Bennett, whose feminine progeny, Joan, Constance, and Barbara, would become prominent in the talkies. The director was Rouben Mamoulian and it opened at the Lyceum on October 14, 1930. On this occasion the critics were not so kind, and the play closed in November.

By this time Davis had already made a screen test, for Samuel Goldwyn's company, which had required her to venture across the East River to the Astoria Studios. Talkies were established, and stage-trained Broadway actors were in demand for their voices. The British actor Ronald Colman had survived the transition satisfactorily, but the heavily accented Vilma Banky, often his costar, had not. Davis went up for *Raffles,* to play the

Bette Davis in 1929, the year of her Broadway debut.

girlfriend of an English gentleman thief, but she was badly lit and ill-prepared. When she saw the rushes she was horrified to note that a crooked tooth seemed to be her most salient facial feature, and she immediately arranged orthodontic treatment. Failing to get the part did not bother her unduly, though, as she was by this time secure in her Broadway career.

In fact, *Solid South* was her last appearance on the Broadway stage until the 1950s.

PART 2
HOLLYWOOD INGÉNUE 1931–36

by George Perry

Bette Davis, a Hollywood blonde, and pets.

Opposite: Conventional pose for a new screen actress, 1931.

DAVIS was offered another screen test, this time by Universal, which was looking for someone to appear in the movie of the Preston Sturges comedy *Strictly Dishonorable*. Davis took rather more care to ensure that she looked good, and gave an excellent reading of the chosen scene. David Werner, Universal's New York talent spotter, was impressed enough to offer her a six-month contract at $300 a week. Although Davis hesitated, Ruthie persuaded her that the money was well worth giving up grimy, wintry Manhattan for a sojourn in the Californian sun. It was a path many New York actors had followed, and had found that whatever was lacking in artistic fulfillment was more than made up by superior pay. There had been the small matter of her name, which Universal's man did not like. He had urged her to call herself "Bettina Dawes." Davis had retorted that she had no intention of being called "between the drawers" for the rest of her days, so Bette Davis she stayed.

When Ruthie and Bette arrived, after days of train travel in uncomfortable conditions and delays caused by poor weather, they looked in vain for the publicity man from Universal who was supposed to meet them. Eventually they gave up and took a taxi to the Hollywood Plaza Hotel, squandering almost every dollar they had. It seemed that the person who was meant to greet them at the station had scanned the arriving passengers and failed to discern anyone resembling an actress. Wrongly concluding she was not on the train he had gone back to the office.

Davis and her mother stayed at the hotel until they found a house to rent on Alta Loma Terrace in the hills. Ruthie borrowed the advance rent and more from a former Maine governor and family friend, as Davis was not due her first Universal paycheck for two weeks. Interestingly, in spite of the common view that the 1930s were the Golden Age of Hollywood, it seemed that fresh talent was often treated with a casualness bordering on indifference. It was and remains to this day a tough town.

The domestic touch, a front-door portrait.

The lead in *Strictly Dishonorable* went to Sidney Fox, who was also to play the lead in *Bad Sister.* Davis's first picture was not a promising debut, and she gained the nickname "Little Brown Wren." Worse, Carl Laemmle, Jr.—who occupied a senior position by virtue of being the studio founder's son rather than for his own capabilities—declared that she had as much sex appeal as Slim Summerville, a comic actor of the day with a fixed hangdog expression.

Universal kept her busy during her contract, and she made five more films, always in mediocre parts. After *Seed* and *Waterloo Bridge* in a minor role, she was loaned out to Radio for *Way Back Home,* to Columbia for *The Menace,* and to Benjamin F. Zeidman for *Hell's House.* The

production line was constant in the age of double-feature programs, and cheap "B" pictures were churned out to fill the bill. Davis found that she had not earned enough of a reputation on Broadway to demand better treatment. There were family anxieties, too. Her sister had been hospitalized for manic depression, and her mother had taken to the California high life and was spending Davis's money as fast as she could earn it. Davis considered returning to New York, but was aware that working on Broadway would not bring in enough to pay the bills.

Predictably, but devastatingly, Universal failed to renew her contract, leaving her in despair and with no option but to pack her bags and to go back as a failure. "I obviously would have to return to New York with my tail between my legs. I hadn't made it," she wrote in her autobiography. Then, on the eve of departure, she took what was to be the most important phone call of her career, and nearly rejected it because she suspected a hoax. It was from George Arliss, a distinguished British stage actor who had started his career in the reign of Queen Victoria and who had established himself in Hollywood on the strength of his classy talent. He was asking her to drop everything to go to see him at the Warner Bros. studio to discuss the role of the girl in *The Man Who Played God,* a talkie remake of one of his celebrated silent pictures. She was in his office within two hours of the call.

Arliss explained how she had come to his notice, and how in spite of her appearances in indifferent roles in second-rate films he had discerned her talent. She was captivated by his courtliness, his caring solicitude, and his respect for her skills, then still in the formative process. Her three years on stage were, he considered, just enough to rub the edges off. The interview was a success. Satisfied, Arliss told her to report to wardrobe as the part was hers. The fact that it was a one-picture deal at a salary less than she had been getting at Universal did not matter. She had a leading role in a George Arliss production, and such was his stature that he had autonomy, and even Jack L. Warner himself would not interfere with his casting choice. She found herself working with a disciplined actor who cared as much for the art as she did, and who was able to impart to her some of his gifts. It was as if she had found a father figure at last.

The success of the film and the praise of critics propelled Davis into a Warner Bros. contract and a tenure at Burbank that was to last eighteen years. Warner Bros. was a much more demanding place than Universal, however unlikely the proposition seemed. Schedules were tight, budgets tighter, everyone pulled their weight, and the production line kept going relentlessly. Warner Bros. seemed to have its finger on the public pulse more than any other studio, and under the hand of its young production head, Darryl F. Zanuck, was not afraid to tackle social-issue stories, often critical of the nature of society and government. Other studios had glamour, glitz, and glossy stars. Warner Bros. concentrated on actors with whom the public could identify.

In the first year of her new contract Davis appeared in eight films, and found that the pace was so frenetic there was little chance to modify

Glamour shots abounded in the 1930s.

"If Hollywood didn't work out, I was prepared to be the best secretary in the world."

In *20,000 Years in Sing Sing*—her only film with Spencer Tracy—she was obliged to occupy a hospital bed, done up after a car accident, in tasteful designer bandages that evoked ridicule in some quarters, a lesson that she took to heart.

Meanwhile Harman Nelson, her beau from Cushing days, came back into her life, migrating to California to pursue a musical career. Ruthie was eager that her daughter should marry, especially as she was still a virgin in spite of a number of romances. The situation was complicated by her sister's illness, however, and her mother wanted to devote more time to her. They were married on August 18, 1932, in Yuma, Arizona, where the waiting period was minimal. Back in Los Angeles the newlyweds occupied the same home as mother and ailing sister.

The marriage was doomed from the start. Their careers were separate and largely incompat-

Blonde Bette and vintage projector in the Warner screening room.

or refine the material. Sometimes she was making films back-to-back, beginning a new one on the Monday when work on the previous film had finished only the week before, or even dovetailing scenes during overlapping productions. Warner Bros. owned a considerable chain of movie theaters, which had to be kept in regular supply, so the maintenance of output was important.

The films came thick and fast: *So Big!, The Rich Are Always With Us, The Dark Horse.* In *The Cabin in the Cotton* she played a platinum-haired Southern vamp. In *Three on a Match* one of her co-players was Humphrey Bogart, who had been laid off from Universal at the same time she had.

Bette and Nelson outside her Warner dressing room, 1932.

ible, since Ham's was a nocturnal calling and Davis's began at dawn and could continue long into the evenings. Her earnings were ten times his. Ruthie was not an easy mother-in-law for Ham. Bobby's insecurities multiplied. Additionally, Ham found himself sometimes referred to in print as "Mr. Davis."

Work nevertheless continued at a relentless pace. Her five films in 1933 included *Parachute Jumper*, a starring role in *Ex-Lady*, and *Bureau of Missing Persons*. She was happy to appear in another film with George Arliss, *The Working Man*. For *Fashions of 1934* her hair was bleached to give her a Jean Harlow look. She partnered James Cagney in *Jimmy the Gent*, was a crime wife in *The Big Shakedown*, and an early victim in *Fog over Frisco*. Yet although she was working steadily and had become established with the public, she felt that most of her roles barely stretched her and were inadequate. She was determined to be cast as the wanton Mildred in *Of Human Bondage*, scheduled to be made by RKO with John Cromwell as director. W. Somerset Maugham had written the novel two decades earlier, and the part of the woman who does her best to destroy a club-footed medical student who has been kind to her was regarded as too loathsome for most Hollywood stars. Davis felt that she had a special propensity to rise to the challenge, and badgered Jack Warner without pause until he finally gave in, warning her that she was placing her career on the chopping block. Mildred was a working-class Londoner, and Davis spent hours studying the accent through an English cleaning woman she had specially hired. The woman had no idea she was being used in this

Bette in 1932, the year of her first marriage.

way and it is interesting to conjecture how Davis had dealt with her employment agency.

Leslie Howard, her British costar, was initially apprehensive that an American could play the part convincingly, but changed his view after a few days on the set. Davis actually manages to make the dreary cockney accent interesting by careful tonal emphases in which her vocal creativity is brilliant. The speech that ends, "You know what you are, you gimpy-legged monster? You're a cripple. A cripple. A cripple!" is spine-chilling the way she delivers it. Howard's fears that she would steal the picture turned out to totally justified.

Even her death scene was emotionally shocking, as Davis eschewed any attempts by the makeup department to sanitize and prettify her; hence the sallow skin, the brittle hair, the black, sunken eyes of a victim of consumption about to depart the earthly world. With Mildred, Davis proved to the world that she was not a mere movie star, but an actress of outstanding ability. In spite of the acclaim, an Academy Award nomination eluded her, and the ensuing controversy caused a fundamental change to the rules. The 1934 Best Film was Frank Capra's comedy *It Happened One Night* with Clark Gable and Claudette Colbert.

On Davis's return to the Burbank fold, Jack Warner seemed to be the only person in Hollywood unmoved by her success, putting her in an undistinguished and formulaic film called *Housewife,* in which she played a marriage breaker. Following this dire anticlimax she was assigned to *The Case of the Howling Dog,* an early

Perry Mason melodrama in which she was to be Della Street, his loyal legal assistant. She refused and was suspended. There was a change of heart, however, and she was taken off suspension to play opposite Paul Muni in *Bordertown.* Muni was a considerable actor, although too mannered and intense to do as well in films as he could on stage (a conclusion he eventually worked out for himself). The director, Archie Mayo, was of lesser caliber and kept urging Davis to make her performance obvious rather than subtle. She was required to disintegrate into madness during a courtroom scene, and Mayo wanted the full works—with eye-rolling and a foaming mouth, screams, and violence—and Davis wanted simply to become distracted and obtuse. The producer Hal Wallis had to arbitrate, and Davis won.

A small film followed, *The Girl from 10th Avenue,* in which she was a shop girl helping a jilted society lawyer, played by Ian Hunter. Her next, with George Brent, an actor of whom she was fond and with whom she often costarred, was in a way a prototype for the 1940 Howard Hawks newspaper film, *His Girl Friday.* It was called *Front Page Woman,* and was about a pair of reporters who allay their love by outdoing each other in scoops and use dirty tricks to get them. The director was Michael Curtiz, the most versatile on the Warner Bros. lot, but a taskmaster who was hard to please. Davis was cast with George Brent again in *Special Agent,* in which her character kept the books for a mobster, and was inveigled by Brent to spill the beans for the Treasury's benefit, which also ensured that at the end of the film she went unpunished, in

Finely lit studio portrait, 1932.

Davis, Jack L. Warner, and her Oscar for *Dangerous.* His immaculate evening clothes contrast with her low-key outfit that attracted criticism.

spite of the strictures of the Production Code Administration.

The slight the Academy had given her at the 1934 Awards was made up the following year. In *Dangerous* her costar was Franchot Tone (another affair that concluded unsatisfactorily when he married Joan Crawford), and she played a languishing stage actress in an alcohol-induced career hiatus who is given a sharp jolt by a wealthy architect. His designs on her are thwarted when a forgotten husband turns up refusing her a divorce. She takes him for a drive and wraps the car around a tree, not caring if one, the other, or both are killed. Her performance finally secured her an Oscar. Davis used to claim that the term "Oscar" derived from her assertion that the Academy Award statuette reminded her of Ham, whose middle name was Oscar. There are,

however, other theories on the derivation. Controversy even surrounded her outfit on the night. Some stars are disparaged for the ostentation of their dresses, but for Davis it was the exact opposite. She attracted scorn from the couture critics for turning up in a print dress with wide white lapels, a garment deemed suitable perhaps for a family occasion but hardly for Hollywood's greatest night out. It was a deliberate statement, her message to the industry and the world at large that she did not rate the Academy Awards too highly in the scale of things.

Leslie Howard had achieved considerable success on Broadway in Robert E. Sherwood's *The Petrified Forest,* in which he played an English romantic wandering the lonely desert highways of the Southwest, philosophically meditating on the fate of mankind, which in the 1930s in the

She would have made a better impression on Oscar night gowned like this, *Ex-Lady.*

that Bogart landed the first decent part in his film career. Davis was cast as Gabby, an unlikely waitress in such a place, who yearns to visit her mother's native France and there gaze at paintings and tour medieval cathedrals.

The film has not worn particularly well. Howard's languid musings, which in the 1930s may have suggested high seriousness, now look theatrical and indulgent, and Archie Mayo's

Humphrey Bogart and Bette Davis, New Year's Day, 1937.

On set with Leslie Howard in The Petrified Forest, *Archie Mayo directing.*

aftermath of one devastating world war and the potentiality of another was an abiding preoccupation. He pauses at an isolated gas station and diner and engages in dialogue with its denizens. The place is seized by runaway convicts, led by a notorious gangster said to be modeled on John Dillinger and played by Humphrey Bogart. When the film version was scheduled Warner Bros. wanted Edward G. Robinson for the part, but Howard indicated that if it did not go to Bogart he would withdraw. It was thus thanks to Howard

direction fails to lift the piece from its proscenium setting, with Arizona's wide-open spaces mostly represented by a painted background diorama. It was additionally ironic that Mayo had transported the cast to the real place in order to acclimatize them, and had succeeded in making some of them, including Davis, ill long before the soundstage wind machines started blowing dust all over them.

More trouble ensued after production of *The Petrified Forest* had ended. Davis was supposed to start immediately on a Dashiell Hammett thriller, *The Man in the Black Hat.* She claimed that she was ill and exhausted and needed time off to recover. She refused permission for the Warner Bros. doctor to examine her, and was suspended. After a few days, during which time she presumably rested, she agreed to start wardrobe discussions.

Davis, desperate for better parts, had hoped that Warner Bros. would permit her to be loaned out again to RKO, where Katharine Hepburn was to play the title role in *Mary of Scotland,* with John Ford directing. The role Davis coveted was that of Elizabeth. Warner Bros. refused to consider it and the part was given to Florence Eldridge. Instead, Davis was pushed into another screwball role in *The Golden Arrow* alongside George Brent.

After several misfires, *The Man in the Black Hat* was finally re-titled *Satan Met a Lady,* and was a revisit to Hammett's *Maltese Falcon* plot, a Sam Spade thriller of 1931 with Ricardo Cortez and Bebe Daniels. Under William Dieterle's direction the undistinguished result was something approaching a screwball comedy, with Davis in an approximation of the role that Mary Astor would fulfill so well in John Huston's 1941 film.

There then came a demand that she play a female lumberjack in a film called *God's Country and the Woman.* She was told that not only would it costar her favorite, George Brent, but would be made in Technicolor, an expensive innovation that Warner Bros. had been slower than the other major studios to adopt. She read the script and was unimpressed. Even the lure of Scarlett O'Hara in

A studio portrait highlights 1930s elegance in an Art-Deco setting.

Gone with the Wind, the filming rights of Margaret Mitchell's novel having been acquired by the studio, was insufficient to persuade her. She was placed on a three-month suspension. At the same time she discovered that the time would be added to her contract, which had another five years to run. In spite of expensive preproduction sorties to Oregon, Davis retreated in dudgeon to Laguna

A 1934 studio pose.

Beach. The film was made with a lesser actress, Beverly Roberts. The Scarlett O'Hara bait proved to be ineffective when the rights to *Gone with the Wind* were passed on to David O. Selznick.

Her differences with Warner Bros. were not over financial terms, although their publicity machine attempted to promote a public impression that this was the case, even allowing her salary to be elevated in print to $5,000 a week, a fictitious figure, but one that would register with the millions of hungry and jobless Americans who had suffered through the Great Depression. The substance of her complaint was that she had little control over the progress of her career. She had to rely on management from her employers, and she maintained that they had no idea how to do it. She was expected to do any job that was thrown at her, and she believed that her worth to the studio was measured not in terms of her artistic fulfillment, but in the financial return expected from any picture that had her name on the credit titles. Her stand was in fact causing her financial hardship as she was overextended, having to maintain the trappings and appearance expected of a star—an expensive home not only for her, but also now for Ruthie, and to provide monetary support for her husband, mother, and to a large extent her sister. A breaking point had been reached.

"What a fool I was to come to Hollywood, where they only understand platinum blondes and where legs are more important than talent."

The eyes are carefully accentuated in this studio still.

THE BAD SISTER

Bette Davis with Conrad Nagel at a dramatic moment.

Universal (1931)

Credits

Director: Hobart Henley
Producer: Carl Laemmle, Jr.
Screenplay: Raymond L. Shrock and Tom
Reed; additional dialogue by Edwin Knopf;
based on *The Flirt* by Booth Tarkington
Cinematographer: Karl Freund

Cast

**Conrad Nagel, Sidney Fox, Bette Davis,
ZaSu Pitts, Slim Summerville,
Charles Winninger, Emma Dunn,
Humphrey Bogart, Bert Roach,
David Durand**

Running time: 68 minutes

At the start of her $300 a week contract with Universal, Davis had hoped to star in *Slightly Dishonorable* under the direction of Preston Sturges. She was elbowed aside in favor of Sidney Fox, another Hollywood newcomer from Broadway, who also played the lead in what was to be Davis's first film under her short Universal contract. In *The Bad Sister*, Sidney Fox plays a spoiled rich girl in Indiana who rejects her dull suitors for an oily conman (Humphrey Bogart). He skips town, having duped its businessmen, taking her with him. Davis plays Fox's virtuous, wallflower sister who takes up with a decent young doctor (Conrad Nagel) after he has been discarded by the flighty older sister.

Both Davis and Bogie were subsequently informed that they were lackluster performers who could not expect a future with Universal, and were both to move on to become the leading artists at Warner Bros.

Lovers clinch: Nagel and Davis.

SEED

Davis plays a minor figure in the cast of this drama and she made little impression. John Boles plays a clerk who strives to become a novelist with the encouragement of his wife (Lois Wilson), who cares more for their home and five children (Davis plays the girl with four brothers). A former girlfriend (Genevieve Tobin) persuades a publisher (Richard Tucker) to back the book, and having achieved success, the author divorces his wife to marry the girlfriend. Years later his talents are wasted on potboilers, and his ex-wife confronts him with the grown-up children, forcing a crisis of conscience. So insignificant was Davis's role that her name did not appear on advertisements, critics completely overlooked her, and even she often omitted *Seed* from her filmography.

Bette Davis, in a minor role, faces John Boles.

Universal (1931)

Credits
Producer and Director: John M. Stahl
Screenplay: Gladys Lehman;
based on a novel by Charles G. Norris
Cinematographer: Jackson Rose

Cast
John Boles, Genevieve Tobin, Lois Wilson,
Raymond Hackett, Bette Davis,
Frances Dade, ZaSu Pitts, Richard Tucker,
Jack Willis, Bill Willis, Don Cox,
Dick Winslow, Kenneth Seiling, Terry Cox,
Helen Parrish, Dickie Moore

Running time: 96 minutes

WATERLOO BRIDGE

The star is Mae Clarke (left). Davis plays the hero's sister.

Universal (1931)

Credits

Director: James Whale
Producer: Carl Laemmle, Jr.
Screenplay: Benn W. Levy; continuity and additional dialogue by Tome Reed; based on a play by Robert E. Sherwood
Cinematographer: Arthur Edeson

Cast

Mae Clarke, Kent Douglass, Doris Lloyd, Ethel Griffies, Enid Bennett, Frederick Kerr, Bette Davis, Rita Carlisle

Running time: 72 minutes

Again Davis is a junior cast member in the first of three screen versions of Robert Sherwood's poignant story set in World War I of an encounter, in a London air raid, between a girl who has fallen on hard times (Mae Clarke) and a Canadian officer (Kent Douglass, later known as Douglass Montgomery), which becomes a doomed romance. Davis plays his sister, briefly seen during a sad weekend at his mother's (Enid Bennett) country house, before he returns to the trenches. Clarke later dies in another air raid at the place they first met, Waterloo Bridge.

WAY BACK HOME

The source was a popular NBC radio program of the day, a homespun saga set in Maine, in which a minister (Phillips Lord) is the center of the community, attending to and solving the problems that beset his flock. A youth (Frankie Darro) takes refuge from a brutal father (Stanley Fields) and the good pastor hopes to adopt him. Davis, in another secondary role, befriends the boy. She is attacked by his evil parent but saved by her boyfriend (Frank Albertson). The preacher pursues the villain, who has reclaimed his son, then a train brings his dastardly existence to an end. The simplistic, painful yarn set movie narrative back twenty years or more, and the film was poorly received. Albertson became smitten with Davis, who later said that the cinematographer J. Roy Hunt was the first to light her in such a way that she looked attractive.

Radio (1931)

Credits
Director: William A. Seiter
Producer: Pandro S. Berman
Screenplay: Jane Murfin; based on radio characters by Phillips Lord
Cinematographer: J. Roy Hunt

Cast
Phillips Lord, Effie Palmer, Bennett Kilpack, Raymond Hunter, Frank Albertson, Bette Davis, Oscar Apfel, Stanley Fields, Dorothy Peterson, Frankie Darro

Running time: 81 minutes

Davis with Frank Albertson, who became infatuated in real life.

Columbia (1932)

Credits

Director: Roy William Neil
Producer: Sam Nelson
Screenplay: Dorothy Howell, Charles Logue; dialogue by Roy Chandler; based on *The Feathered Serpent* **by Edgar Wallace**
Cinematographer: L. William O'Connell

Cast

H. B. Warner,
Bette Davis,
Walter Byron,
Natalie Moorhead,
William Davidson,
Craufurd Kent,
Halliwell Hobbes,
Charles Gerrard,
Murray Kinnell

Running time: 64 minutes

With her Universal contract about to be terminated, Davis made another loan-out for a hastily made pot-boiler set in England, in which Walter Byron plays a man framed by his stepmother for murdering his father. He escapes from prison, flees to the US, has plastic surgery, and returns posing as a potential buyer of the ancestral home. Neither his stepmother (Natalie Moorhead) nor his ex-fiancée (Davis) recognizes him. However, a canny Scotland Yard man does, but before he makes his arrest the real killers are tricked and exposed.

Bette Davis was on a loan-out to Columbia for this indifferent thriller set in England.

HELL'S HOUSE

In Davis's last film before the end of her Universal contract she plays the girlfriend of a bootlegger (Pat O'Brien). An orphaned youth (Junior Durkin) is sent to reform school after refusing to incriminate him. As he faces brutal treatment in a savagely managed institution, promised help never materializes. The boy escapes, and still trusts Pat O'Brien. Davis persuades him to contact an influential newspaperman (Morgan Wallace) who has been trying to expose the sadistic condition, but the boy's only hope of freedom depends on Pat O'Brien giving himself up. Junior Durkin, who was killed in 1935 at twenty in an automobile crash, like Frank Albertson in *Way Back Home*, became infatuated with Davis, a fact of which she was unaware until O'Brien set her wise.

Pat O'Brien plays a shady bootlegger and dangerous boyfriend.

Capital Films Exchange (1932)

Credits

Director: Howard Higgins
Producer: Benjamin F. Zeidman
Screenplay: Paul Gangelin,
B. Harrison Orkow; based on a story
by Howard Higgins
Cinematographer: Allen S. Siegel

Cast

Junior Durkin, Pat O'Brien, Bette Davis, Junior Coughlan, Charles Grapewin, Emma Dunn, James Marcus, Morgan Wallace, Wallace Clark, Hooper Atchley

Running time: 72 minutes

Davis comforts Junior Durkin, a fugitive from reform school.

THE MAN WHO PLAYED GOD

Warner Bros. (1932)

Credits

Director: John Adolphi
Producer: Jack L. Warner
Screenplay: Julian Josephson, Maude Howell; adapted from a short story by Gouverneur Morris and the play *The Silent Voice* by Jules Eckert Goodman
Cinematographer: James Van Trees

Cast

George Arliss, Violet Heming, Ivan Simpson, Louise Closser Hale, Bette Davis, Donald Cook, Paul Porcasi, Oscar Apfel, William Janney, Grace Durkin, Ray Milland, Dorothy Libaire, Hedda Hopper, Andre Luguet, Charles Evans, Murray Kinnell, Wade Boteler, Alexander Ikonnikoff

Running time: 80 minutes

Violet Heming, Davis, the masterly George Arliss, and Louise Glosser Hale.

Davis was eternally grateful to George Arliss, who had seen her in *Hell's House* and, recognizing her talents, cast her in *The Man Who Played God*. Reprising his role from a silent picture of 1922, he plays Montgomery Royale, a concert pianist whose hearing is damaged in an explosion. Unable to continue his career, he retreats to an apartment overlooking Central Park, and whiles away time by watching life from his window. Having become a lip reader, he is aware of what people are saying to each other. He sees his young fiancée, Grace (Davis), telling a young man, Harold (Donald Cook), with whom she is in love, that she cannot leave him because of his affliction. Appreciating her sacrifice he terminates their engagement, and a happy ending is achieved when Mildred (Violet Heming), a friend of his sister, is revealed to have always loved him.

Arliss, whose antecedents went back to late-Victorian British theater, was the most distinguished stage actor to flourish in the new talking pictures, and could be relied on to deliver crowd-pleasing performances with gusto. Davis herself later observed that at sixty-three, and forty years her senior, he was by then too old to play Royale, but the public seemed not to mind. Platinum-coiffed and bubbly, she projected a fresh-faced, youthful energy, and delivered her lines in the clipped, incisive manner that became one of her most distinctive characteristics (although her speech was occasionally too fast for the sound equipment of the time to cope with adequately). She always regarded *The Man Who Played God* as one of the most important films she ever made, and although she was paid considerably less on a one-picture deal than she had been getting on her now-terminated Universal contract, the experience of working under Arliss's tutelage and encouragement led to her new career at Warner Bros.

GEORGE ARLISS

Arliss, convinced of Davis's ability, secured her a contract with Warner Bros.

An established stage actor long before the invention of cinema, George Arliss (1868–1946) was one of Hollywood's most unlikely big names. Born George August Andrews in London in 1868, he made his debut in 1887. In 1902 he toured the US as a member of Mrs. Patrick Campbell's theater company, and decided to stay. American audiences were entranced by his carefully enunciated, declamatory manner. He played many historical figures on Broadway, including Disraeli, Voltaire, and Richelieu, all of whom he would later portray on screen. He was fifty-three when he made his film debut, *The Devil*, in 1921 (repeating his 1906 appearance in a Molnar play), followed by the first version of *Disraeli*, his most famous role. The 1929 sound remake of *Disraeli* brought him an Academy Award.

Arliss was granted complete control of his ten Warner Bros. films, setting up his own production unit, and for *The Man Who Played God* in 1932, another silent-picture remake, he cast a little-known actress as the female lead. She was Davis, and ever afterward she acknowledged that he had been responsible for the career break that led to her stardom. Arliss was an old-school actor with a huge following, and balanced his portrayals of historic figures with lighter, mildly satirical comedies, one of which starred Davis, *The Working Man*. His reign at Warner ended when the production head, Darryl F. Zanuck, left for Twentieth Century-Fox. Arliss went with him to make the very successful *House of Rothschild*, before retiring and returning to London. He survived the war, dying a few months after it ended.

Hardie Albright with Bette Davis in the first screen version of Edna Ferber's novel.

Warner Bros. (1932)

Credits
Director: William A. Wellman
Producer: Jack L. Warner
Screenplay: J. Grubb Alexander, Robert Lord; based on the novel by Edna Ferber
Cinematographer: Sid Hickox

Cast
Barbara Stanwyck, George Brent, Dickie Moore, Bette Davis, Guy Kibbee, Mae Madison, Hardie Albright, Robert Warwick, Arthur Stone, Earle Foxe, Alan Hale, Dorothy Peterson, Dawn O'Day, Dick Winslow, Elizabeth Patterson, Rita LaRoy, Blanche Friderici, Lionel Bellmore

Running time: 82 minutes

Publicity still of Davis and Albright.

Edna Ferber's novel was first filmed as a silent in 1925, with Colleen Moore and Phyllis Haver, and for a third time in 1953, with Jane Wyman and Nancy Olsen. This second version starred Barbara Stanwyck as Selina, a woman left penniless by her gambling father, who becomes a schoolteacher in a rural Dutch community in Illinois. She marries a farmer (Earle Foxe) but is quickly widowed. She has high hopes that their son (Hardie Albright) will become an architect but he turns to selling bonds. A sculptor she encouraged in childhood (George Brent) returns as her new love, and meanwhile her son has fallen for Dallas (Davis), an artist. Davis was jittery in Stanwyck's presence and was attracted to Brent. A critic in the *New York Times* called her performance "unusually competent."

Warner Bros. (1932)

Credits
Director: Alfred E. Green
Producer: Samuel Bischoff
Screenplay: Austin Parker; based on the novel by E. Pettit
Cinematographer: Ernest Haller

Cast
Ruth Chatterton, George Brent, Adrienne Dore, Bette Davis, John Miljan, Mae Madison, John Wray, Robert Warwick, Virginia Hammond, Walter Walker, Eula Guy, Edith Allen, Ethel Kenyon, Ruth Lee, Berton Churchill

Running time: 73 minutes

Davis became an Orry-Kelly clothes horse in a showy role.

Ruth Chatterton played the lead as a stockbroker's wife, Caroline, whose husband Greg (John Miljan) has an affair with Allison (Adrienne Dore) and precipitates their divorce. A star newspaperman, played by Brent, falls in love with her but she is too concerned about the plight of her ex-husband's firm to return his affection, and he eventually takes up with a flashy blonde, Malbro (Davis). In an automobile accident, Allison is killed and Greg badly injured. Caroline rushes to his side, Julian drops Malbro, realizing that he will never love anyone but Caroline.

As it was filmed back-to-back with *So Big!* it was as well that Davis's parts were small in both productions, and Chatterton inhibited her as much as Stanwyck. On this, the first of Davis's ten films with Brent, she watched Chatterton fall in love and make a husband of him in real life.

THE DARK HORSE

Fooling around with Warren William in a political comedy.

Warner Bros. (1932)

Credits
Director: Alfred E. Green
Producer: Samuel Bischoff
Screenplay: Joseph Jackson, Wilson Mizner
Cinematographer: Sol Polito

Cast
Warren William, Guy Kibbee, Bette Davis, Frank McHugh, Vivienne Osborne, Sam Hardy, Robert Warwick, Harry Holman, Charles Sellon, Robert E. O'Connor, Berton Churchill

Running time: 75 minutes

For this comedy with a political theme, Davis moved into a costarring role, where she acquitted herself well. Guy Kibbee plays a feeble gubernatorial candidate, and party worker Kay (Davis) suggests that Hal (Warren William), who has a winning track record, be appointed as campaign manager. She is in love with him, but he is jailed for missing alimony payments to his ex-wife (Vivienne Osborne). The committee, aware of his skills, pay up so that he can be released. He reworks an Abraham Lincoln speech for the nominee to deliver on a combined platform, but the opposing candidate uses the same source, enabling Hal to denounce him for plagiarizing the utterances of a great president. In revenge after the debacle, the opposition smears him and forces a remarriage to his former spouse to avoid scandal, much to Kay's disgust. Nevertheless, it all works out to her satisfaction. In spite of the lightweight material, the movie reinforced Davis's position at Warner Bros.

THE CABIN IN THE COTTON

Warner Bros. (1932)

Credits
Director: Michael Curtiz
Executive producer: Jack L. Warner
Screenplay: Paul Green; based on the
novel by Harry Harrison Kroll
Cinematographer: Barney McGill

Cast
Richard Barthelmess, Bette Davis,
Dorothy Jordan, Henry B. Walthall,
Berton Churchill, Walter Percival,
William LeMaire, Hardie Albright,
Edmund Breese, Tully Marshall,
Clarence Muse, Russell Simpson,
John Marston, Erville Alderson,
Dorothy Peterson, Snow Flake,
Harry Cording

Running time: 79 minutes

Bette Davis and Richard
Barthelmess ignite
Southern passion.

This was the first time Davis worked with Michael Curtiz and he typically gave her an exacting time, although she acknowledged that he was one of the most capable filmmakers she ever encountered. She plays Madge, a southern belle and the sexually charged daughter of wealthy cotton planter Norwood (Berton Churchill). She takes a shine to Marvin (Richard Barthelmess), the son of a poor sharecropper who is promoted by her father to the position of bookkeeper. His ulterior motive is uncovering and thwarting a sharecroppers' rebellion, but Marvin finds evidence of swindling. During a riot, the store is burned down and with it the incriminating records, but Marvin has a duplicate set that forces Norwood's hand. He returns in triumph to his former girl-friend (Dorothy Jordan), but Madge optimistically believes that she can still win him over.

In spite of the often audible doubts of the director, Davis reveled in the role of the voracious Madge, and her showy performance turned out to be the liveliest in the film. It also gave her the chance to deliver what was perhaps the earliest of her immortal screen utterances: "Ah'd like t'kiss ya, but ah just washed mah hair."

Warner Bros. (1932)

Credits

Director: Mervyn LeRoy
Producer: Samuel Bischoff
Screenplay: Lucien Hubbard; original story by Kubec Glasmon and John Bright
Cinematographer: Sol Polito

Cast

Joan Blondell, Warren William, Ann Dvorak, Bette Davis, Grant Mitchell, Lyle Talbot, Sheila Terry, Glenda Farrell, Clara Blandick, Buster Phelps, Humphrey Bogart, John Marston, Patricia Ellis, Hale Hamilton, Frankie Darro, Dawn O'Day, Virginia Davis, Dick Brandon, Allen Jenkins, Jack La Rue, Edward Arnold

Running time: 63 minutes

Three school friends reunite and catch up on events in each other's lives. Mary (Joan Blondell) has spent time in reform school but has become an entertainer. Vivian (Ann Dvorak) is married to Robert, an attorney (Warren William), and has a son (Buster Phelps). Ruth (Davis) is a stenographer. Vivian plans a cruise as respite from her failing marriage, but before sailing she meets Mike (Lyle Talbot), a gambler, and runs off with him. Her husband divorces her, wins custody, falls in love with Ruth, and marries her. Mike, stuck with impossible gambling debts and a now-alcoholic wife, tries to blackmail Robert, and when this fails he sends a trio of thugs (Humphrey Bogart, Allen Jenkins, and Jack La Rue) to kidnap the boy. Vivian saves the day at terrible cost to herself.

Davis, Joan Blondell, and Ann Dvorak tempt fate.

There is a considerable amount of plot to squeeze into a film lasting just over an hour, and at times the pace is too much for coherence. Untypically, Davis plays the least interesting of the three women, and her ability is barely tested. The title, based on the World War I superstition that three cigarettes lit from the same match gave time for a sniper to draw a bead, refers to the pact the girls make at the beginning, with three on a match.

"It must be a grand feeling to get everything you want."

20,000 Years in Sing Sing

Davis pays a visit to Spencer Tracy serving time in Sing Sing.

This prison drama was the only film in which Davis ever costarred with Spencer Tracy, who took the role originally intended for James Cagney, at that time in dispute with the studio. He plays Tom Connors, a tough guy and career criminal who draws a long sentence but behaves cockily in the expectation that his associates will soon have him sprung. He eventually realizes he has been deserted. Davis plays his girlfriend Fay, who tries to persuade a mobster (Harold Huber) to help. In parrying his advances she falls from a speeding automobile and is seriously injured. The warden (Arthur Byron), in a rare act of compassion, gives Tom an unescorted day release to visit her, expecting him to honor his word to return that night. At her apartment he finds Joe Finn (Louis Calhern), the man responsible for his sentence. He comes off worst in the ensuing fight, but Fay grabs a gun and kills Finn. Tom escapes, but when he hears that the warden may face dismissal he gives himself up. At the trial Fay testifies that she fired the fatal shot, but no one believes her and Tom goes to the electric chair.

A bitter story that would have ended differently had the Production Code Administration been enforced at that time (Fay would not have been allowed to go free), the film is one of the first to show the workings of the penal system in vivid and realistic detail, and the scenes within the prison are much better that those outside its walls.

It was the only time she appeared on screen with Tracy.

Warner Bros. (1933)

Credits
Director: Michael Curtiz
Associate producer: Robert Lord
Screenplay: Wilson Mizner, Brown Holmes; adaption by Courtney Terrett and Robert Lord from the book by Lewis E. Lawes
Cinematographer: Barney McGill

Cast
Spencer Tracy, Bette Davis, Arthur Byron, Lyle Talbot, Sheila Terry, Edward McNamara, Warren Hymer, Louis Calhern, Spencer Charters, Sam Godfrey, Grant Mitchell, Nella Walker, Harold Huber, William LeMaire, Arthur Hoyt, George Pat Collins

Running time: 77 minutes

Warner Bros. (1933)

Credits

Director: Alfred E. Green
Executive producer: Jack L. Warner
Screenplay: John Francis Larkin; based on
Some Call It Love by Rian James
Cinematographer: James Van Trees

Cast

Douglas Fairbanks, Jr., Leo Carrillo,
Bette Davis, Frank McHugh, Claire Dodd,
Sheila Terry, Harold Huber, Thomas E.
Jackson, George Pat Collins, Pat O'Malley,
Harold Healy, Ferdinand Munier,
Walter Miller

Running time: 65 minutes

In spite of her pure Yankee background, Davis often played southerners, and here she is Alabama, the girlfriend of a former marine pilot who has problems finding a job after his discharge. Because of his steely indifference to danger he is hired by a racketeer (Leo Carrillo) to fly liquor in from Canada, eluding government interceptors. He later discovers he has unwittingly been smuggling drugs. With his copilot (Frank McHugh) he outwits the criminal, turns him over, and convinces the authorities that he was innocent. This is somewhat surprising considering he has actually shot an official plane out of the sky, something that would not be condoned once the Production Code was in place. Davis deployed her southern drawl with captivating ease, but had little to do in what was essentially a swift-paced buddy movie, a clip from which was to be used with other clips of her early work in *Whatever Happened to Baby Jane?* to demonstrate that Baby Jane's films were on the whole terrible.

Davis with Douglas Fairbanks, Jr., and Frank McHugh.

THE WORKING MAN

George Arliss with Davis and Theodore Newton, spoiled children of his business rival.

Davis was pleased to be teamed once again with Arliss after a succession of second-rate films that hardly taxed her talent. In real life, her father had worked for a famous Boston shoe company, and in *The Working Man*, George Arliss took on the role of the shrewd John Reeves, a successful footwear manufacturer. He retires, handing his company to his smug nephew Theodore (Hardie Albright). On a vacation he meets Jenny and Tommy Hartland (Davis and Theodore Newton), the spoiled children of a rival company on the slide. He dislikes their indulgent lifestyle and, unrecognized, takes a job in their factory, which he soon reorganizes so that it is competitive once again. He is even appointed their guardian, and teaches them to give up their indolent ways and make a success of the business. Such is their eternal gratitude that Jenny falls in love with him. For Arliss it is a lighter vehicle than usual, and it gives him a chance to display his good humor and sharp wit.

Warner Bros. (1933)

Credits
Director: John Adolphi
Executive producer: Jack L. Warner
Screenplay: Maude T. Howell, Charles Kenyon; based on *The Adopted Father* by Edgar Franklin
Cinematographer: Sol Polito

Cast
George Arliss, Bette Davis, Hardie Albright, Theodore Newton, Gordon Wescott, J. Farrell MacDonald, Charles Evans, Frederick Burton, Edward Van Sloan, Pat Wing, Claire McDowell, Harold Minjir, Douglass Dumbrille

Running time: 73 minutes

EX-LADY

Warner Bros. (1933)

Credits

Director: Robert Florey
Production supervisor: Lucien Hubbard
**Screenplay: David Boehm, based on an
original story by Edith Fitzgerald and
Robert Riskin**
Cinematographer: Tony Gaudio

Cast

**Bette Davis, Gene Raymond,
Frank McHugh, Monroe Owsley,
Claire Dodd, Kay Strozzi,
Ferdinand Gottschalk, Alphonse Ethier,
Bodil Rosing**

Running time: 62 minutes

Davis with Gene Raymond as a couple with
modern ideas of marriage.

The theme was one that the Production Code, had it been working at that point, would have instantly suppressed: a couple who take a calculated decision to live together without being married. The fury of the Legion of Decency at the film's release hastened the day of enforcement.

Gene Raymond plays Don, an adman, and Davis plays Helen, a commercial artist who has the advanced notion that marriage stifles romance. When Don starts his own agency she has, for the sake of their clients, to acquiesce in matrimony. The business flourishes until they go on a belated honeymoon to Cuba and return to find they have lost important accounts, essential to their financial success. Don goes after a wealthy potential client (Kay Strozzi), who inflames Helen's jealousy by implying an affair is taking place. They row, but accept a looser arrangement akin to their earlier status. Then Helen appears to be having a dalliance, upsetting Don. When she convinces him that it was only to get his attention they go back to conventional marriage in a copout finale that showed a distinct lack of courage in pursuing the risqué theme.

Bette Davis was required to be a fashionable clothes horse, in sophisticated gowns and peignoirs for much of the time, her platinum blonde hair adding to the allure. It was not the outspoken theme that caused her to dislike the film, but the fact that she was playing a part that could have been fulfilled by any number of Hollywood actresses. A clip from the film was used in *Whatever Happened to Baby Jane?*

BUREAU OF MISSING PERSONS

Davis had top billing but a small part.

Warner Bros. (1933)

Credits

Director: Roy Del Ruth
Producer: Henry Blanke
Screenplay: Robert Presnell; based on
the book *Missing Men* by John H. Ayers
and Carol Bird
Cinematographer: Barney McGill

Cast

Bette Davis, Lewis Stone, Pat O'Brien,
Glenda Farrell, Allen Jenkins,
Ruth Donnelly, Hugh Herbert,
Alan Dinehart, Marjorie Gateson,
Tad Alexander, Noel Francis, Wallis Clark,
Adrian Morris, Clay Clement,
Henry Kolker, Harry Beresford,
George Chandler

Running time: 75 minutes

Pat O'Brien plays a police detective who has been relegated from street duties because of his extreme toughness, and now works in the Police Department's "kindergarten." Under the captain, played by Lewis Stone, positive results in locating missing people are achieved by patience and reasoning. In what the critic Alexander Walker called "Poverty Row's answer to *Grand Hotel*," Davis, although she had top billing, appears in only one part of the film and does not make her entrance until halfway through. She goes to the bureau to seek her missing husband but, as O'Brien discovers, she is in fact a missing person herself, wanted in Chicago for her husband's murder. She disappears, but O'Brien traps her by claiming the corpse has been found, tempting her to visit the morgue, where amazingly her husband is alive and among the mourners. She has been the victim of a plot involving his dimwitted twin brother. It was yet another un-taxing part, but she found a good friend in Pat O'Brien.

Pat O'Brien as hardnosed cop, Davis as murder suspect.

Warner Bros. (1934)

Credits

Director: John Francis Dillon
Producer: Samuel Bischoff
Screenplay: Niven Busch, Rian James;
original story by Sam Engels
Cinematographer: Sid Hickox

Cast

Charles Farrell, Bette Davis, Ricardo Cortez, Glenda Farrell, Allen Jenkins, Henry O'Neill, Philip Faversham, Robert Emmett O'Connor, John Wray, George Pat Collins, Adrian Morris, Dewey Robinson, Samuel S. Hinds, Matt Briggs, William B. Davidson, Earle Foxe, Frederick Burton

Running time:
64 minutes

In another insipid role, Davis appears in a crime programmer as the wife of a neighborhood druggist (Glenda Farrell) who has been inveigled by a post-Prohibition gangster (Ricardo Cortez) into faking patent medicines. When she becomes pregnant she tries to persuade her husband to relinquish his criminal activity. Her life is threatened, she is beaten, and ordered to dilute the drugs to cut costs. In premature labor, she is treated with counterfeit medication, loses the baby, and nearly dies herself. Her husband goes to kill the racketeer, only to find that the ruined president of a legitimate pharmaceutical company (Henry O'Neill) has got there ahead of him. Davis would have preferred Glenda Farrell's role as the villain's wisecracking moll.

Charles Farrell as an underworld patsy, Davis as loyal wife.

FASHIONS OF 1934

Above: Davis in a role calling for total elegance. Right: Davis and William Powell.

Songs by Sammy Fain and Irving Kahal, choreography by Busby Berkeley, and Davis in a blonde wig that transformed her into a mix of Garbo and Harlow are just some of the highlights of *Fashions of 1934*. Once again Davis was marooned in a part that gave her too little to do, and required her to be garbed up to the nines in slinky gowns from the imagination of Orry-Kelly. William Powell is an immaculate fashion thief who snatches Paris designs as soon as they are paraded on the catwalk, and then sells them on the mass market. Davis and Frank McHugh are accomplices—she is a fashion artist pretending to be a wealthy customer and he is a surreptitious snapper with a miniature camera hidden in the head of his cane. Verree Teasdale is a bogus duchess and Reginald Owen a celebrated couturier. The finale is a dazzling eruption of Busby Berkeley spectacle, replete with ostrich-plumed chorus girls, that would have sent the public away satisfied. All, that is, except Bette Davis fans.

Warner Bros. (1934)

Credits
Director: William Dieterle
Producer: Henry Blanke
Screenplay: F. Hugh Herbert,
Gene Markey, Kathryn Scola,
Carl Erickson; original story by
Harry Collins and Warren Duff
Cinematographer: William Rees

Cast
William Powell, Bette Davis, Frank McHugh, Verree Teasdale, Reginald Owen, Henry O'Neill, Phillip Reed, Hugh Herbert, Gordon Westcott, Nella Walker, Dorothy Burgess, Etienne Girardot, William Burress, Spencer Charters, Jane Darwell, Arthur Treacher, Hobart Cavanaugh, Albert Conti

Running time: 77 minutes

ORRY-KELLY

Orry-Kelly and Bette Davis discuss her *Jezebel* dress over cigarettes.

George Orry Kelly, usually known as Jack, was born in 1897 at Kiama, New South Wales, the son of a tailor from the Isle of Man and a Sydney woman. He studied acting and dance as well as art, worked briefly in a bank, and migrated to New York in 1921, where he painted murals for nightclubs and stores. He met a young Englishman, Archibald Leach, and they shared an apartment with another Australian, Charles Spangles. Kelly moved into films, designing title cards, and then costumes and sets for the New York theater, while Leach, reborn as Cary Grant, moved to Hollywood. In 1931 he was instrumental in getting Kelly, by now known professionally as Orry-Kelly, entry into First National Pictures.

From 1932 to 1944 Orry-Kelly was chief costume designer for Warner Bros., responsible for hundreds of films. His flair and skill swiftly pushed him into the top echelon and enhanced the charms of many great stars. Davis claimed to have owed much of her success to his brilliant costumes, the most famous of which was the vivid scarlet ball gown (actually bronze, which photographed better in black-and-white) she wore in *Jezebel*.

Jack Warner eventually fired Kelly because of his chronic alcoholism, but he went on to win three Oscars for other studios, for *An American in Paris, Les Girls,* and *Some Like It Hot*. Small, blue-eyed, charming when sober, irascible when drunk, a multitalented and moody perfectionist, he never married, and died from cancer in 1964, leaving an unfinished memoir, *Women I Have Undressed.*

An Orry-Kelly creation for *Fashions of 1934*.

JIMMY THE GENT

Warner Bros. (1934)

Credits

Director: Michael Curtiz
Executive producer: Jack L. Warner
Screenplay: Bertram Milhauser; original
story by Laird Doyle and Ray Nazarro
Cinematographer: Ira Morgan

Cast

James Cagney, Bette Davis, Alice White,
Allen Jenkins, Arthur Hohl, Alan Dinehart,
Phillip Reed, Hobart Cavanaugh,
Mayo Methot, Ralfe Harolde, Joe
Sawyer, Philip Faversham, Nora Lane,
Howard Hickman, Jane Darwell,
Joseph Crehan, Robert Warwick,
Harold Entwhistle

Running time: 66 minutes

Right: Davis and Cagney: dream-teaming for
Warner Bros.

The teaming of Cagney and Davis looked promising, and was certainly anticipated with relish by the two Warner Bros. stars themselves. The result was disappointing, but the resulting film has its admirers, who enjoy the breakneck pace of this screwball comedy. Cagney, sporting perhaps the worst haircut of his career, plays a corner-cutting, unscrupulous seeker of missing heirs to intestate dead persons. Davis is his disillusioned girlfriend, who goes to work for a smoother, more gentlemanly rival (Alan Dinehart) in disgust. Endeavoring to woo her back, Cagney unconvincingly adopts a similar polish and dress style, but only succeeds when he is able to reveal the other to be even more of a rogue than he is.

"You're the kind of guy that would steal two left shoes!"

The role called for Cagney to project high style.

FOG OVER FRISCO

Warner Bros. (1934)

Credits

Director: William Dieterle
Production supervisor: Robert Lord
Screenplay: Robert N. Lord, Eugene Solow;
based on an original story by George Dyer
Cinematographer: Tony Gaudio

Cast

Bette Davis, Donald Woods, Margaret
Lindsay, Lyle Talbot, Arthur Byron,
Hugh Herbert, Douglas Dumbrille,
Robert Barrat, Henry O'Neill, Irving Pichel,
Gordon Westcott, Charles Wilson,
Alan Hale, William B. Davidson,
Douglas Cosgrove, George Chandler,
Harold Minjir, William Demarest

Running time: 67 minutes

In this fast-paced thriller, Davis plays a society good-timer who keeps racy company and eventually comes to a bad end. Margaret Lindsay is her forgiving stepsister constantly excusing her behavior. In fact, although billed below Davis, Lindsay has the larger part, her character surviving kidnap and cracking a gang of thieves specializing in stolen bonds, in which Davis and Lyle Talbot (playing her fiancé) are implicated.

Davis made the most her amoral role, in which the frisson of engaging in crime gives her a sexual charge. So much plot is crammed into the tight running time that there is little room for clear characterization, however, and the roles are generally stereotypes. In retrospect, Davis claimed to have enjoyed her participation, mainly because William Dieterle, an exile from Germany, was sensitive to his actors' needs.

Davis with Lyle Talbot as her foolish fiancé.

OF HUMAN BONDAGE

To become properly recognized as an outstanding actress, Davis had to persuade Jack L. Warner to lend her to RKO to play Mildred in *Of Human Bondage.* She claimed that she pleaded with him daily until he relented. He had initially opposed her taking on such an unsympathetic character, believing that a negative public response would damage a valuable Warner Bros. property. John Cromwell had wanted her for the part, though, and to be fair there were few actresses in Hollywood who would have gone anywhere near it. Mildred is a monster, conceived in misogynistic venom by Somerset Maugham for his 1915 novel, a slatternly low-class London waitress who takes an inadequate man to hell. There were some who felt that an American would be unable to handle the mangled vowels of a semiliterate Cockney, but Davis hired an English maid who turned out to be a proficient voice coach (had she sprung from Mildred's milieu?), and managed to make as good a job of it as any middle-class British actress from Kensington.

Leslie Howard was apprehensive that Davis would steal the picture. Rightly.

RKO Radio (1934)

Credits
Director: John Cromwell
Producer: Pandro S. Berman
Screenplay: Lester Cohen; based on the novel by W. Somerset Maugham
Cinematographer: Henry W. Gerrard

Cast
Leslie Howard, Bette Davis, Frances Dee, Kay Johnson, Reginald Denny, Alan Hale, Reginald Owen, Reginald Sheffield, Desmond Roberts

Running time: 83 minutes

Davis confounded Howard by applying a lower-class London accent she learned from a cleaning woman.

It is a story of obsession. Leslie Howard plays the club-footed Philip Carey who, having failed as an artist, takes up medical studies. He meets Mildred and, mesmerized by her superficial flirtatiousness, is soon hopelessly infatuated. He is irrationally jealous when she goes out with a coarse salesman (Alan Hale) and she retaliates by berating him for being a cripple. Rejected and despairing he returns to his studies, scraping through an examination.

Nora (Kay Johnson), a romantic novelist, becomes interested in Carey, but the shadow of Mildred looms. She returns to him, pregnant and abandoned by her salesman lover, and Philip pays for an apartment for her, intending to marry her and take the child as his own. Understandably, Nora bows out. Having taken his money and his kindness, Mildred once more betrays him, this time by running off to Paris with another medical student (Reginald Denny).

At a hospital where he works as an intern, a patient introduces Carey to his daughter Sally, who develops a genuine regard for him. Once more the vile Mildred appears, along with her baby, and this time he allows her to stay, albeit against his better judgment. She offers him sex, but he refuses, at which point she launches into a vitriolic diatribe, concluding, "You know what you are, you gimpy-legged monster? You're a cripple. A cripple! A cripple!" In her rage she trashes his apartment, destroys his paintings, and burns the securities that pay for his progress through medical school. He is forced to drop out and work in a lowly sales job, but loses it in his clinical depression. Sally nurses him back to health and a legacy allows him to have corrective surgery on his foot and return to medicine. He learns that Mildred has died miserably in a charity ward, and he is at last released from his obsession, with the possibility that he can make a life with Sally.

Impressively, Davis rejected any Hollywood attempt to make her look pretty in her death scene, insisting on doing her own makeup. John Cromwell was so shocked when she walked on set that he asked her to modify it, but she refused, and audiences saw, in as unglamorous a guise as

"Funny-looking little thing, isn't it? I can't believe it's mine."

Mildred on the slide. Davis was keen to let her looks go for art.

any star had ever allowed, a woman in the grip of mortal illness. In *The Lonely Life,* she wrote: "I made it very clear that Mildred was not going to die of a dread disease looking as if a deb had missed her noon nap. The last stages of consumption, poverty, and neglect are not pretty, and I intended to be convincing-looking."

It is a melodramatic and overwrought work, and in spite of two remakes it remains rooted in the early part of the twentieth century. Davis's

performance retains its power, however, and the dire fears of Leslie Howard that she would steal the show were wholly realized. Although regarded as a certainty for an Academy Award she was inexplicably not nominated, the three contenders for 1934 being Claudette Colbert (who won for *It Happened One Night*), Norma Shearer, and Grace Moore. Conservatism prevailed in the Academy, and Davis's performance was adjudged too shocking to be rewarded.

George Brent was Davis's favorite leading man in all senses.

Warner Bros. (1934)

Credits

Director: Alfred E. Green
Executive producer: Jack L. Warner
Screenplay: Manuel Seff, Lillie Hayward;
original story by Robert Lord
and Lillie Hayward
Cinematographer: William Rees

Cast

Bette Davis, George Brent, Ann Dvorak,
John Halliday, Ruth Donnelly,
Hobart Cavanaugh, Robert Barrat,
Joe Cawthorne, Phil Regan, Willard
Robertson, Ronnie Cosbey, Leila Bennett,
William R. Davidson, John Hale

Running time: 69 minutes

Back at Warner Bros. after her triumph in *Of Human Bondage*, Davis was rushed into another programmer in a marriage-wrecking role. George Brent plays a copywriter who starts his own advertising agency, urged on by his wife (Ann Dvorak). It languishes for lack of clients, but his ambitious former girlfriend, played by Davis, who has traveled to Europe and returned as a sophisticate, writes a brilliant, catchy jingle for a cosmetics manufacturer (John Halliday) that is a hit with the public, and soon attracts other advertisers. Her initially successful attempts to destroy the marriage are eventually thwarted by the power of true love and the triumph of family over the female predator.

A black background enhances her features in a stylish portrait.

BORDERTOWN

Warner Bros. (1935)

Credits

Executive producer: Jack L. Warner
Director: Archie Mayo
Screenplay: Laird Doyle, Wallace Smith;
adapted by Robert Lord from a novel by
Carroll Graham
Cinematographer: Tony Gaudio

Cast

Paul Muni, Bette Davis, Margaret Lindsay,
Gavin Gordon, Arthur Stone, Robert
Barrat, Soledad Jiminez, Eugene Pallette,
William B. Davidson, Hobart Cavanaugh,
Henry O'Neill, Vivian Tobin, Oscar Apfel,
Samuel S. Hinds, Chris-Pin Martin,
Frank Puglia, Jack Norton

Running time: 90 minutes

Her status enhanced by *Of Human Bondage*, Davis was teamed with Paul Muni.

Having been suspended for refusing to appear in *The Case of the Howling Dog,* Davis was facing a bleak future at Warner Bros. Her rave reviews for *Of Human Bondage* changed all that and she was cast opposite Paul Muni, regarded as the studio's prestige actor, in a melodrama that bore resemblances to the 1941 Bogart-Raft-Lupino film *They Drive by Night.*

Muni plays Johnny Ramirez, a lawyer disbarred for throwing punches in court, who becomes a bouncer in a casino on the Mexican border, run by Charlie Roark (Eugene Pallette), and quickly works his way up to partnership. Davis is Roark's flashy wife Marie, who takes an interest in Ramirez but is rebuffed when he pays more attention to Dale Elwell (Margaret Lindsay), a society woman attracted to lowlife haunts. Marie dispatches Charlie by leaving him drunk and unconscious on the back seat, then shutting the garage door with the motor running. Even with a verdict of accidental death Johnny is unimpressed, and she accuses him of abetting murder. Things look black for Johnny until she goes on the stand and is revealed to the jury as a self-absorbed psychotic fantasist. Archie Mayo wanted Davis to play the scene in a state of total hysteria, but she wisely resisted, allowing her deranged condition to become apparent rather more subtly. She told the director that if he wanted her to act like it was silent picture they should have titles, not dialogue.

THE GIRL FROM 10TH AVENUE

Wrongly thought a working girl on the make, Davis with Alison Skipworth.

A 1914 theatrical piece that had been filmed as a silent three times—in 1917, 1922, and 1928—*The Girl from 10th Avenue* features Davis as Miriam Brady, a working girl who meets Geoffrey Sherwood (Ian Hunter), a jilted lawyer acting up alcoholically in front of the church where his ex-fiancée (Katherine Alexander) is marrying another man (Colin Clive). On a drunken rebound, the lawyer marries the working girl in one of those binges after which the groom wakes up in a different state not remembering anything.

Class intrudes. She is not up to being the wife of an attorney, and his friends think she is a gold digger. With her encouragement Geoffrey starts his own law firm, and she tries hard to become more refined. Alexander resurfaces, claiming she made a big mistake. Miriam offers Sherwood a divorce, but changes her mind when she meets her rival and sees her as a shallow, selfish opportunist. Sherwood thinks he has to divorce Miriam, but eventually realizes that she is worth far more than the woman who so callously dumped him.

The story plods a predictable path; it is obvious that it will all work out well in the end, in spite of the short running time.

Warner Bros. (1935)

Credits
Director: Alfred E. Greene
Production supervisor: Robert Lord
Screenplay: Charles Kenyon; based on the play *Outcast* by Hubert Henry Davies
Cinematographer: James Van Trees

Cast
Bette Davis, Ian Hunter, Colin Clive, Alison Skipworth, John Eldredge, Phillip Reed, Katherine Alexander, Helen Jerome Eddy, Gordon Elliott, Adrian Rosley, Andre Cheron, Edward McWade, Mary Treen, Heinie Conklin

Running time: 69 minutes

George Brent, Davis, and Roscoe Karns as eager newshounds.

Right: Davis is out to prove that newspaper-women can flourish beyond the women's page.

Warner Bros. (1935)

Credits

Director: Michael Curtiz
Producer: Samuel Bischoff
Screenplay: Laird Doyle, Lillie Hayward,
Roy Chanslor; based on *Women are Bum*
Newspapermen **by Richard Macauley**
Cinematographer: Tony Gaudio

Cast

Bette Davis, George Brent, June Martel,
Dorothy Dare, Joseph Crehan,
Winifred Shaw, Roscoe Karns, Joseph King,
J. Farrell MacDonald, J. Carroll Naish,
Walter Walker, DeWitt Jennings,
Huntley Gordon, Adrian Rosley,
Georges Renavent, Grace Hayle,
Selmer Jackson, Gordon Westcott

Running time: 82 minutes

"You make me so mad I could ... well, I could spit!"

The hardboiled world of scoop-hungry newspaper reporters is the basis of this Michael Curtiz film, a precursor of *His Girl Friday* five years later, which was another version of Ben Hecht and Charles MacArthur's *The Front Page*, filmed in 1931.

George Brent, a favorite costar, is a top newsman on one paper, Davis a career woman on another. They are lovers, but also dedicated rivals, and she is particularly intense because he regards women as poor at the job. She strives hard to prove him wrong, and is not going to give up everything for marriage until she has made her point. Her zeal gets her fired, but she saves herself by enabling an innocent man to be spared the chair against all odds.

SPECIAL AGENT

In the 1930s, Washington found it more effective to convict notorious gangsters for failing to pay their taxes than for their bloodier crimes, and the Internal Revenue Service became a dominant factor in removing them from the scene (the most notable scalp being Al Capone, who was sent to Alcatraz in 1931 for tax evasion). In this fast-paced thriller, newspaperman Bill Bradford (George Brent) is recruited as an undercover agent and sent to discover the financial secrets of a justice-eluding racketeer, Alexander Carston (Ricardo Cortez). He charms the bookkeeper (Davis), and, in keeping with the new Production Code, she is depicted as wholly innocent of all involvement in her boss's shady undertakings, although judging by her Orry-Kelly costumes it must have been a very well-paid post. Her revelations bring about Carston's indictment, but when he finds out that she has been working with a G-man, he has his thugs kidnap her so she cannot testify. Bradford rides to the rescue, and they marry after Carston is safely imprisoned.

The story and dialogue are ridden with clichés and obvious twists, and the movie represented yet another programmer for Davis, who had little opportunity to demonstrate her acting capabilities.

Warner Bros. (1935)

Credits
Director: William Keighley
Producer: Martin Mooney
Screenplay: Laird Doyle, Abem Finkle; based on an idea by Martin Mooney
Cinematography: Sid Hickox

Cast
Bette Davis, George Brent, Ricardo Cortez, Jack LaRue, Henry O'Neill, Robert Strange. Joseph Crehan, J. Carroll Naish, Joseph Sauers, William B. Davidson, Robert Barrat, Paul Guilfoyle, Irving Pichel, Douglas Wood, James Flavin, Lee Phelps, Loiuis Natheaux, Herbert Skinner, John Alexander

Running time: 76 minutes

George Brent goes undercover to pump information from Davis.

DANGEROUS

Warner Bros. (1935)

Credits

Director: Alfred E. Greene
Producer: Harry Joe Brown
Screenplay and original story: Laird Doyle
Cinematographer: Ernest Haller

Cast

Bette Davis, Franchot Tone,
Margaret Lindsay, Alison Skipworth,
John Eldredge, Dick Foran, Walter Walker,
Richard Carle, George Irving,
Pierre Watkin, Douglas Wood,
William Davidson, Frank O'Connor,
Edward Keane

Running time: 78 minutes

Davis won her first Academy Award for this performance, although it was regarded generally as a "guilt" Oscar, the industry's belated recognition that she should have won for *Of Human Bondage* the year before, when she had not even been nominated. Even Davis felt her win for *Dangerous* was unjustified and that it should really have gone to Katharine Hepburn for *Alice Adams.* She underestimated her skills.

Here she plays Joyce Heath, an alcoholic actress on the slide and broke, befriended by an architect, Don Bellows (Franchot Tone), who whisks her off to his country acres for rehabilitation, an uphill struggle given her ability to get her hands on a drink in spite of the housekeeper (Alison Skipworth). Her benefactor falls in love with her and ditches his fiancée (Margaret Lindsay). He backs Joyce's theatrical comeback, then

Davis in a *Dangerous* portrait still.

discovers that she is already married, and her husband (John Eldredge) will not offer her a divorce. Resourcefully, she takes her awkward spouse for a night drive in Don's car, deliberately crashing into a tree. Quite apart from the curiously lax authorities who allow a full-grown tree in the middle of a highway, this melodramatic moment results in an unpredictable outcome. Davis gives a remarkably mature performance for a twenty-seven-year-old.

A more elegantly costumed Davis in *Dangerous*.

Warner Brothers (1936)

Credits

Director: Archie Mayo
Producer: Henry Blanke
Screenplay: Charles Kenyon, Delmer Daves;
based on the play by Robert E. Sherwood
Cinematographer: Sol Polito

Cast

Leslie Howard, Bette Davis, Genevieve
Tobin, Dick Foran, Humphrey Bogart,
Joseph Sawyer, Porter Hall, Charley
Grapewin, Paul Harvey, Eddie Acuff,
Adrian Morris, Nina Campana,
Slim Thompson, John Alexander

Running time: 83 minutes

Davis with her costar Leslie Howard, an itinerant thinker.

Left: Dreaming of medieval Europe in an Arizona diner.

Robert Sherwood's play had been a huge success on stage for Leslie Howard and Humphrey Bogart. Warner Bros. intended Edward G. Robinson to appear with Howard, but he loyally cabled to say, "No Bogart, no deal." The setting, which contains almost all the film's action, is a gas station and diner located deep in the Arizona desert—a dusty service stop where few passersby pause. Jason Maple (Porter Hall) runs the place, aided by his waitress daughter Gabby (Davis) and Boze (Dick Foran), a former football player who has a yearning for her—understandably as there seem to be no other nubile females within tens of miles. There is also the loquacious Gramps (Charley Grapewin) who, in his aspiration to be the resident grizzled old-timer, talks endlessly of the days of Billy the Kid.

Leslie Howard plays Alan Squier, an itinerant philosopher from across the ocean who, in the grip of a miasma of detestation at the way

Humphrey Bogart challenges Howard and Davis against the Painted Desert.

the world is going, is drifting slowly across America. To Gabby he represents an opportunity to quit her claustrophobic life and satisfy an atavistic urge to see France, the country of her late mother's birth, and study art in Paris. They fall in love. Her dreams are shattered with the incursion of Duke Mantee (Humphrey Bogart) and accompanying hoods, who have broken jail and are making a murderous cross-country escape. They are all held hostage along with a rich couple and their black chauffeur. Squier is fascinated by Mantee, admiring him as a man who knows what he wants and achieves it, and he enters into a pact with the gangster that will enable Gabby to fulfill her ambition.

In Archie Mayo's hands this is a leaden production, with overblown dialogue, photographed in a stagy manner so that the climactic moment— the police ambush—is merely heard off-screen, as though the film has not escaped the shackles of Broadway. Even supposedly outdoor shots reek of the soundstage, with painted backdrops and the wrong sort of cactus for that part of Arizona. Davis, reunited the second time with Howard, gives a restrained performance, emphasizing Gabby's vulnerable naivety. Although billed fifth, Bogart more or less walks away with the film, and his hunched, twitchy Duke is one of his finest characterizations ("Great to have a real killer around here again," says Gramps).

Warner Bros. (1936)

Credits

Director: Alfred E. Greene
Producer: Samuel Bischoff
Screenplay: Charles Kenyon; based on a play by Michael Arlen
Cinematographer: Arthur Edeson

Cast

Bette Davis, George Brent, Eugene Pallette, Dick Foran, Carol Hughes, Catherine Doucet, Craig Reynolds, Ivan Lebedeff, G. P. Huntley, Jr, Hobart Cavanaugh, Henry O'Neill, Eddie Acuff, Earle Foxe, E. E. Clive, Rafael Storm, Sarah Edwards, Bess Flowers, Mary Treen, Selmer Jackson

Running time: 68 minutes

Bette Davis, now an Oscar winner, found herself playing a madcap heiress in this screwball comedy, except that she is actually the product of a publicity man's imagination to keep a cosmetic company, whose name she has adopted, in the public eye. In reality she is a cafeteria cashier. A reporter (George Brent) is sent by his New York newspaper to interview her in Florida when she is believed to be marrying an impecunious count. A suspicious rival (Carol Hughes) has her investigated. Somehow it is the newspaperman who marries Davis, another ploy to ward off fortune hunters, and the honeymoon generates an ocean of publicity. Brent, however, resents his position and she is terrified he will learn the truth about her. She rescues him from a jail sentence for drunken driving, and makes him attend all her functions in her custody. He retaliates by going after Hughes, who reveals the deception. At that point he realizes Davis is his true love and hijacks her to a remote cabin so he can write his novel. It is absurd, but innocuous.

Davis acting a madcap heiress, with George Brent as a newsman.

SATAN MET A LADY

A screwball version of *The Maltese Falcon*, this is the second of the three films from Dashiell Hammett's novel—and the least of them. William takes the part of the San Francisco private eye Sam Spade, although here he is called Ted Shayne. Here it is not a black falcon that is sought by a picaresque troupe of shady operators, but a ram's horn rich with gemstones. The role of the rotund adventurer played in John Huston's film by Sydney Greenstreet has a gender change here, taken on by Alison Skipworth. Davis fulfils the *femme fatale* role played by Bebe Daniels in the first film and Mary Astor in the third.

Director William Dieterle had probably seen *The Thin Man*, which successfully applied screwball to thriller, but as he had been in America only a short time, his command of English may have resulted in a less than complete comprehension of it. Davis does her best, but it is an uphill job. Bosley Crowther, complaining in the *New York Times* about the monstrous lunacy, said, "One lives through it in a constant expectation of seeing a group of uniformed individuals appear suddenly from behind the furniture and take the entire cast into protective custody."

Davis and Warren William in a screwball take on *The Maltese Falcon*.

In the *femme fatale* role, anticipating Mary Astor.

"*Do you mind very much, Mr. Shane, taking off your hat in the presence of a lady with a gun?*"

Warner Bros. (1936)

Credits
Director: William Dieterle
Producer: Henry Blanke
Screenplay: Brown Holmes;
based on the novel *The Maltese Falcon*
by Dashiell Hammett
Cinematographer: Arthur Edeson

Cast
Bette Davis, Warren William, Alison
Skipworth, Arthur Treacher, Winifred Shaw,
Marie Wilson, Porter Hall,
Maynard Holmes, Olin Howland,
Charles Wilson, Joe King,
Barbara Blane, William Davidson

Running time: 76 minutes

PART 3
SWEEPING TO THE TOP
1937–45

by George Perry

N 1936, an Italian producer based in England, Ludovico Toeplitz, whose credits had included *The Private Life of Henry VIII* and *Catherine the Great,* entered Davis's world. His lawyers, he told her, had assured him that she could not be enslaved by Warner Bros. and he offered her $60,000 twice over, a remarkable figure for the time, to make a couple of films in Europe. One was *I'll Take the Low Road* and was to be directed by Monty Banks, with Douglass Montgomery and Nigel Bruce costarring. Maurice Chevalier was expected to star alongside her in the other.

At the time, Davis had never left the US. She decided that to avoid any attempt by Warner Bros. to prevent her traveling to England she would embark from Montreal after a Saturday-night flight to Vancouver (process servers did not work on Sundays), and then take a lengthy cross-Canada train journey. She and Ham sailed on the RMS *Duchess of Bedford* from Montreal to Greenock, near Glasgow, Scotland, and arrived on their fourth wedding anniversary, August 18, 1936.

The voyage had been fraught with paranoia lest Warner Bros. should find out, but the first her employers knew of her departure was when her arrival on British soil hit the press. She and Ham embarked on a second honeymoon, renting a car to tour Scottish castles, glens, and braes, sniff the heather and dine on pheasant and grouse. They went on to Wales in the hope of finding her Davis roots, a fruitless task as it is such a common name there. Before serious business in London they spent time at the popular south coast resort of Brighton, and stayed in the nearby village of Rottingdean at the Tudor Close Hotel.

Toeplitz then sent her to Paris for costume fittings, giving her an opportunity to look for her mother's Huguenot roots and the surname Favor, a no more successful task. She admired the boulevards and the architectural landmarks, as well as the cuisine—so much lighter and more imaginative than the stodgy fare she had encountered in Britain. On her return to London she found that an angry Jack Warner had been to

Davis as *Jezebel*, a defining role (and Academy Award winner).

Opposite: Portrait by George Hurrell, doyen of studio photographers.

October 1936: Davis leaves her London hotel for her court hearing.

Venice to confront Toeplitz, the upshot of which was a lawsuit, Warner Bros. Pictures, Inc. vs. Nelson, to be held in the High Court with Sir William Jowitt appearing for the plaintiff, and Davis, Sir Patrick Hastings, and Norman Birkett for the studio. Ham meanwhile returned to seek work in New York.

The courtroom atmosphere, with its legal performers in gray wigs and black gowns, and the unctuous formality with which counsel addressed the judge, was intimidating to Americans. Hastings was a renowned barrister, given to barnstorming eloquence that often had little relevance to the case but was nevertheless persuasive. He dismissed Jowitt's arguments that the contract was a form of well-paid slavery, and declared that "this is the action of a very naughty young lady," a remark so patronizing that now it would be regarded as scandalously inappropriate. He also made much of the fact that whatever the servitude under discussion, it was so well-paid that he would consider it himself on the same basis of remuneration. He was echoing public

sentiments. The case had attracted huge press publicity, and Davis was presented as a spoilt, pampered movie star who was not content with a wage a thousand times higher than the British average.

Her counsel never called her to the stand, much to Hastings' chagrin as he would have enjoyed publicly shredding such a famous dramatic actress. She lost anyway, the judge enforcing contract law to the letter. Toeplitz vanished from view. Davis retreated to Brighton feeling bitterly the severity of her chastisement. Jowitt moved to appeal. She cabled her mother to come and join her in England, but just as Ruthie was about to travel Davis sent another message to say that she was dropping the appeal and coming home.

Two factors had persuaded her. The first was that she had been ordered by the court to meet Warner Bros.'s costs on top of her own, a total of $15,000. By the time the appeal process had been exhausted, with no firm hope of winning, she was likely to be out of pocket by $50,000. The second factor had been some wise words from George Arliss, who had made a point of visiting her in Brighton, with Jack Warner's knowledge. He told her to concede gracefully and go back. He assured her that things would improve at the studio. He admired her courage but told her to face her employers proudly. It was the last time she saw him, but she always acknowledged the strength he had given her. Soon afterward she left for New York aboard the *Aquitania*.

Ham had already made a record with Tommy Dorsey, and it was mutually decided that he should stay in Manhattan in the hope that something else would turn up, so Davis and Ruthie returned to California alone. There Davis found Arliss's predictions to be sound. Warner Bros. absolved her of the responsibility to meet their legal costs. She also learned that her salary was to be given a healthy increase. The gesture was just as well, since the promise to pay for the trial turned out to be empty, and she soon had to resort to paying back a Bank of America loan in monthly installments.

The first film she was offered, *Marked Woman*, met with her approval, a hard-hitting "torn-from-the-headlines" melodrama in the Warner Bros. tradition. It was based on the Lucky Luciano case, in which a notorious mobster ran a prostitution ring from a shady nightclub and was successfully prosecuted by an up-and-coming district attorney, Thomas A. Dewey, who eventually ran for president. Humphrey Bogart was cast on the right side of the law in the attorney role and Davis was the leader of the girls, renamed "hostesses" to meet the susceptibilities of the PCA. In the course of the film Davis's character was severely beaten by henchmen for betraying the gang boss, and was scarred by a cross slashed on to her face. The usual Hollywood makeup department's idea of chic medical dressings did not appeal, and Davis went to her own doctor, informed him of the injuries she was supposed to receive, and asked that he bandage her accordingly. On her return to the studio the gate guard took one look at her horrifying appearance and reported that Davis had been seriously injured in some accident. The director, Lloyd Bacon, deemed the bandaging

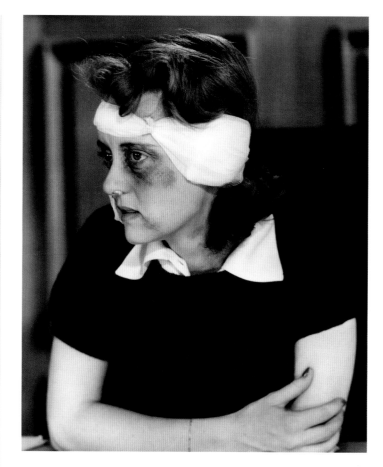

excessive and producer Hal B. Wallis was obliged to arbitrate. He did so, in her favor.

Marked Woman was followed by *Kid Galahad*, a fight picture directed by Michael Curtiz, with Edward G. Robinson and Humphrey Bogart as business rivals and shady operators, Davis as Robinson's girl, and Wayne Morris as a young and exploited boxer. Then Edmund Goulding gave her a starry lift in *That Certain Woman*, a stereotypical women's picture rooted in the *Stella Dallas* mode of sacrifice and suffering. In *It's Love I'm After* she played opposite Leslie Howard as half of a theatrical couple whose apparent onstage chemistry is contrasted with their vicious battles off. Archie Mayo directed the screwball comedy, and its impact was heightened by the inside knowledge that offscreen Davis and Howard did not get on.

Bandaged by a professional medic for her *Marked Woman* appearance.

Davis with sometime lover, Howard Hughes, 1936.

At this point, Davis's marriage fell apart. In fact, it was surprising that it had lasted so long, given the incompatibilities between Davis and Ham Nelson. There were rumors that she had been having an affair with the millionaire aviator-turned-movie mogul Howard Hughes, and that Ham had bugged one of their liaisons, but Hughes was not cited as co-respondent when Ham filed for divorce in November 1937. Curiously, his grounds included Davis's "excessive reading" habits, a charge that she was unable to deny, and the judge approved the petition.

Her personal troubles were exploding while she was shooting *Jezebel*. Davis always maintained that the most coveted role in Hollywood history, Scarlett O'Hara, did not go to her because George Cukor, her nemesis from Rochester days, was the original *Gone with the Wind* director and had persuaded Selznick to pass on her. It is much more likely that she was rejected because her Julie Marsden was too striking a southern belle to be eclipsed by Scarlett. In William Wyler, Davis found a director whose intelligence, taste, and authority far outstripped hers, and whose painstaking dedication to his work was renowned. "I'd met my match," she claimed. He patiently coaxed a great performance from her and she fell in love. Her costar was Henry Fonda, the young man who had attended Ruthie and Bette's unsuccessful dinner at Cape Cod. Wyler, too, had encountered Davis at an early stage of her career when she was at Universal and was given a test for his first big directing job, *A House Divided*. She had been outfitted in a totally unsuitable dress with a low neckline, which she found embarrassing. She heard a small, dark man standing by the camera say: "What do you think about these dames that come onstage and show their chests, and think they can get jobs?" It was a job she did not get, but it was her first meeting with William Wyler.

During the making of *Jezebel* her long-estranged father died in Massachusetts from a heart attack. She did not break off to go to his funeral, although she requested a day or two to mourn. Then it was time to move on.

Wyler's pace of shooting was slow and painstaking, and forty takes before he was satisfied were by no means unusual. Huge conflicts raged with Jack Warner's office, and there were serious threats to remove Wyler and install

William Dieterle in his place. There are some second-unit shots in the finished film—in the trek through the swamps to reach New Orleans, isolated by yellow fever—that were actually directed by John Huston, who was then officially still a writer. Another serious problem concerned the availability of Henry Fonda, who was intent on honoring a promise to be with his wife in New York when she was due to give birth, and who found the date looming dangerously close with many of his scenes still unfinished.

Davis was to regard Wyler as the greatest love of her life whom she never married, but the affair ended when *Jezebel* wrapped. She even had his baby aborted. The relationship had been stormy, and it is possible that pragmatism prevailed, as each was clearly capable of destroying the other's career. She would nevertheless make two more films with him. When *Jezebel* opened in March 1938 Davis had her face on the cover of *Time,* and the film took $1.5 million at the box office.

Davis makes the cover of America's top picture weekly.

After *Jezebel* she costarred with Errol Flynn in *The Sisters.* She found his approach to acting frivolous and casual, and only appreciated his gifts when she saw how well he came across onscreen. It was a noble, self-sacrificing role—a loyal mistreated wife standing by a feckless man, and getting caught up in the 1906 San Francisco earthquake. Davis had an affair with Anatole Litvak, the director, with the full knowledge that he was married to her *bête noire* Miriam Hopkins. In 1939, the applause of Oscar night still ringing in her ears, she was the star of *Dark Victory,* arguably one of the greatest women's pictures of all time. She played Judith Traherne, a wealthy socialite whose hedonistic existence embraces her gilded circle of friends, horses, and shopping, and was scarcely a worthy role model for all those women in the audience who had lived through the hard times of the Depression. She learns that she has a brain tumor and has only months to live. She marries her doctor (George Brent) and

Fay Bainter and Davis flank a beaming studio head, Jack L. Warner, on winning Oscars for *Jezebel.*

Big at the box-office but could Flynn keep up with Davis?

retreats to an idyllic New England cottage where in due course the sunlight fades for her. She dies peacefully and prettily, her husband having left for a conference, unaware (although he is meant to be a brilliant practitioner) that her end is nigh. The Vienna Boys' Choir swells on the soundtrack. Director Edmund Goulding shamelessly milks the emotional thrust of the mawkishness, and the undertaking is saved from bathos by Davis's magnificent performance, stimulating huge box-office returns.

Her part as the Empress Carlotta of Mexico in *Juarez*, a Paul Muni vehicle, was relatively small. In her big scene she rants at Claude Rains, playing Napoleon III, for his betrayal of her husband, who he had installed as his puppet ruler. She goes mad in an effective performance, but it is not at the center of the story. In *The Old Maid*, once

again under the direction of Edmund Goulding, she costarred with Miriam Hopkins, cast in the queen bitch role. There was little regard between them. Hopkins had played *Jezebel* on Broadway in 1934 and it flopped, while Davis had filmed it with considerable box-office success and an Oscar to boot. Davis had also bedded Hopkins' husband. In *The Old Maid*, Hopkins is a jealous cousin who thwarts Davis's marriage when she discovers that she had a child from her jilted fiancé who was later killed in the Civil War. She raises the girl as her own and Davis's character is forced into the role of spinster aunt. In her eagerness to upstage Davis, Hopkins turned up on set wearing one of her *Jezebel* dresses, and was frustrated when her gesture was ignored. Frustration turned to rage when Davis walked away with the picture and was the focus of the reviewers' attentions.

When Davis made her first film in Technicolor, *The Private Lives of Elizabeth and Essex*, a historical epic based on a poetic play by Maxwell Anderson, she had hoped for Laurence Olivier to be her leading man. Instead she got Errol Flynn. She was even more aware than before of his cavalier attitude toward acting, and how seriously he took to carousing and womanizing. He was at that time an extraordinarily powerful box-office draw, and the front office was adamant that he could pull in audiences who might otherwise have been put off by Davis's deglamorized portrait of the queen, with her hairline shaved back to reveal an enormous forehead. She was not happy with the choice of director either, the do-anything, highly talented Michael Curtiz, who believed that success depended on getting his own way in every conflict. The film was a hit when it opened, and Flynn's performance was regarded as charmingly self-effacing in the presence of Davis's crushing talent.

Exhausted after shooting, she retreated to her beloved New England and toured the places of her younger days, which she found changed, smaller, and disappointing. At a favorite spot, Peckett's Inn at Sugar Hill, New Hampshire, she met Arthur Farnsworth, the colorful thirty-one-year-old host. A powerful rapport developed between them, which soon evolved into a full-fledged affair. The studio accepted that she needed a break and agreed to a new deal limiting the number of films she had to make, allowing for lengthy vacations, and also raising her money. She wanted a home away from Hollywood, so she bought a late-eighteenth-century farmhouse and 200 acres, and named it Butternut. On New Year's Eve, 1940, Arthur "Farney" Farnsworth became her second husband.

Davis and Arthur Farnsworth, her second husband.

At home at Butternut, her cozy home in New Hampshire.

By then she had made another costume drama, *All This, and Heaven Too*, with Charles Boyer, in which she played a governess to the children of an unhappily married French nobleman. Davis's role was another display of saintly self-sacrifice, and an enormous box-office success. It was followed by a new version of W. Somerset Maugham's steamy tropical melodrama, *The Letter*, with William Wyler as director. Davis played a Singapore rubber planter's wife who shoots her lover to death on the verandah steps, and deceives her husband, lawyer, judge, and jury

William Wyler and Davis at the time of *The Little Foxes*.

into believing that he was making advances to her, with only a hard-to-explain letter likely to contradict her story. She received an Oscar nomination for her portrayal of the conflicted woman.

The next of her pictures was *The Great Lie*, in which George Brent again costarred, with Mary Astor as the third part of a triangle involving a child. It was a melodrama with comic overtones and an ending that seemed to turn off conflict like a tap to evoke the kind of tear-jerking conclusion that was becoming a Davis hallmark. Farnsworth had accompanied her to California and at the conclusion of shooting they had slipped off to Arizona to seal their union and confound the gossip columnists who had been left in the dark.

The Bride Came C.O.D., her next film, with James Cagney, was a screwball comedy in the *It Happened One Night* mold, in which she played an eloping heiress hijacked by a penniless aviator at the behest of her millionaire father. It was neither memorable nor funny, in spite of several moments where she landed inopportunely on cactus plants and had to have Cagney remove the spikes from her rump. Far more suitable to her talents was her loan-out to Samuel Goldwyn for *The Little Foxes,* in the role that Tallulah Bankhead had filled in Lillian Hellman's play on Broadway. A story of entrepreneurial greed in a backwoods town in the Deep South, it was the last film she shot under the direction of William Wyler. The fact that they were former lovers hindered rather than helped the atmosphere, which was thick with artistic disagreement. Davis even left the production after a vicious argument. She remained absent for three weeks after being diagnosed with nervous exhaustion, and the studio pondered whether to replace her with Bankhead or even Miriam Hopkins, who had coveted the role of Regina Giddens. In the end, scenes were shot round Davis until she could return. Strife notwithstanding, *The Little Foxes* was another outstanding hit, and Davis regretted that she never had an opportunity to make another film with Wyler.

Although it was a secondary role, she was keen to play Maggie, the secretary to the national arch-bore Sheridan Whiteside, in the film of George S. Kaufman and Moss Hart's hit Broadway comedy *The Man Who Came to Dinner.* She had hoped that John Barrymore could play the irascible leading character, but his alcohol-fuddled memory let him down when he was tested, and he died not long afterward. Other names entered the frame, including Cary Grant, who was prepared to offer his salary to British War Relief, and Orson Welles, who might not only have played Whiteside but directed as well. Eventually Monty Woolley, the toast of Broadway but unknown in middle America, was cast and the directing assignment was handed to William Keighley who had recently made the lamentable Davis-Cagney pairing, *The Bride Came C.O.D.* Unimaginative direction lets down what should have been a sparkling film comedy, and Davis's romantic interest, a newspaper editor played by Richard Travis, is so unappealing one wonders why he and not Ronald Reagan, another contender, was given the part. Production was delayed after Davis was bitten on the nose by a dog, and had to wait until the wound healed.

With *In This Our Life* she was back into southern melodrama in a good-sister bad-sister story based on a Pulitzer novel by Ellen Glasgow. Olivia de Havilland contrasted with saintly behavior the unredeemed selfishness, narcissism, and duplicity of Davis's character. It was John Huston's second directorial assignment after *The Maltese Falcon,* and production was delayed because Farney had fallen ill in Minnesota. With the assistance of Howard Hughes, who lent a plane, Davis rushed off to be at his bedside. One explanation for the frenzied, unshaded performance of the final cut is that de Havilland was having a romantic fling with Huston at the time, usurping what Davis saw as her privilege, and it may have sapped her confidence. In spite of all shortcomings and the total detestability of the screen persona, the movie made $1.7 million, marking Davis's biggest success to date, and more than enough

In contemplative mood: a general publicity portrait.

to satisfy Jack Warner that she had the best bankability of any star on the studio roster. She was aware enough to demand more money, a raise to $5,500 a week, and to insist that she be asked to make no more than two films a year. She won the concessions.

An interesting interlude occurred when Davis, now at the height of her profession, was made president of the Academy of Motion Picture Arts and Sciences, the first time the post had been filled by a woman. She went along to the first meeting with a portfolio of resolutions, and was surprised to find that she was expected to be merely a figurehead; the last thing the conservative organization wanted was for her to come in

Hair test for
Now, Voyager.

and start changing things. In spite of warnings that she was biting the hand that fed her, she resigned almost immediately and was delighted to find that several of her suggestions were later adopted.

Her next film was her most popular, and made $2.38 million. In *Now, Voyager,* directed by Irving Rapper (chosen by her because he was more amenable than the earlier proposition Michael Curtiz), she played opposite Paul Henreid, an émigré and refugee from Hitler with a dignified continental bearing that propelled the studio into thinking it had found a new Boyer. Based on an Olive Higgins Prouty novel, this was a classic ugly-duckling story, in which a young woman is kept in purdah by her wealthy Bostonian mother so that she can serve her old-age needs. An eminent progressive psychiatrist, played by Claude Rains, rescues her from a nervous break-down, and gives her the confidence to don

fashionable clothes and take a South American cruise. She meets a man who gives her love but cannot marry her as he has a dependent wife and a disturbed daughter. So Davis's character adopts the daughter and bestows on the father unlimited visiting rights. The film ends with her most cele-brated curtain line: "Oh Jerry, don't let's ask for the moon—we have the stars."

America had entered World War II in December 1941, after the Japanese attack on Pearl Harbor. Davis flung herself wholeheartedly into selling war bonds on promotional tours, and made many speeches urging Americans out of complacency and into committing themselves to the struggle. Her first film after the PCA had lifted its absurd restrictions on criticism of the Nazi regime was *Watch on the Rhine,* from Lillian Hellman's play, in which she was the wife a refugee, played by Paul Lukas, who is a prominent figure in the antifascist underground movement. The propaganda motif was that even within the US, Nazis were present, working covertly to undermine and destroy democracy.

Davis was a passionate supporter of President Roosevelt, and was profoundly anti-Hitler. Her most significant contribution to the war effort was the creation of the Hollywood Canteen. She had seen how successful and popular the Stage Door Canteen in New York had been, and felt that a similar club for uniformed forces could work in Los Angeles, which was a stepping-off point for service personnel embarking for duty in the Pacific and elsewhere. Abetted by John Garfield, who shared her enthusiasm, she enlisted the backing of studio chiefs and industry heads, notably Jules Stein of MCA, as well as the multiplicity of craft unions representing Hollywood's labor force. Premises at 1415 Cahuenga Boulevard, between Hollywood and Sunset, were taken over and transformed.

The Hollywood Canteen opened on October 3, 1942, and remained in business until the end of hostilities in 1945. Famous stars washed dishes, served tables, and danced with ordinary GIs, while the biggest names in show business provided constant entertainment. Davis reverted to her Girl Scout bossiness, and whipped up a dazzling level of enthusiasm, even persuading Joan Crawford to tackle mountains of unwashed plates without a grumble. Kay Kyser and his band made a point of performing every Saturday night, even when they had to return from out-of-state engagements. Nobody was paid, and no serviceman had to put his hand in his pocket to savor the delights on offer. There was, of course, a film to be made, although by the time it came out in early 1945 the war was nearly over. In *Hollywood Canteen,* Davis appears as herself, emceeing and making forceful speeches. Joan Leslie recalled that she seemed to find it much harder to be simply Bette Davis than she did to adopt a fictional persona.

Portmanteau revue films with a patriotic theme and all-star casts were popular wartime musical entertainment in theaters, and most studios produced their versions. Warner Bros. had three: *This is the Army, Thank Your Lucky Stars,* and *Hollywood Canteen*, with Davis in the latter two. In *Thank Your Lucky Stars* she even performed a musical number, a song by Frank

At the opening of the Hollywood Canteen, Davis hands out Camel cigarettes to servicemen.

Loesser, words by Arthur Schwartz, in which she laments the absence of datable men as a consequence of the draft—"They're Either Too Young or Too Old"—and was briefly flung around by a jitterbug expert.

She played in a film with Miriam Hopkins called *Old Acquaintance,* directed by Vincent Sherman, who had replaced a sick Edmund Goulding. They appeared as dubious lifelong best friends, a relationship fraught with one-sided jealousy. Sherman later claimed he was not directing the film, he was refereeing it. Davis's most satisfying moment came when she was called on to shake Hopkins vigorously until her teeth rattled.

Just before she was due to start *Mr. Skeffington,* word reached her that Farney had collapsed on Hollywood Boulevard. He died shortly afterward. Wild theories abounded, one of which suggested that he had been assassinated by fifth columnists (as the enemy spy network was designated) because he was working in the aviation industry on high-security projects. In spite of conflicting testimony, evidence that a fall two months earlier at Butternut could have been salient, and a number of curiously unexplained factors, the jury returned an inquest verdict of accidental death.

Work began on *Mr. Skeffington* when Davis had recovered from the tragedy. Director Vincent Sherman was added to the list of Davis's lovers, partly at his request. He said later: "The only way I could finish the picture was by having an affair with her." Allegedly she so imposed her views on him that she was all but directing the film herself, and he claimed that he slept with her because his extraordinarily understanding wife gave him permission for the sake of his career and their mortgage.

The narrative of the movie concerns a bankrupt heiress whose brother has squandered their late parents' fortunes and who has been discovered embezzling his employer's funds. To save him from prison bars she marries the victim, a decent, considerate, and honorable Jewish man. It is not much of a marriage, as she continues to maintain a stable of admirers, and eventually her husband returns to Europe to raise their daughter, in whom she has little interest. The girl grows up to be as compassionate as her father and arrives back in the US to tell her mother that he has been sent to a concentration camp. Davis made much of the illness that then strikes her character—a strain of virulent diphtheria that ravages her features. With so much makeup she managed to look like the prototype of Baby Jane years later. Her old suitors take one look and flee.

Then her ex-husband (Claude Rains) returns, somehow liberated from hell. He is totally blind but still loves her and so she has no need to worry about being hideous.

The young actor who played her brother, Richard Waring, was hailed as an impressive new talent and was signed to have a pivotal role in the next Davis film, *The Corn Is Green*. Sadly Waring was denied his opportunity by the draft board, which insisted on his enlistment no matter how hard the studio pleaded for a deferment. He had to forego the plum part of a young Welsh coalminer in a poverty-stricken valley, who is found to have a gift for words and is coached by a formidable teacher to pass the examination for Oxford. Waring's place was taken by John Dall. *The Corn Is Green* is a stagy film, set in a Welsh village that only Hollywood could visualize, where the mists swirl and miners return from their shift at the pit singing with concert-hall perfection. Davis went to great lengths to look like a frumpy English schoolmarm—overdoing it in the view of the director, Irving Rapper. Her severe appearance aside, it was a part that suited her well, that of a woman who was not going to give up no matter the opposition, and whose manner conveyed such an assertive sense of authority that she was bound to get her own way. At the time of filming she was thirty-six years old. Ethel Barrymore had played the same role on the New York stage at sixty-five.

The time had arrived when she could no longer play younger roles. It was a crucial moment for an actress at her career peak, as Davis was in 1945.

Davis, befurred, for studio publicity shot.

Overleaf: Bette Davis, cover girl in the age of the fan magazine.

SCREEN
Romances

JANUARY
25 CENTS

15
complete screen
romances include

Joan Crawford
and
Clark Gable in
"Forsaking
All Others"

Paul Muni and
Bette Davis in
"Bordertown"

Francis Lederer
and Ginger
Rogers in
"Romance In
Manhattan"

Claude Rains
and Joan
Bennett in
"The Man Who
Reclaimed His
Head"

Bette Davis

Motion Picture

DECEMBER

15¢
FORMERLY
25 CENTS
IN CANADA 20¢

NRA
MEMBER

BETTE DAVIS
by
MARLAND STONE

HUNDREDS OF INTIMATE PICTURES!

Modern Screen

AUGUST
10
CENTS

THE LARGEST
CIRCULATION
OF ANY SCREEN
MAGAZINE

BETTE
DAVIS

JACKIE COOGAN'S
OWN STORY
"I WANT MY MONEY!"

SCREEN
Romances

MAY
25¢
NOW
10¢

BETTE DAVIS

SCREEN
HITS INCLUDE:

JUAREZ—*Starring* **BETTE DAVIS** *and* **PAUL M**
THREE SMART GIRLS GROW UP—*Starring* **DEANNA DU**

movie MIRROR

BETTE DAVIS

JOAN CRAWFORD WITHOUT FRANCHOT TONE
A Revealing Glimpse Into The Future

Picture Play

DECE...

**BETTE DAVIS—
HER RETREAT
FROM FOLLY**

PHOTOPLAY

/6

BEAUTIFUL BRAT *Beginning* the Story of Margaret Sullavan's Rebelliou
Start Now—THE CASE OF THE HOLLYWOOD SCANDAL By Erle Stanley Ga

MOVIES
Hollywood's 4-in-1 magazine
P.D.C.

TELLING ON TYR

HILARIOUS HONEYM

WHAT YOUR LIPS REV

Bette D

December **10** cents
in U.S.A. and Canada

MARKED WOMAN

Warner Bros. (1937)

Credits

Director: Lloyd Bacon
Producer: Lou Edelman
Screenplay: Robert Rosson, Abem Finke;
additional dialogue by Seton I. Miller
Cinematographer: George Barnes

Cast

Bette Davis, Humphrey Bogart, Eduardo Ciannelli, Jane Bryan, Lola Lane, Isabel Jewell, Rosalind Marquis, Mayo Methot, Ben Welden, Henry O'Neill, Allen Jenkins, John Litel, Damian O'Flynn, Robert Strange, Raymond Hatton, William B. Davidson, Frank Faylen, Jack Norton, Kenneth Harlan

Running time: 96 minutes

The second phase of Davis's career—after her court case in London against Warner Bros.—began auspiciously with a tough "torn-from-the-headlines" thriller in the hardnosed manner the studio had made its own. It is based on the real-life infamy of the gangster Lucky Luciano, and his successful prosecution by the attorney Thomas E. Dewey (who later stood as Republican presidential candidate against Truman).

Humphrey Bogart plays the prosecutor, David Graham, Davis plays Mary Dwight, the leader of the "hostesses" (the Hays office was never going to allow the girls to be called prostitutes, as the very notion had now been abolished from the screen) who service the Club Intime, a clip joint—another Hollywood euphemism. The owner is Johnny Vanning (Eduardo Ciannelli), an Italian-accented racketeer, who does not hesitate to maim or murder anyone who crosses him. When a defaulting gambler brought by Mary into the club is killed after failing to meet his losses, Graham has Mary held as a material witness. Vanning goes to trial but she reneges on her word to testify, and without her evidence the case collapses and he is acquitted.

Informal publicity pose, 1937.

Bette Davis, Mayo Methot, Rosalind Marquis, and Humphrey Bogart on the right side of the law.

Right: Davis as clip-joint hostess, Bogart as crusading district attorney.

"I'll get even if I have to crawl back from the grave to do it."

Mary's young college-girl sister (Jane Bryan) has come to New York, and is bewildered by the scene she finds. She is murdered by one of Vanning's men after she resists his charms. Mary threatens to tell all, and is badly beaten and scarred by Vanning's thugs. Davis, remembering the cosmetic neatness of her death's-door makeup in *20,000 Years in Sing Sing*, was appalled by the glamorous job made of her injuries, and went off to be bandaged by a real medical practitioner. The result caused consternation among the gate staff when she drove back to the studio. Wisely, Hal Wallis, the head of production, allowed her to have her way.

Davis's great line in the film is, "I'll get even if I have to crawl back from the grave to do it," and from the hospital bed she is able to conspire with the other girls to bring Vanning to justice. Bogart, playing the man on the right side of the law, is a patient, almost plodding figure. Although he clearly respects Mary's courage, there is no attempt to turn it into a love match—a brave step that might have been different in lesser hands. The memorable ending of the film shows them returning possibly reluctantly but inevitably to their separate worlds, the girls marching defiantly in line to be swallowed by the night.

KID GALAHAD

Warner Bros. (1937)

Credits

Director: Michael Curtiz
Executive producer: Hal B. Wallis
Screenplay: Seton I. Miller; based on a novel by Francis Wallace
Cinematographer: Tony Gaudio

Cast

Edward G. Robinson, Bette Davis, Humphrey Bogart, Wayne Morris, William Haade, Jane Bryan, Harry Carey, Soledad Jiminez, Veda Ann Borg, Ben Welden, Joseph Crehan, Harland Tucker, Frank Faylen, Joyce Compton, Horace McMahon

Running time: 102 minutes

Bette Davis played the part of "Fluff."

Edward G. Robinson plays fight promoter Nick Donati and Davis is his mistress Louise Phillips, known as "Fluff." Donati throws a party, at which a bartender called Ward Guisenberry (Wayne Morris) gets into a spat with the champion Chuck McGraw (William Haade) and floors him with one punch. He is hired as a contender, and Fluff nicknames him Galahad. Humphrey Bogart plays Donati's rival and the champ's manager, Turkey Morgan—this is the kind of film where almost everyone has a nickname—and when the Kid, who trusts Nick implicitly, is ready to face Chuck in the ring, he is unaware that Turkey has done a deal requiring him to lose. The fix is dependent on the fighter following Nick's instructions, which he does. He is savagely pummeled to pulp, much to Fluff's horror, as she has fallen in love with him. Nick suddenly realizes he has a genuine great fighter under his wing, tells him to cut loose and win, leaving Turkey with heavy losses. He goes after Nick with murderous intent and both men shoot each other fatally, leading to a bitter-sweet ending.

Davis did not get on with Robinson, who felt she had been miscast. Michael Curtiz was his usual irascible self, once bawling out a recumbent bit player who was supposed to have been knocked out by Morris for badly faking the fight. The actor did not hear him. He had been knocked senseless.

Connoisseurs of boxing movies are usually approving of *Kid Galahad,* and it certainly has an exceptional cast. Davis does not have much of a chance to shine, although she does at one point sing "The Moon Is in Tears Tonight" in elegant black with sequins. In fact she was dubbed by an unknown singer.

Davis in the back seat with Edward G. Robinson.

Warner Bros. (1937)

Credits

Director: Edmund Goulding
Executive producer: Hal B. Wallis
Screenplay: Edmund Goulding, based in his
original screenplay *The Trespasser*
Cinematographer: Ernest Haller

Cast

Bette Davis, Henry Fonda, Ian Hunter,
Anita Louise, Donald Crisp,
Katherine Alexander, Mary Phillips,
Minor Watson, Ben Welden, Sidney Toler,
Charles Trowbridge, Norman Willis,
Herbert Rawlinson, Rosalind Marquis,
Frank Faylen, Willard Parker

Running time: 93 minutes

Gloria Swanson starred in *The Trespasser* in 1929, written and directed by Edmund Goulding, with the intention of recouping some of the money she had lost on her aborted project with Erich Von Stroheim, *Queen Kelly*. Goulding also wrote and directed the remake eight years later, with Davis as the secretary of an unhappily married lawyer (Ian Hunter). She is the widow of a gangster to whom she was forcibly married while still a teenager. Her boss loves her but has not pressed it, and she elopes with the weakling son (Henry Fonda) of one of his richest clients (Donald Crisp). His tyrannical father tracks them down and calls for an annulment, so she returns to her old job. Later there is a baby to be reckoned with, and Fonda marries again, Hunter dies, Fonda learns that it is his child, Davis learns that Fonda's wife was maimed for life in an automobile accident on their honeymoon … and so it goes on to a conclusion that is pure soap opera. Davis handles what seems to be a sort of *Stella Dallas* role as a fate-ridden heroine with her customary emotional power, but the material is unpromising, even if it turned out to be a successful "women's picture."

Henry Fonda tries persuasion on Davis.

It's Love I'm After

Leslie Howard and Davis as a sparring stage couple.

This is a screwball comedy, performed by expert practitioners who actually elevate the material into something more sophisticated than it would otherwise have been. Leslie Howard and Bette Davis are a celebrated acting couple, adored in Shakespeare by the public, who envisage them as a great romantic match. Offstage they bicker and fight and scream, are jealous of each other's success, and constantly defer their marriage, exasperating all who have to deal with them. Olivia de Havilland is a starstruck socialite who forms a passion for Howard, much to the chagrin of her fiancé (Patric Knowles). He asks Howard to behave badly during the New Year holiday as a guest at her parents' home in Pasadena. Davis is left in a Los Angeles hotel. In spite of his excessive display of boorishness, Olivia de Havilland's infatuation is actually enhanced, leading Davis, in a mood of feminine rationality in dealing with the absurdities of men, to take more drastic measures. She may have felt that it was not her sort of film, but she played the part supremely well.

Warner Bros. (1937)

Credits
Director: Archie Mayo
Executive producer: Hal B. Wallis
Screenplay: Casey Robinson; based on a story by Maurice Hanline
Cinematographer: James Van Trees

Cast
Leslie Howard, Bette Davis, Olivia de Havilland, Patric Knowles, Eric Blore, George Barbier, Spring Byington, Bonita Granville, E. E. Clive, Veda Ann Borg, Valerie Bergere, Georgia Caine, Sarah Edwards, Lionel Belmore, Irving Bacon

Running time: 90 minutes

Warner Bros. (1938)

Credits

Director: William Wyler
Executive producer: Hal B. Wallace
Screenplay: Clement Ripley, Abem Finkel,
John Huston; contributor Robert Bruckner;
based on the play by Owen Davis
Cinematographer: Ernest Haller

Cast

Bette Davis, Henry Fonda, George Brent,
Donald Crisp, Fay Bainter,
Margaret Lindsay, Henry O'Neill,
John Litel, Gordon Oliver, Spring Byington,
Margaret Early, Richard Cromwell,
Theresa Harris, Janet Shaw, Irving Pichel,
Eddie Anderson

Running time: 104 minutes

The monumental success of Margaret Mitchell's epic of the Old South *Gone With the Wind* in 1936 ensured a favorable reception for *Jezebel*, in spite of its earlier incarnation as a play lasting a mere thirty-four performances in New York in 1934. The star was Miriam Hopkins, who had hopes for the film when Warmer Bros. optioned the rights cheaply in 1935. Eventually the project was steered toward Davis and placed in the hands of William Wyler, one of the most accomplished directors in Hollywood. Davis would win her second Oscar for her performance as the willful, headstrong Julia Marsden, a reigning beauty in mid-century New Orleans.

This is the Southland in its full antebellum glory, a romantic lotus land dripping with Spanish moss and magnolia blossom, where the stifling humidity is assuaged by abundant mint juleps. It is a place where chivalry and old-world courtesies prevail, where correctness and etiquette are pre-eminent, and gentlemen's codes of honor require transgressors to defend themselves at dawn, and where contented black slaves gather in front of the plantation house after dinner to serenade the white folk.

Henry Fonda plays Pres Dillard, a young banker who with his advanced idea represents the new South, and urges the burghers of New

Davis reads her cues while a close-up is lined up.

The infamous scarlet dress was actually bronze-colored, which photographed better in black and white.

"This is 1852 dumplin', 1852, not the Dark Ages. Girls don't have to simper around in white just because they're not married."

Orleans to face the fact that the world is changing, that the industrialized North is surpassing the southern states, that King Cotton is being usurped by coal and steel. He is engaged to Julie, but it is a tempestuous match as she feels she comes second to his career, and consequently thinks little of trying to persuade him to abandon a crucial directors' meeting in mid-flight to go with her to the fitting of a new dress. He refuses and she punishes him by determinedly wearing a vivid scarlet creation to the Olympus Ball, at which unmarried young women traditionally wear white. He retaliates by insisting on dancing with her after she realizes the severity of her gaffe and simply wants to be taken home. The other dancers leave the floor in disgust and they end up as a solo act. Her humiliation is completed when he terminates their engagement and leaves New Orleans to work in a northern branch of the family bank. Julie withdraws, hurt and angry with herself.

A year later Pres returns to cope with staff shortages at the bank. Yellow fever has erupted in the city and Julie has retreated to the family plantation, ready to beg his forgiveness. Her reconciliation scene, rehearsed for months, is aborted when she learns that he has brought with him a Yankee wife, Amy (Margaret Lindsay), who finds southern ways quaint and alien. Pres goes to the chaotic city, now under martial law, but succumbs to the fever that is scything through the population. Julie makes a perilous, clandestine journey through the bayou to nurse him, followed by Pres's wife with a governor's pass. Pres must be taken to quarantine on an island of lepers, and Julie pleads with Amy to be allowed to accompany him so that he has a bare hope of survival, promising that she will send him back to her. As she rides away on the plague cart, cradling the comatose Pres, her eyes gleam because she has her man, albeit it at terrible cost.

Julie Marsden is one of Davis's most bravura creations. Her first appearance—riding a spirited horse into the courtyard of the townhouse, dismounting, flicking up the trailing hem of her riding habit with her crop, and striding exceptionally late into her own party in such inappropriate clothing—sets the tone for what is to follow. From her cascading curls and flushed cheeks to her supreme self-confidence, she is a true southerner to the core, but she is also a rebel who wants to challenge hidebound conventions and in that respect Pres is an excellent counterpart. His admiration for the northern way of doing things is regarded as treachery by the old guard, with Buck Cantrell (George Brent), his rival in affection for Julie, as its keenest adherent who at one point accuses Pres of the most heinous of all offenses to the southern cause, that of being an abolitionist.

There is something distasteful about the way black people are presented. The white folk live surrounded by an army of servants who unhesitatingly leap to perform every task, fulfill every whim, no matter how selfish or illogical. Chief among them is Uncle Cato (Lew Paton), the family retainer who is as cherished as a favorite piece of furniture, and knows his place exactly.

Shooting the Olympus Ball sequence on Warner Bros.'s biggest sound stage.

When the liberal-minded Pres suggests that they drink a mint julep together in honor of his bride, Cato mutters that is hardly proper but that he will gladly take it to the pantry to toast the couple in private.

William Wyler was a stately director, renowned for his patience, and the bane of the front office, who watched the mounting production bills and lengthening schedule with horror. He would often require his actors to endure take after take. To carry out the trick with the riding crop lifting her hem, Davis practiced hard to achieve it in one easy movement, but nevertheless found that she had to endure forty-eight takes before the director was satisfied. Puzzled, she asked to sit through the rushes, and finally saw what Wyler had seen. The chosen shot had exactly the casual confidence of a gesture that would establish her role. It had ceased to be a polished, calculated trick, and was something entirely natural to the character.

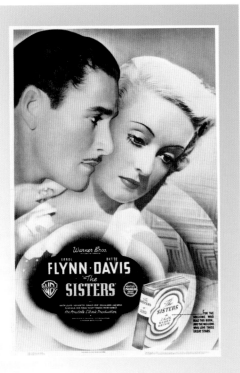

Warner Bros. (1938)

Credits

Director: Anatole Litvak
Producer: Hal B. Wallis, in association with
Favid Ledwis
Screenplay: Milton Krims; based on the
novel by Nyron Brynig
Cinematographer: Tony Gaudio

Cast

Errol Flynn, Bette Davis, Anita Louise,
Ian Hunter, Donald Crisp, Beulah Bondi,
Jane Bryan, Alan Hale, Dick Foran,
Henry Travers, Patric Knowles, Lee Patrick,
Laura Hope Crews, Janet Shaw,
Harry Davenport, Ruth Garland,
John Warburton, Paul Harvey,
Mayo Methot, Irving Bacon, Arthur Hoyt

Running time: 99 minutes

Flynn the feckless husband, Davis the determined wife.

Many of Warner Bros.'s leading men were small, aggressive, and compensating in energy and charisma for their unremarkable looks. Errol Flynn—an enormous star after his 1936 film *Captain Blood*—was the exception. Tall, handsome, graceful, and superbly photogenic, he could overcome his limited acting range by his athletic physicality and prowess as a lover on- and offscreen (particularly the latter, where his excessive private life made him notorious). In spite of their obvious differences in approach—Davis was dedicated and professional, Errol Flynn was devil-may-care and undisciplined—in their first film together they got on well.

Davis plays Louise, the eldest of the three Elliott sisters, belles of the ball at a Montana celebration for the presidential election of Theodore Roosevelt in 1904. She meets Frank (Flynn), a good-looking, charming newspaperman, and runs off with him to San Francisco, where they are quickly married. He is always restless, aspiring to write a novel while scratching a low-paid living as a sportswriter, and seeking solace in alcohol. She finds herself pregnant, loses her baby, then wanders the city seeking her husband, not knowing he is on a boat to the Far East. She is caught in the 1906 earthquake (presented with special effects to rival W.

Davis wore 1900s costumes for *The Sisters*.

S. Van Dyke's 1936 MGM film *San Francisco*), rescued by a neighbor (Lee Patrick), works in a department store where her boss (Ian Hunter) falls in love with her, and goes back to Montana in time for the 1908 Taft election. One of her sisters, Helen (Anita Louise) is now a rich widow, and her other, Grace (Jane Bryan) is having problems with her husband. Her siblings run the interloper out of town. Frank reappears, asking for another chance, and Louise agrees, still in love with him after all she has been through.

The story is novelettish, one of those women's pictures in which a heroine undergoes several fates that strain credulity, but Davis is effective as the put-upon Louise, even seen in one earthquake shot as being in considerable danger of injury and without sign of a stunt double. Davis always felt that she had somehow incurred Anatole Litvak's animosity, and this was his revenge. It is much more likely that he had seen the possibilities of a great shot.

DARK VICTORY

Warner-First National (1939)

Credits

Director: Edmund Goulding
Producers: David L. Lewis, Hal B. Wallis
Screenwriters: George Emerson Brewer, Jr.,
Bertram Bloch (play), Casey Robinson
Cinematographer: Ernest Haller

Cast

Bette Davis, George Brent,
Humphrey Bogart, Geraldine Fitzgerald,
Ronald Reagan, Henry Travers,
Cora Witherspoon, Dorothy Peterson

Running time: 104 minutes

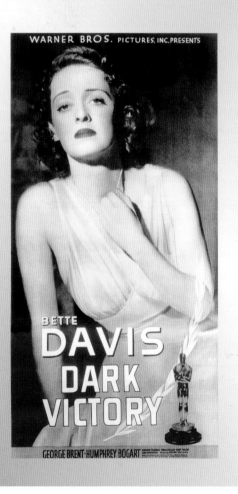

Davis with Humphrey Bogart as her Irish stable manager.

A curious phenomenon of the Depression years was the propensity of the movie-going masses to lap up unsatirical depictions of the domestic life of the mega-rich who, as far as they were concerned, might have existed on another planet. Davis plays a pampered young heiress whose central passions are horses on the Long Island family acres, shopping for the latest fashions, and the eternal cocktail circuit. Her hedonistic lifestyle is clouded by the onset of inexplicable headaches and double vision, and she is persuaded to be examined by a smooth but skilled specialist (George Brent). She has a brain tumor, but he removes it and life resumes … except that she discovers the secret the medical people have dared not tell her: surgery has come too late and she has only a few months to live. At only twenty-three, such a revelation is heartbreaking, and brings a radical rethink to her existence. Having fallen in love with her doctor, she marries and moves to a quiet, idyllic country home, where eventually she expires gracefully, makeup and beauty intact, in a misty finale. Her last words to her husband as he leaves the house—unaware that her last moments are nigh—are: "Nothing can hurt us now. What we have can't

"I think I'll have a large dose of prognosis negative."

be destroyed. That's our victory—our victory over the dark. It is a victory because we're not afraid."

Inevitably, such mind-numbing sentimentality deeply affected audiences. It was seen as a superior "women's weepy," became an enormous box-office success, and only failed to win Oscars because it was the year of *Gone With the Wind.* Davis excelled in the role, largely because she played it in a completely uncompromising way, not allowing the screenplay's encouraging tendencies to self-pitying indulgence to impede her performance.

Humphrey Bogart appears in a strange role as an Irish trainer and stable manager who has a brief symbiotic moment with her, as if to demon-

strate that a flighty socialite can still make sympathetic contact with the common herd. Ronald Reagan also breezes in as a party-going idler whose trivial values soon oust him from the direction the remainder of her life will take. Geraldine Fitzgerald—beautiful in her Hollywood debut—plays the sympathetic friend and confidante, with the unspoken hint that Davis's widower will soon find an accommodating haven in his grief.

This is a prime example of the polished commercial studio picture of the 1930s at its professional best, one that delivered excellent box-office results, enhancing the careers of those concerned.

JACK WARNER

Bette Davis with Jack L. Warner in 1945.

With his brothers Harry, Albert, and Sam, Jack Warner (1892–1978) founded Warner Bros. Pictures in 1923, and it was he who shrewdly ran the studio and controlled production until it was sold to Seven Arts in 1967. Under his rule the studio had made a dog (Rin Tin Tin) a world star in the 1920s, had successfully launched sound films with Al Jolson and *The Jazz Singer*, and had created a raft of tough male stars, including James Cagney, Humphrey Bogart, Edward G. Robinson, and Paul Muni. The hallmark of Warner Bros. output was its close contact with public taste, and its addressing of social-issue topics in hard times when most other studios only focused on escapist entertainment.

Jack Warner hired Bette Davis after her unpromising debut at Universal, with the enthusiastic approval of George Arliss, but initially failed to give her proper opportunities. After her unsuccessful lawsuit she achieved rapprochement and better roles, winning Oscars for *Dangerous* and *Jezebel,* and becoming the highest-paid actress in Hollywood. She and Jack Warner were locked in a volatile professional relationship for years, their many conflicts tempered by a mutual acknowledgment of their capabilities. Her films always made money for Warner until *Deception* in 1946, and their ways parted with *Beyond the Forest* three years later, after eighteen years.

JUAREZ

Warner Bros. (1939)

Credits

Director: William Dieterle
Producer: Hal B. Wallis, in association with
Henry Blanke
Screenplay: John Huston, Aeneas
MacKenzie, Wolfgang Reinhardt; partly
based on the play *Juarez and Maximilian*
by Franz Werfel, and a book *The Phantom
Crown* by Bertita Harding
Cinematographer: Tony Gaudio

Cast

Paul Muni, Bette Davis, Brian Aherne,
Claude Rains, John Garfield, Donald Crisp,
Joseph Calleia, Gale Sondergaard, Gilbert
Roland, Henry O'Neill, Harry Davenport,
Louis Calhern, Walter Kingsford,
Georgia Caine, Montagu Love, John Miljan,
Vladimir Sokoloff, Irving Pichel,
Pewdro de Cordoba, Gilbert Emory,
Monte Blue, Manuel Diaz, Hugh Sothern,
Mickey Kuhn

Running time: 125 minutes

Juarez was made in the period before World War II, when the Hays Office refused to allow any criticism of Nazi Germany lest it upset American trade prospects there. Ingeniously, Warner Bros. resorted to historical subjects as a way of making critical comment that would satisfy MPAA strictures. *Juarez* was intended to counter fascist influence in Latin America, a cause for concern in the State Department, and was one of the most elaborate productions of its day, requiring thousands of drawings and blueprints to make the settings look as authentic as possible.

The film was a vehicle for Paul Muni as the Zapotec Indian Benito Juarez, who is elected president of Mexico and advocates democracy for the people against the power of Napoleon III of France (Claude Rains). In the ensuing conflict, Maximilian von Hapsburg (Brian Aherne), the liberal archduke of

Davis as Empress Carlotta, Brian Aherne as
Emperor Maximilian.

Davis as Carlotta loses her mind when she realizes her husband is doomed.

Right: Costumed by Orry-Kelly to look like the nineteenth-century Empress of Mexico.

Austria is appointed emperor, and finds himself in the position of defending the indefensible when required to sign edicts seizing land from the poor. The situation is made worse for him because the US, under President Lincoln, is financing Juarez in accordance with the Monroe doctrine. Maximilian's wife Carlotta (Davis) goes to France to plead with Napoleon III to remove his troops, but all help is refused. Knowing that her husband is doomed, she loses her reason. In Mexico Maximilian is seized and executed. Belatedly Juarez appreciates that he has been killed unjustly.

Davis's part is relatively small but registers an impact in what is in general a tiring plot and not the most effective of Muni performances, weighted as he is by extensive latex makeup. Her mad scenes are vivid, and are orchestrated to a climax where they are intercut with her husband's death thousands of miles away. The Max and Carlotta story that could have been was consigned to the cutting-room floor, as the emphasis misguidedly swung toward Muni to make it more of a history lesson than a great romance.

THE OLD MAID

Warner Bros. (1939)

Credits

Director: Edmund Goulding
Producer: Hal B. Wallis, in association with Henry Blanke
Screenplay: Casey Robinson; based on the play by Zöe Atkins, adapted from the novel by Edith Wharton
Cinematographer: Tony Gaudio

Cast

Bette Davis, Miriam Hopkins, George Brent, Donald Crisp, Jane Bryan, Louise Fazenda, James Stephenson, Jerome Cowan, William Lundigan, Rand Brooks, Cecelia Loftus, Janet Shaw, DeWolf Hopper

Running time: 95 minutes

BETTE DAVIS MIRIAM HOPKINS
The Old Maid
George BRENT

presented by Warner Bros.

Philadelphia 1861. On the morning of Delia's (Miriam Hopkins) marriage to the socially desirable Joe (Jerome Cowan), her long-term, feckless, but attractive fiancé Clem (George Brent) turns up after two years without contact. Horribly torn, Delia asks her cousin Charlotte (Davis) to meet him at the railroad depot and break the news that he has been jilted. Charlotte and Clem fall in love and agree to marry after his return from the Civil War. He is killed at Vicksburg, and Charlotte, with the conspiratorial assistance of the family doctor (Donald Crisp), becomes the mother of a little girl. She starts a nursery for war orphans. On her own wedding day to Joe's brother Jim (James Stephenson) she confesses that one of the children, little Clementina, is hers. The happily married yet mean-spirited Delia contends that the wedding cannot take place, and tells Jim that Charlotte has a terminal illness and can never bear children. In compassion, he releases Charlotte. Delia's Joe dies after a riding accident, and Charlotte learns of her falsehood. Nevertheless she and Tina will live under the same roof, as Delia promises to raise the girl alongside her own children. However, the little girl calls Delia "mommy" and her real mother "Aunt Charlotte."

The years pass, and Tina grows into vivacious young womanhood while Charlotte has become a sour, thin-lipped spinster with a frumpy hairdo. Delia, the surrogate mom, is relaxed, but "Aunt" Charlotte is a disciplinarian, constantly scolding and admonishing the girl for her bubbly behavior. Tina loves Delia and detests Charlotte as a shriveled, bitter, miserable old maid. Inevitably she falls in love and wants to marry into a good family, but Charlotte knows that it cannot happen because the boy's people will never accept his union with a penniless foundling. Delia formally adopts Tina, giving her a name and inheritance so that she can marry.

The mores of nineteenth-century society regarded a woman who bore a child out of wedlock as irredeemably beyond the pale, and the unfortunate infant would carry the stigma of illegitimacy throughout life. Extreme it may have been, but nevertheless it was a commonplace of social conduct, hence the lengths to which Charlotte goes to conceal Tina's parentage. If he had been given the facts it is likely that Jim would have forgiven his bride and continued the stratagem by adopting Tina after their marriage, but Delia, motivated by an irrational jealousy that Charlotte had somehow taken Clem from her, destroys her impending marriage at the last moment and condemns her to spinsterhood.

Hopkins and Davis were rivals, and detested each other in real life. Their co-stardom amounted to a duel of acrimonious heavyweights. The acting mettle of each was severely tested, and in the contest Davis was the outstanding winner. Hopkins played Delia as shallow and petty, fluttering her eyelashes and shaking her curls like an unsubtle *ingénue* even as the years advance. Davis, on the other hand, gives appropriate shading to every stage of Charlotte's development, from youthful exuberance to the final scene of reconciliation, when the wrong she has endured no longer has relevance. Her power to convey emotion by the subtlest of glances, the tilt of her head, the angle of her hands, the stiffness of her carriage, was much in evidence, leaving no doubt as to which of them dominated the screen. Even her makeup, in which she ages more noticeably than her rival, was simple, with no prosthetics or heavy lining, just a pale wash that drained her face and gave it a harsh pallor under a cushion of gray hair.

Gowned for the wedding that never was, the bride "released" from her vows.

THE PRIVATE LIVES OF ELIZABETH AND ESSEX

Warner Bros. (1939)

Credits

Director: Michael Curtiz
Producer: Hal B. Wallis, in association with Robert Lord
Screenplay: Norman Reilly Raine, Aeneas MacKenzie; based on the play *Elizabeth the Queen* by Maxwell Anderson
Cinematographer: Sol Polito

Cast

Bette Davis, Errol Flynn, Olivia de Havilland, Donald Crisp, Vincent Price, Alan Hale, Henry Stephenson, Henry Daniell, Leo G. Carroll, Nanette Fabares (later Fabray), Rosella Towne, Maris Wrixon, Ralph Forbes, Robert Warwick, John Sutton, Guy Bellis, Doris Lloyd, Forrester Harvey

Technicolor

Running time:105 minutes

Above: Errol Flynn, Davis as Elizabeth, and dialogue director Stanley Logan.

Right: Davis resisted Flynn's sexual appetite and worried about his acting.

Bette Davis's first film in color is a Tudor extravaganza in which she plays Queen Elizabeth, by then a sexagenarian, dallying with her favorite, the swashbuckling, seafaring adventurer Robert Deveraux, Earl of Essex (Errol Flynn). The role was a considerable challenge for her at the age of thirty, requiring makeup that removed her eyebrows and shaved back her hairline to give her a bulging forehead. Weighted by Orry-Kelly's intricately brocaded dresses, huge and elaborate ruffs, and strands of heavy jewelry, her range of movement was restricted, requiring her to command regal authority by bearing and posture alone. She would have liked Laurence Olivier to play Essex, feeling that Flynn was far too lightweight even to speak Maxwell Anderson's poetic lines with conviction, but he was busy elsewhere, making *Wuthering Heights* for William Wyler.

Essex has returned a hero of Cadiz, where he won a famous sea victory over the Spanish. However, the queen is displeased because she feels he has put personal glory ahead of national interest. In any case, her

A triumph of costuming in the most sumptuous of Warner's "Merrie England" pictures.

court swarms with enemies who resent his position. One, Sir Walter Raleigh (Vincent Price) is promoted above him, and Essex goes off in dudgeon to his country retreat, vowing not to return until the queen apologizes. She does, but is unable to prevent him taking a force to Ireland to fight a rebellion led by the Earl of Tyrone (Alan Hale), who outsmarts him. Essex cannot understand why his letters asking for assistance have been ignored by the queen, not realizing that they

have been intercepted by her lady-in-waiting Lady Penelope (Olivia de Havilland) on the instructions of Francis Bacon (Donald Crisp). On his return to London, the furious Essex seizes the palace but is mollified when Elizabeth appears to concede. As soon as his troops stand down, though, she has him consigned to the Tower for treason. She offers to share the throne with him, but he refuses—it is all or nothing—and stands by tearfully as she allows him to go to the executioner's block.

Anton Grot's art direction was magnificently imaginative, with vast, sparsely furnished sets that gave an impression of space and allowed the elaborate costumes to be properly displayed. Particularly striking was the Throne Chamber at the Tower of London, with its surprising concealed staircase in the center of the floor, which opened to give direct access to the dungeon of the condemned below. The score by Erich Wolfgang Korngold was as rich and exciting as those he had supplied for other Flynn films, including *Captain Blood* and *The Adventures of Robin Hood*.

The Private Lives of Elizabeth and Essex (the title was changed from *Elizabeth the Queen* in order to give Flynn's role more prominence) fits into a genre of 1930s Warner Bros. films that has been defined by the critic Nick Roddick as "Merrie England," historical pageants of medieval and Tudor times, which provided opportunities for spectacle, action, and sumptuous settings to gratify audiences who at the same time may have felt that they were soaking up a little culture and educational knowledge, albeit carefully distilled by Hollywood.

Flynn's dashing demeanor contrasted with Davis's starchy monarch.

Davis would play the first Queen Elizabeth again in 1955, when she was sixteen years older but the character twelve years younger. If there was a challenge to be faced she invariably made a point of facing it. When filming *Elizabeth and Essex* she was delighted when Charles Laughton, who had played Elizabeth's father in *The Private Life of Henry VII,* visited the set.

Although she never had an opportunity to work with him, she gleaned a valuable nugget of advice, which she imparted to her biographer Charlotte Chandler: "Never not dare to hang yourself. That's the only way you can grow in your profession. You must continually attempt things that you think are beyond you, or you get into a complete rut."

"He was just beautiful ... Errol. He himself openly said I don't know really anything about acting, and I admire his honesty because he's absolutely right."

ALL THIS, AND HEAVEN TOO

Boyer as the tormented Duc, Davis as the gentle governess.

Warner Bros. (1940)

Credits
Director: Anatole Litvak
Producer: Hal B. Wallis, in association with David Lewis
Screenplay: Casey Robinson; based on the novel by Rachel Lyman Field
Cinematographer: Ernest Haller

Cast
Bette Davis, Charles Boyer, Jeffrey Lynn, Barbara O'Neill, Virginia Weidler, Helen Westley, Walter Hampden, Henry Daniell, Harry Davenport, George Coulouris, Montagu Love, Janet Beecher, June Lockhart, Ann Todd, Richard Nichols, Fritz Leiber, Ian Keith, Sibyl Harris, Mary Anderson, Edward Fielding, Ann Gillis, Peggy Stewart, Victor Killian, Mrs. Gardner Crane

Running time: 143 minutes

The novelist Rachel Field was descended from the central figure in this reality-based account of a mid-nineteenth-century scandal in France. Davis plays Henriette Deluzy Desportes, hired as governess to the four children of the Duc and Duchesse de Praslin (Charles Boyer and Barbara O'Neill). While Henriette proves exemplary in her duties, the Duchesse, a dark, statuesque Corsican beauty, is consumed with irrational jealousy, accusing her of alienating the children from her and stealing her husband's affections. The mother's shortcomings are highlighted when against all advice she insists on taking the youngest, a four-year-old boy who has a chill, out in poor weather. He contracts diphtheria, and his life is saved by Henriette's patient nursing.

Eventually the Duchesse forces Henriette's resignation, after spies within the home and gossipmongers without falsely allege that she has been having an affair with the Duc, and she retreats with the promise that she will at least be given a letter of commendation. Unknown to the Duc, his wife reneges and Henriette is forced into poverty. When he finds out and confronts his wife, her triumphant and callous gloating inflames him into killing her. Henriette is arrested and imprisoned as an accomplice, but the Duc because of his rank is held in his home. After his friend King Louis Philippe is forced to sign a trial order, the Duc takes poison and Henriette is acquitted for lack of evidence. She makes her way to the US, where a kind young minister, Rachel Field's great uncle, the Rev. Henry Field (Jeffrey Lynn) has arranged a teaching post in a girls' school. The story is told in flashback to a classroom of initially hostile girls who have discovered she has been in prison, but who are overwhelmingly won over after her tale is told.

Although Davis acknowledged Litvak's directorial skill, she felt the fundamental flaw in this lengthy and ambitious film (according to Warner Bros., with more sets than in *Gone with the Wind*) was that the Duchesse should be portrayed as a fastidious, groomed beauty rather than as an unsavory harridan. Davis, drably dressed, with an unflattering and severe hairstyle, is outclassed by the chic Duchesse and her elegant couture. A tall woman, Barbara O'Neill towers over Davis in their scenes together, emphasizing the employee's petite size. Her obsessive rants against her children's governess do not convince, and Davis felt that the Duchesse should have been physically repellent rather than a good-looking neurotic. The motivation for her murder, she felt, was not convincing, but she also thought that, in spite of the novelist's contention that the attraction never went beyond expressions of friendship, the Duc and Henriette had been lovers and that she was guilty of complicity.

Charles Boyer, a popular romantic actor, never actually plays a love scene here, but his performance is compellingly passionate nonetheless. There is about the Duc an entirely appropriate air of worry and foreboding, and it is perhaps pertinent to refer to Boyer's acute anxiety at the time of filming, in the spring of 1940, when his beloved homeland of France was being ravaged by Hitler's Nazi hordes. All he could do was to listen to broadcast communiqués between takes, until Anatole Litvak had the radio removed because it was interfering with his concentration.

Davis does her best with a role that is extraordinarily virtuous, and Henriette is drawn as a flawless, irreproachable character who never reacts in anger, even when tormented beyond normal endurance. Even so, her saintliness is eclipsed by that of the Rev. Field, who has met her only once before, fleetingly on a ferryboat crossing the English Channel. As

A studio portrait while Davis was making *All This, and Heaven Too*.

"Happiness isn't a little cake which we can cut up to fill our appetites."

her Samaritan he rescues her from a grim future after her release, arranges her passage to America and employment as a teacher in a good school, then dedicates the rest of his life to her.

WILLIAM WYLER

Davis and Wyler, 1940.

Willi Weiler was born in Mulhouse, Alsace, in 1902 when the region was part of the German Empire. He moved to New York in 1921, where he worked as a messenger boy for Universal. He went to Los Angeles two years later, and by 1925 was the youngest director on the Universal lot, churning out innumerable westerns and learning his craft. As William Wyler he was naturalized in 1928, and talking pictures established him as one of Hollywood's finest directors.

Davis first met Wyler briefly and disastrously in 1931 when he was casting *A House Divided*, but seven years later, when she had become a leading star, she took on the main role in his *Jezebel*, winning her second Best Actress Oscar. Wyler had been married to the actress Margaret Sullavan

Wyler, seated, supervises the dress-fitting sequence in *Jezebel*.

from 1934 to 1936, but he and Davis embarked on an intense affair, and he exerted a huge influence on her emotional and professional life.

Their amorous liaison ended with the completion of the film and he married Margaret Tallichet, eventually having four children. Wyler made two more films with Davis, *The Letter* and *The Little Foxes*, for which Warner Bros. loaned her to Samuel Goldwyn, the studio with which he was associated for many of his great successes, including the Oscar-winning *The Best Years of Our Lives*.

Wyler's films won more Oscars for performers than those of any other Hollywood director, including Greer Garson for *Mrs. Miniver*, Audrey Hepburn for *Roman Holiday*, Olivia de Havilland for *The Heiress* and Barbra Streisand for *Funny Girl*. He was Best Director three times—for *Mrs. Miniver*, *The Best Years of Our Lives*, and *Ben-Hur* ("It took a Jew to make a really good movie about Christ"), all of which were also Best Films. In World War II he flew combat missions with the USAAF and suffered loss of hearing in one ear. His documentary *The Memphis Belle: a Story of a Flying Fortress* was the outcome. Wyler died in 1981, his greatness ranking alongside that of Griffith and Ford.

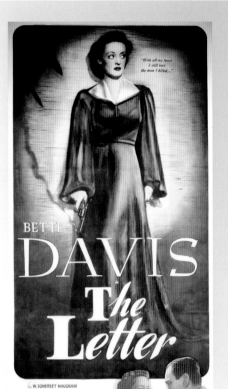

Warner Bros. (1940)

Credits

Director: William Wyler
Producer: Hal B. Wallis
**Screenplay: Howard Koch; adapted from
the play by W. Somerset Maugham**
Cinematographer: Tony Gaudio

Cast

**Bette Davis, Herbert Marshall, James
Stephenson, Frieda Inescourt, Gale
Sondergaard, Bruce Lester, Elizabeth Earl,
Doris Lloyd, Sen Yung, Willie Fung, Tetsu
Konai, Roland Got, Otto Hahn, Pete
Katchenaro, David Newell, Ottola Nesmith,
Lillian Kemble-Cooper**

Running time: 95 minutes

In a celebrated atmospheric opening sequence, the moon is seen against scudding clouds and a rubber tree oozes its sap into little cups attached to the bark. The camera tracks through the open shelters where plantation workers slumber in hammocks. A gunshot is heard in the bungalow across the compound. A white man appears in the doorway and staggers to the verandah steps. A woman shoots him from behind. In a closer shot she is revealed to be the planter's wife Leslie Crosbie, played by Davis, and she empties her revolver into what is now a recumbent corpse. Later she recalls how the man had called uninvited and made sordid advances, forcing her to defend herself with the gun her husband had thoughtfully provided for her protection when he was away shipping rubber.

Somerset Maugham's *The Letter,* a story of adultery, deceit, and murder in colonial Singapore, was staged in 1927 with Gladys Cooper in the lead, and filmed in 1929 with Jeanne Eagels. By the time of William Wyler's version, the Production Code was rigidly enforced, transforming the victim's Chinese mistress into a formidably elegant Eurasian wife, and ensuring that even if a murderess is acquitted, eventual justice prevails.

Herbert Marshall who had played the lover in the Eagels film here plays the role of the husband Robert, a decent, hardworking man

The dramatic opening killing in *The Letter.*

Davis and Herbert Marshall as her foolish, trusting husband.

devoted to his wife and completely taken in by her version of events. The superior male role, that of the defense lawyer Howard Joyce, is played by James Stephenson. Never totally convinced by her explanation, his misgivings are confirmed when his sycophantic Chinese assistant (Sen Yung) tells him that a letter written by Leslie on the day of the killing proves that she is lying. It is now in the possession of the victim's widow (Gale Sondergaard) and can be bought for $10,000.

In prison, Leslie confesses that the letter is genuine and that the man had been her lover for years, an affair discreetly conducted during her husband's long absences. The sparking point had been his marrying the Eurasian woman. She begs her attorney to buy and suppress the letter so that she will not hang, but he refuses, arguing that his professional duty to the law outweighs friendship. He later tells Robert about the letter, without revealing its true meaning, but says that

it would be sufficient in court to secure her conviction. Robert instructs him to buy it "at any price" so that it will not fall into the hands of the prosecution. Reluctantly, the evidence is suppressed, and Joyce is able to achieve an acquittal, after which Robert plans to move from Singapore to Sumatra, buying his own plantation so that he and Leslie can begin life anew, unaware that his life savings have been used to save her neck.

During the celebration party Leslie finally tells Robert the truth, but he tries to forgive her and begs for her love. She breaks off the embrace and says that she is unable to go on with a pretense. He withdraws and she walks out into the moonlight. Waiting for her is the widow with a dagger. The deed is accomplished while party noises and dance music waft from the house into the evening air.

In the second of the three films that William Wyler made with her, Davis gives one of her finest and most restrained performances, and her

Davis, magnificent as cool, mendacious, manipulative Leslie Crosbie.

British accent is completely convincing. Her Leslie is cool, poised, and confident as she deceives her questioners after the murder, even preparing a meal before she accompanies them to town to be charged. She diffuses her tension by quietly crocheting a lace bedcover, donning unglamorous spectacles to concentrate on the detail. One of the conditions imposed by the owner of the letter is that she has to accompany her lawyer to a den in Chinatown to retrieve it, a setting modified by the Breen office from the Chinese brothel in the Eagels film, but nevertheless a sinister, alienating slice of the Orient, laced with opium fumes and shadowy onlookers, glass decorations tinkling in the breeze of a hastily opened window. Sondergaard appears through a

bead curtain and stands motionless, insisting that the white woman approach her. She drops the letter on the floor, necessitating Leslie to kneel before her to retrieve it, as though an old culture is triumphing over the interloper.

This is a Singapore that no longer exists—where British expatriates exert effortless superiority, referring to the local inhabitants as "natives," the workers as "boys." Even when charged, Leslie is treated with careful deference, with a prison matron fawning over her as though she is a royal visitor. In the courtroom all faces are white, with wigs and gowns worn by judge and barristers. Were it not for the ceiling fans and linen suits it could have been London's Old Bailey. Her acquittal is quickly reached with heartfelt relief all round. This is a world that Somerset Maugham understood better than anybody.

Wyler's direction is at its most accomplished, often using long, flowing takes, and if Warner Bros. were worried that he should repeat the budget overruns and schedule slippages of *Jezebel* he confounded them by finishing not only under budget, but only three days past the due date. The film, with its evocative Max Steiner score, the crisp yet delicate lighting of Tony Gaudio, and the elegant gowns of Orry-Kelly, firmly represents the classic high-style period of Warner Bros.

Wyler fretted about the ending, and even prepared an alternative version that eliminated the final scene between Robert and Leslie. If that had prevailed it would have robbed filmgoers of one of the most famous lines uttered by Davis throughout her career: "With all my heart I still love the man I killed."

THE GREAT LIE

Uneasy triangle: Davis, George Brent, and Mary Astor.

The opening bars of Tchaikovsky's Piano Concerto No. 1 replace the familiar Warner Bros. fanfare, and after the opening credits a disgruntled maid contemplates a luxurious Manhattan apartment that has been soundly trashed after a prolonged binge. It belongs to Sandra Kovak (Mary Astor), a world-famous concert pianist, now unconscious in the bedroom. A playboy with a passion for flying, Pete Van Allen (George Brent), is up and about, having married her a few days earlier. He learns that the marriage is invalid as she had not finalized a divorce in time, and a new date is set. In the interim he takes off in his light plane to a farm in Maryland where his former fiancée, Maggie Patterson (Davis), is distraught because she thought she was still engaged to him. They both realize they have made a mistake, and are reunited while Sandra gets on with her scintillating career.

Post-nuptial bliss at the farm is curtailed when, at Maggie's instigation, Pete accepts an aviation job from Washington that involves piloting a mission to Brazil. His plane goes down somewhere in the Amazon rainforest and a search for survivors is fruitless. Sandra tells Maggie that

Warner Bros. (1941)

Credits
Director: Edmund Goulding
Producer: Hal B. Wallis, in association with Henry Blanke
Screenplay: Lenore Coffee; based on the novel *January Heights* by Polan Banks
Cinematographer: Tony Gaudio

Cast
Bette Davis, George Brent, Mary Astor, Lucile Watson, Hattie McDaniel, Grant Mitchell, Jerome Cowan, Sam McDaniel, Thurston Hall, Russell Hicks, Charles Trowbridge, Virginia Brissac, Olin Howland, J. Farrell MacDonald, Doris Lloyd, Addison Richards, Georgia Caine, Alphonse Martell

Running time: 102 minutes

Wardrobe test shot for Davis in *The Great Lie*.

she is carrying Pete's child. The women have little in common except their grief, but Maggie suggests that they move to a remote place so that Sandra can have the baby, which Maggie will then raise as her own. In return she will share Pete's inheritance with the pregnant woman. They depart to an isolated, desolate Arizona, and spend months on their own until the delivery. Maggie fiercely ensures throughout that Sandra sticks to a Spartan regime. Maggie then returns to Maryland with Pete Jr. who is universally hailed as her son. Then his father is found alive, and returns, slightly gray about the temples, to pick up the threads of his life. A brief idyll is shredded when Sandra appears intent on taking the child, claiming that the deal was only feasible if Pete had been dead. Maggie has to decide how she is going to deal with her great lie.

Mary Astor has the sharp super-bitch role, with the elegant dresses, sophisticated mien, and quick retorts, while Davis is a wholesome country-woman, given to mooching around her rural Maryland home in jodhpurs, and who looks dowdy in a metropolitan setting. The juxtaposition works, but the plot is full of credulity-straining holes. How come the newspapers have not latched on to the marriage that never was? How could Sandra, in the face of her fans, the media, and the unfortunate concertgoers who have bought advance tickets, suddenly disappear without explanation for several months in the midst of an intense musical career? And why should money have been a factor in the deal when she is meant to be one of the best-paid women in America? Was Arizona so primitive in 1941 that a birth goes unregistered and a certificate is not issued even when professionals—doctor and midwife—are in attendance? What exactly had Pete been doing in Brazil all the months he was missing? Why are the legal complications of a man who has risen from the dead, such as wills, probate, and taxes not even given a mention, even though his reappearance has made headlines?

The fact is that it is a lazily constructed work which, had lesser performers than Astor and Davis been involved, would probably have been quickly forgotten. Hattie McDaniel and her brother, Sam McDaniel, as Maggie's retainers, are dreadful racial stereotypes, the first a devoted Aunt Jemima-like housekeeper, the other a servile, ingratiating handyman at everyone's beck and call. As great kitsch *The Great Lie* has the redeeming asset of being highly entertaining, but without profundity.

Outdoor portrait of Davis, more elegant than she appears in *The Great Lie*.

The Bride Came C.O.D.

Warner Bros. (1941)

Credits

Director: William Keighley
Producer: Hal B. Wallis, in association with
William Cagney
Screenplay: Julius and Philip Epstein;
based on a story by Kenneth Earl and
M. M. Musselman
Cinematographer: Ernest Haller

Cast

James Cagney, Bette Davis, Stuart Erwin,
Jack Carson, George Tobias,
Eugene Pallette, Harry Davenport,
William Frawley, Edward Brophy,
Harry Holman, Chick Chandler,
Keith Douglas, Herbert Anderson,
Creighton Hale, Frank Mayo,
DeWolf Hopper, Jack Mower,
William Newell

Running time: 92 minutes

James Cagney as indigent aviator, Davis as abducted heiress.

James Cagney and Bette Davis were teamed for this screwball farce, which echoed *It Happened One Night* but fell a long way short of it. She is the inevitable madcap heiress who elopes with a bandleader (Jack Carson) in a plane chartered from an aviator (James Cagney) on the edge of bankruptcy. Her father (the obese and adenoidal Eugene Pallette, so brilliant in similar roles in *My Man Godfrey* and *The Lady Eve*, which are in a different league of screwball) hires him to deliver her in an unmarried condition to his ranch in Texas, but she thinks she is being kidnapped and offers a counter deal to take her back to Los Angeles. The pilot refuses as he regards her father's offer as more likely, and after a struggle he has to make a forced landing in the desert.

Too often Davis lands on spiky cacti, to be tended by Cagney.

The sole resident of a ghost town, an old-timer (Harry Davenport), believes her kidnap yarn, locks up Cagney, and installs her in the abandoned town hotel. Her prospective bridegroom arrives with a Nevada justice of the peace, who marries them. Then her father arrives, and refuses to pay Cagney the money because he has not delivered. It is revealed that they were really in California so the marriage is not legal. Cagney marries Davis, making sure she appreciates that her father's wealth is the deciding factor, in case she should think he has gone sentimental.

A running gag in the film has Davis constantly landing on prickly cacti, usually requiring the delicate removal of sharp spikes from her rear quarters. She also spends an unconscionable amount of time teetering around the searing desert in a fur-trimmed coat. Clearly the film was intended as a change of pace from her customary heavy dramatics, but while she and Cagney are watchable, comedy was not their *métier*.

Right: Cagney hoists Davis in screwball tradition.

Below: Davis taking a break during filming.

Regina Giddens, one of Davis's most memorable fierce women.

Teresa Wright, William Wyler, and Davis discuss a scene.

RKO (1941)

Credits

Director: William Wyler
Producer: Samuel Goldwyn
Screenplay: Lillian Hellman, based on her
stage play; additional scenes and dialogue
by Arthur Kober, Dorothy Parker,
and Alan Campbell
Cinematographer: Gregg Toland

Cast

Bette Davis, Herbert Marshall,
Teresa Wright, Richard Carlson,
Patricia Collinge, Dan Duryea,
Charles Dingle, Carl Benton Reid,
Jessie Grayson, John Marriott,
Russell Hicks, Lucien Littlefield,
Virginia Brissac

Running time: 116 minutes

Lillian Hellman's study of familial greed in a southern town at the turn of the century transferred to the screen with Bette Davis in the role of Regina Giddens, which Tallulah Bankhead had played on Broadway in 1939.

Regina and her two brothers are the town's leading citizens, and because of their aggressive attitudes the largely black workforce exists on one of the lowest average wages in America. This is reason enough for a Chicago industrialist to go into partnership to build a new cotton mill that will leave the family rolling in obscene wealth. The two brothers, Ben (Charles Dingle) and Oscar (Carl Benton Reid) must each put up $75,000, and a third tranche is expected from Regina, but her ailing, disillusioned husband Horace (Herbert Marshall), who controls their finances, refuses to participate.

At his father's instigation, Oscar's shiftless son Leo (Dan Duryea) steals an appropriate number of bonds from Horace's deposit box at the bank where he works. Horace finds out and tells Regina that he will treat it as a loan to be repaid quickly so that she will not benefit from the larceny. She allows him to have a fatal heart attack without lifting a finger to help, and tells her brothers she wants seventy-five percent of the undertaking, or else they will go to jail. Her daughter Alexandra (Teresa Wright), earmarked by Regina to marry Leo, and who deeply loved her father, overhears and resolves to sever all association with her mother, taking off into a wet night with David (Richard Carlson), an ambitious young local newspaper editor, knowing that their union was her father's last wish.

Regina Giddens is one of Davis's great screen monsters: a glacial, callous, heartless harpy whose concern for the wellbeing of others is almost entirely absent. Bankhead had imbued her with a certain amount of southern charm, but Davis makes no concessions, and presents a figure so formidable that she makes her brothers seem like adolescent weaklings. In the climactic scene, the husband Horace has a heart attack while she sits entirely still, watching him grope for his medicine, break the bottle, beg for another from upstairs, and finally realize that she is never going to help him. Only when he completely collapses on the staircase does she spring to life and call for help, gambling that by then he is beyond recovery.

At the end of the film Regina has won the riches she sought but has lost the respect of everyone who knows her and will face a friendless, lonely future. She stares from an upstairs window as her daughter departs, and the impact of her Pyrrhic victory sinks in. Given the strictness of the Production Code at the time it is remarkable that the storyline was not changed and that she is not facing a charge of murder, but the fact that the stage version was still familiar

was apparently a deciding factor to leave it unchanged. It is the last of the three films that Davis made under the direction of William Wyler, and what had earlier been a positive relationship had by then deteriorated, even though both had initially been eager that she play the part. Samuel Goldwyn had acquired her services from Warner Bros. under a complex deal that in part included his loan to them of Gary Cooper to play *Sergeant York*.

Four members of the Broadway cast appeared in the film. Charles Dingle and Carl Benton Reid, who played the brothers Ben and Oscar, Patricia Collinge as Birdie, Oscar's malleable, well-bred, and ill-used wife, and Dan Duryea, who made his screen debut playing the first of a lengthy gallery of dislikeable human beings.

The cinematography was by Gregg Toland, whose other 1941 film was the unsurpassed *Citizen Kane,* and occasional shots employ similar adventurous use of depth-of-field. This was particularly effective when associated with Wyler's penchant for long takes. In the heart-attack scene, the camera holds Davis in sharp focus while behind her Marshall thrashes about in an increasing blur. There is no need for her to look at him, she simply waits, tight-lipped. On the whole, Davis plays Regina coldly and unemotionally, without heavy histrionics. There is, after all, no need for anything else, it is all there in the screenplay. Wyler actively disagreed with her interpretation and felt it should be more shaded, but she insisted on doing it her way.

George Hurrell's portrait of Davis in *The Little Foxes.*

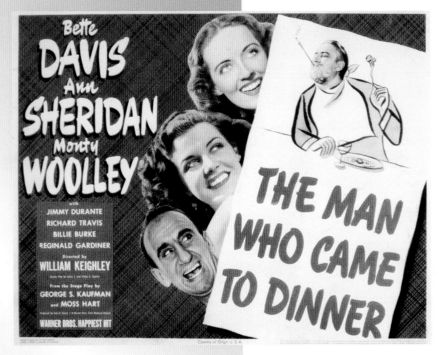

Warner Bros. (1941)

Credits

Director: William Keighley
Producer: Hal B. Wallis
Screenplay: Julius and Philip Epstein; based on the play by George S. Kaufman and Moss Hart
Cinematographer: Tony Gaudio

Cast

Bette Davis, Ann Sheridan, Monty Woolley, Richard Travis, Jimmy Durante, Reginald Gardiner, Billie Burke, Elisabeth Fraser, Grant Mitchell, George Barbier, Mary Wickes, Russell Arms, Ruth Vivian, Edwin Stanley, Charles Drake, Nanette Vallon, John Ridgely

Running time: 113 minutes

By all accounts Alexander Wolcott, the celebrated critic, wit, man-of-letters, and member of the Algonquin Round Table was often regarded as the world's worst house-guest. On a sudden descent on Moss Hart's elegant country home he commandeered the master bedroom, bullied and barked at servants, demanded a chocolate cake at his bedside, and departed with meager thanks for anybody, including his bemused host. "Supposing he had broken a leg and had to stay," said Hart to George S. Kaufman. Their eyes met. They had just dreamed up the plot of one of Broadway's most successful comedies of the 1940s.

To play the acerbic monster, Sheridan Whiteside, they cast Monty Woolley, friend of Cole Porter and at the time a professor of drama at Yale (their first choice, John Barrymore, was too advanced in his alcoholic descent to remember his lines). Woolley would also play the part on film, with Mary Wickes as the long-suffering nurse the only other stage cast player.

Whiteside, a national celebrity and media savant, is visiting Ohio to give an overpaid lecture in the company of his patient secretary Maggie Cutler (Davis). Reluctantly agreeing to dine at the home of a ball-bearing manufacturer (Grant Mitchell) and his fluttering wife (Billie Burke), he slips on the icy stoop and announces his intention to sue for his injury, which necessitates a stay in their home. He is a wheelchair tyrant who turns the entire household upside down, terrorizing the staff, inciting the son to leave home and become a photographer and the daughter to elope with a labor organizer. He takes over the principal rooms of the house, entertains assemblies of strange guests, including

Jimmy Durante and Davis. His role was based on Harpo Marx.

murderers from a nearby penitentiary and an entire delegation of Chinese diplomats. Exotic presents are delivered, including an octopus from Dr. Lucius Beebe and sundry penguins from Admiral Byrd.

When Maggie meets and falls in love with Bert Jefferson (Richard Travis), a local newspaperman and aspiring playwright, Whiteside schemes to separate them by persuading a glamorous actress, Lorraine Sheldon (Ann Sheridan), to break off her Palm Beach sojourn and pursuit of an English lord to lure Bert with promises of working with him on his play. An old Hollywood friend, Banjo (Jimmy Durante) erupts on to the scene with a sense of humor all his own, and removes Lorraine

in an Egyptian mummy case (a present from the Khedive) so that love can find its way.

The pace has to be sustained, and it all moves along at such speed that any plot shortcomings have passed by before there is time to consider them. The cast is well-tuned to farce, although Davis has a relatively sane role compared with the others. The only cast shortcoming is Richard Travis, who lacks the charisma that could convince a hardboiled New Yorker to give up her sophisticated world to become the wife of a smalltown newspaper editor in Ohio. Monty Woolley is brilliant in his role of Whiteside, and although he later made other films this is the one for which he is still remembered.

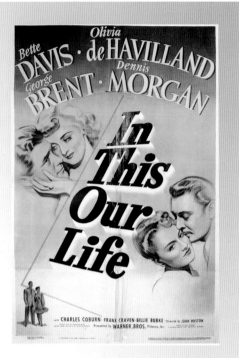

Warner Bros. (1942)

Credits

Director: John Huston
Producer: Hal B. Wallis, in association
with David Lewis
Screenplay: Howard Koch; based on the
novel by Ellen Glasgow
Cinematographer: Ernst Haller

Cast

Bette Davis, Olivia de Havilland,
George Brent, Dennis Morgan,
Charles Coburn, Frank Craven, Billie Burke,
Hattie McDaniel, Lee Patrick, Mary Servoss,
Ernest Anderson, William B. Davidson,
Edward Fielding, John Hamilton,
William Forest, Lee Phelps

Running time: 97 minutes

Davis as the spoiled-rotten Stanley Timberlake.

In John Huston's second film as director, Bette Davis and Olivia de Havilland played two sisters in a southern family named Timberlake that has dropped a few notches down the social ladder because the father (Frank Craven) was outsmarted in the family business by his hardnosed brother-in-law (Charles Coburn). The girls inexplicably have men's names—Davis is Stanley and de Havilland, Roy. Stanley is headstrong, narcissistic, utterly selfish, spoiled rotten by her rich uncle who keeps a special twinkle in his eye for her, while Roy is sweet, kind, and gentle. Stanley jilts an up-and-coming attorney, Craig Fleming (George Brent), just before their wedding and runs off with Roy's surgeon husband Peter Kingsmill (Dennis Morgan). Heartbroken, Roy divorces him so that he and Stanley can marry, but her egotistical behavior soon drives him to drink and suicide.

In the meantime, sharing their victimhood, Craig and Roy fall in love. Stanley returns unfazed by widowhood and tries to win back Craig. Habitually a fast driver, she kills a child, and pins the blame on Parry Clay (Ernest Anderson), a quietly ambitious black teenager who is studying to be a lawyer with Craig's and Roy's help. When Stanley's deception is unmasked and she is facing prison she skips off to her uncle for help, but he is wrapped up in his own plight, having just learned that he is terminally ill. "All you're thinking about is your own miserable life. Well, you can die for all I care. Die!" She runs out of the house, and drives off, pursued by cops, to meet a fiery end.

Davis's performance is restless and unrelenting, with no room for redeeming characteristics. Stanley's bitchery is so acute and obvious that is seems implausible that she can lead Peter to abandon a beautiful, loving wife for her, or for Craig—an upright, decent lawyer—to have ever wanted to marry her. It also seems unlikely that her invalid mother (Billie Burke) would be ever willing to excuse her delinquent ways or for her saintly sister to be so ready to forgive. Only her uncle, played in a splendidly exuberant fashion by Coburn, truly has her measure, because he recognizes in her a similar degree of ruthlessness, but his interest borders on the incestuous.

As torrid southern melodrama, it is at times like a precursor of a Tennessee Williams plot, but where it can be commended is in its portrayal of the black character played by Ernest Anderson, who is seen as not only a deliberate break from the standard servile stereotypes expected in the 1940s, but as a victim of a callous and cynical attempt to have him

Ernest Anderson listens helplessly as Davis blatantly frames him for her crime.

convicted for a crime in order that its true perpetrator can continue her ways unaffected. A scene between Parry and Stanley in the jailhouse, in which she urges him to confess so he can draw a lighter sentence is particularly revealing, with both of them knowing that racial prejudice will ensure any story he tells will routinely be discounted on the word of a white person on the witness stand. So shocking a comment on the absence of justice in sections of the nation was deemed unsuitable for export at the time, and there was a fierce battle to ensure that censorship did not prevail. Even so, scenes between de Havilland and Anderson, in which she talks to him as though he was a normal human being, were removed in prints of the film delivered to southern states on the grounds that they might inflame white audiences. It is hard in modern times to comprehend just how advanced was the notion that a young black youth, the son of a white family's cook, could aspire to a middle-class education and profession.

Now, Voyager

Financially it was the most successful of all Bette Davis's films, and is perhaps the ultimate "ugly duckling" picture.

Charlotte Vale (Davis) is the late child of a wealthy, autocratic Back Bay widow (Gladys Cooper) who exerts a ferocious rule over her ornate mansion, keeping the servants scurrying to enact her every pernickety whim. Charlotte's role in life has been chosen by her mother, who is driven by an overwhelming sense of always being right. Her wish is that Charlotte should look after the old woman's needs in her twilight years. Any suggestion that she might wish for independence, boyfriends and suitors, or even the right to choose her own clothes and reading material, is regarded as a selfish and unreasonable betrayal. The consequence is that Charlotte is a frightened, prematurely aged, unattractive frump with no mind of her own, who spends most of her time closeted in her room.

Paul Henreid as Jerry lights the liberated Charlotte, played by Davis.

Warner Bros. (1942)

Credits
Director: Irving Rapper
Producer: Hal B. Wallis
Screenplay: Casey Robinson; from the novel by Olive Higgins Prouty
Cinematographer: Sol Polito

Cast
Bette Davis, Paul Henreid, Claude Rains, Gladys Cooper, Bonita Granville, John Loder, Ilka Chase, Lee Patrick, Franklin Pangborn, James Rennie, Mary Wickes

Running time: 117 minutes

Her concerned sister-in-law Lisa (Ilka Chase) brings a distinguished psychiatrist Dr. Jaquith (Claude Rains) to visit Charlotte at home, where he sees at once the deleterious effect the mother is having on her. In spite of maternal disapproval, he whisks her off to his country sanitarium, a luxurious retreat nestled in green acres like an elegant country resort. After weeks of careful therapy she emerges into the world as an attractive woman. Rather than return immediately to Boston she embarks on a South American cruise, inspired by Jaquith and his citing of a Walt Whitman couplet ("The untold want by life and land ne'er granted, / Now voyager sail thou forth to seek and find.") In the course of her voyage she meets Jerry (Paul Henreid), with whom she has an immediate rapport that turns

Irving Rapper directs Paul Henreid and Davis.

into love. He is, however, burdened by a loveless marriage to which he adheres out of a sense of duty to his daughters, particularly the younger one, who is disturbed. The couple part, and Charlotte returns to her mother's domain, where she finds herself better equipped to deal with her mania for control. She is almost betrothed to a well-bred Bostonian polo player (John Loder), a match her mother would have approved, but Jerry reappears by chance and she breaks her engagement, realizing that she still loves him.

During a quarrel, her mother has a fatal heart attack. Guilt-ridden and desperate, Charlotte scurries back to Dr. Jaquith and at the sanitarium comes across a little girl in acute depression. Charlotte immediately empathizes, recognizing her former self, and begs the doctor to allow her to help the girl. The child immediately responds as though she has found her lost mother, and

soon becomes happy and normal. She is Jerry's daughter Tina (Janis Wilson). With his consent, Tina goes to live with Charlotte in Boston, where he can visit whenever he wants, sharing Tina as their daughter even if he and Charlotte cannot marry. "Oh Jerry, don't ask for the moon," Charlotte says to him. "We have the stars." Max Steiner's lush theme surges to its climax as the camera pans up to a starry night sky in one of the most famous and lachrymose endings of all time.

It is another example of Davis's characteristic restraint and subtlety of performance. If there is any scenery-chewing to be done it is left to Gladys Cooper as the fearsome matriarch, where it is entirely appropriate. Davis makes her first appearance, heralded by a close-up of her hand stubbing out a cigarette and then emptying a loaded ashtray into a waste basket, looking more dowdy and deglamorized in her drab, baggy dress, and clumping, ugly lace-up shoes than any of her contemporaries would dare. She looks more like Norman Bates's mother than a young woman of marriageable age. The transformation into an elegant, poised, and beautiful woman is made all the more effective. Yet even when she is revealed elegantly shod in the height of fashion, with her hair upswept and her face framed by a chic, broad-brimmed hat, she remains the frightened, tentative Charlotte valiantly embarking on a perilous journey that will take her toward independence and womanly fulfillment. Henreid's Jerry is European, gracious, sensitive,

Jerry and Charlotte face their future.

and as she eventually discovers, vulnerable through his need to conceal the desperate pain of his difficult home life.

Claude Rains as the doctor, not for the first time, has the pivotal role, as the catalyst for change. He gives Charlotte her life, and observes her development not only with clinical interest, but almost as a benign puppet-master, with quiet amusement and pleasure at every positive turn.

There was a vogue for psychiatry in 1940s films, when psychoanalysis was regarded as a new cure-all for inadequacy, as well as a better way for treating shell-shocked soldiers than sending them straight back to face the enemy with a bayonet, standard procedure in World War I, but Dr. Jaquith, with his unflappable refusal to be cowed by the overbearing mother, is seen almost as a superhero, the bringer of hope to hopeless cases, and in the hands of Claude Rains he is both saintly and human.

The one aspect of the film that has dated it more than any other, and which to a modern viewer seems both profligate and shocking, is the amount of smoking that takes place. Jaquith makes his first appearance knocking out the bowl of his pipe under the steely eye of the butler as he waits to be ushered into the presence of the widow Vale, and Charlotte and Jerry seem never to play a scene without first lighting up. He has a particular trick of placing two cigarettes in his mouth, igniting both, and handing one to Charlotte, an intimate little routine that inspired millions of smokers in the 1940s as a way to impress their partners. It was not even a new trick. George Brent had performed it ten years earlier in another Davis film, *The Rich Are Always With Us*, but only with the lovers of *Now, Voyager* did it become a symbolic, tender, romantic gesture.

Sixty-six years after its release, at a private screening, the power of Irving Rapper's direction and Casey Robinson's script, drawn from one volume of a quartet of Bostonian novels by Olive Higgins Prouty, still managed to reduce almost every woman in the audience to tears.

Portrait by Bert Six of the new Charlotte Vale.

WATCH ON THE RHINE

Warner Bros. (1943)

Credits

Director: Herman Shumlin
Producer: Hal B. Wallis
Screenplay: Dashiell Hammett; additional scenes and dialogue by Lillian Hellman; based on the play by Lillian Hellman
Cinematographers: Merritt Gerstad, Hal Mohr

Cast

Bette Davis, Paul Lukas, Geraldine Fitzgerald, Lucile Watson, Beulah Bondi, George Coulouris, Donald Woods, Henry Daniell, Donald Buka, Eric Roberts, Janis Wilson, Mary Young, Kurt Katch, Erwin Kalser, Clyde Fillmore, Robert O. Davis, Frank Wilson, Clarence Muse, Anthony Caruso, Howard Hickman, Elvira Curci, Creighton Hale, Alan Hale, Jr.

Running time: 112 minutes

Donald Woods, Donald Buka, Eric Roberts, Davis, and Paul Lukas.

Lillian Hellman's "enemy within" play ran on Broadway in 1941, a pre–Pearl Harbor propaganda piece denouncing fascism and demonstrating how even the nation's capital was not immune to Nazi incursions. Although Dashiell Hammett's screenplay opens it up cinematically, with their theatrical blocking, expository dialogue, off-screen action, and significant entrances and exits, the direction and pacing betray the stage origins and give the film a dated air. Although Davis had top billing, which apparently she accepted reluctantly, the central performance comes from Paul Lukas, who was awarded an Oscar.

He plays Kurt Muller, seen at the beginning in April 1940, crossing the border from Mexico with his wife Sara (Davis) and three super-intelligent children. She is an American who eighteen years earlier married this German engineer who turned antifascist when the Nazis came to power, since when they have endured an itinerant life while he engages in underground activities. She is bringing her family back to the peace and stability of her childhood home, a mansion near Washington, ruled by her mother Fanny (Lucile Watson), the widow of a distinguished jurist and a powerful matriarch.

An impoverished Romanian count and ex-diplomat (George Coulouris) and his disaffected American wife (Geraldine Fitzgerald) are house guests. The wife loathes his constant poker-playing at the German embassy, where he is ingratiating himself. He realizes who Muller really is, and attempts a squalid blackmail with a fatal outcome. As Fanny observes, the family has been shaken out of the magnolias, with Kurt departing back to Germany to carry on the fight, while his brave wife waits for their elder son to be of an age to follow him.

Davis is loyal, loving, noble, and selfless, a role that allows no flamboyant histrionics, yet she manages to project strength and character. Lukas is a quiet, unassuming hero, burdened by the world's tragedy, and Watson, initially tiresome, shows the mettle of a true believer in democracy. In a subplot, Donald Woods is the son who dotes on Fitzgerald, while Coulouris effectively plays the pathetic, slimy parasite who toadies to the Nazis.

Fugitives from Nazism, Davis and Lukas console each other.

OLD ACQUAINTANCE

Flighty Miriam Hopkins, stable Bette Davis. Best friends?

Warner Bros. (1943)

Credits

Director: Vincent Sherman
Producer: Henry Blanke
Screenplay: John Van Druten, Lenore
Coffee; based on the play by
John Van Druten
Cinematographer: Sol Polito

Cast

Bette Davis, Miriam Hopkins, Gig Young,
John Loder, Dolores Moran, Phillip Reed,
Roscoe Karns, Anne Revere, Esther Dale,
Pierre Watlin, Marjorie Hoshelle,
George Lessee, Ann Doran, Francine Rufo

Running time: 113 minutes

Edmund Goulding was scheduled to direct *Old Acquaintance* but withdrew due to ill-health, so Vincent Sherman stepped in. Davis was reunited with Miriam Hopkins, with whom she had appeared in *The Old Maid*, and once again their edgy rivalry came into play. The story spans nearly twenty years, from 1924 to the middle of World War II, but the friendship of Kit Marlowe (Davis) and Millie Drake (Miriam Hopkins) was forged in childhood. Kit pays a visit to their hometown as an accomplished author and stays with Millie, a new and pregnant housewife. Her husband Preston (John Loder) seems already to be feeling the strain of married life, and takes an obvious shine to Kit who is a paragon of calmness and common sense compared with the highly strung Millie.

Millie, jealous of Kit's success, has embarked on her own writing career and produces a manuscript, asking for her friend's help in finding a publisher. The years pass and Millie has become a prolific writer of bestselling romantic novels, managing with facile skill to deliver one every year, in contrast with Kit's painstaking and disciplined approach, which produces results at a much slower pace. She does not have a husband, and Millie cannot keep hers. Having first declared his love to Kit, who rejects him only from loyalty to Millie, Preston walks out.

The third act takes place in wartime. Now a major, Preston reappears and Kit, vacillating over the possibility of marrying Rudd (Gig Young), a pleasant young man ten years her junior, reunites Millie's now-grown daughter Deirdre (Dolores Moran) with her father. He is shortly going to remarry, but Millie mistakenly believes that he has come back to her. Kit discovers that Deirdre and Rudd are in love. The two women, now in advanced middle age, are left only with themselves and their memories.

It is a skillfully contrived women's story, and its principal flaw is that the roles Davis and Hopkins play are extremes. Kit is kind, forgiving, and nobly

"There comes a time in every woman's life when the only thing that helps is a glass of champagne."

self-sacrificing. Millie is a selfish, manipulative, self-pitying neurotic. The Davis character is more intelligent, level-headed, and reasonable, and it is hard to understand why she has tolerated Millie's very different temperament since childhood.

Hopkins allegedly resorted to many tricks to gain the advantage over Davis, to little effect, except to add to the irritation Millie generates. But the lack of redeeming features adds neither plausibility nor depth to the character.

Davis adopts a mature look for a studio portrait.

THANK YOUR LUCKY STARS

Warner Bros. (1943)

Credits

Director: David Butler
Producer: Mark Hellinger
Screenplay: Norman Panama, Melvin Frank,
James V. Kern; based on a story by Everett
Freeman and Arthur Schwartz
Cinematographer: Arthur Edeson

Cast

Dennis Morgan, Joan Leslie, Edward Everett
Horton, S.Z. Sakall, Richard Lane, Ruth
Donnelly, Don Wilson, Henry Armetta,
Joyce Reynolds plus as themselves
Humphrey Bogart, Eddie Cantor,
Bette Davis, Olivia de Havilland,
Errol Flynn, John Garfield, Ida Lupino,
Ann Sheridan, Dinah Shore, Alexis Smith,
Jack Carson, Alan Hale, George Tobias,
Hattie McDaniel, Willie Best, Spike Jones
and his City Slickers

Running time: 124 minutes

A slender plot involving a songwriter (Joan Leslie) and a singer (Dennis Morgan) angling for their breakthrough is a peg for parading a comprehensive roster of Warner Bros. stars performing a succession of set-piece numbers in a huge wartime extravaganza for a charity benefit. To see the likes of Olivia de Havilland, Ida Lupino, Errol Flynn, and John Garfield in a song-and-dance context would be of sufficient novelty to attract audiences. Davis made a contribution now more memorable than the film itself, expertly delivering ("singing" would not be so appropriate a word) a mordant song by Frank Loesser and Arthur Schwartz, lamenting the acute lack of available men as a consequence of the draft.

Davis is required to act as a parody of herself, and even participate in a whirlwind jitterbug interlude, for which she is spun through the air on the first take by Conrad Wiedel, a champion dancer. The result is so convincing that she later said: "He made me look like the dancer I distinctly was not."

As the stars who took part were donating their $50,000 fees to the Hollywood Canteen (itself the subject of a subsequent film revue) the loss of dignity was fully excusable, and appreciated.

"Bette cuts a rug—and steps with a hepcat" said the original caption.

BETTE'S WAR EFFORT

Immediately after the surprise Japanese attack on Pearl Harbor in December 1941 the US entered World War II. As one of his most loyal supporters, Davis instantly wrote to President Franklin D. Roosevelt, pledging any help she could give. He welcomed her initiative, and instead of vacationing in New Hampshire, she embarked on a grueling war-bonds tour that lasted many weeks, in which she visited factories, state fairs, shopping centers, schools, clubs, and even private homes across America. Her enthusiasm was reminiscent of her zeal as a Girl Scout, and she cajoled millions of dollars from the public, at one time selling $2 million worth of bonds in two days. It was not until April that she was back in Hollywood to make *Now, Voyager*. Later she toured army bases with Lena Horne and Ethel Waters, the only white member of Hattie McDaniels' troupe entertaining segregated black units.

Her greatest wartime achievement was the establishment of the Hollywood Canteen, in partnership with John Garfield, who had been rejected by the Draft Board as 4-F. It was to be a club for servicemen offering free food,

With sailors at a benefit show in New York's Madison Square Garden.

dancing, and top-line entertainment. Los Angeles was a railhead and staging post for the Pacific war, and thousands of soldiers were transiting at any one time, so the Canteen became a magnet for them. The premises, housed in a former nightclub that had been built as a livery stable, were on Cahuenga Boulevard in Hollywood, and with the help of the craft unions, who fitted it out, and industry executives, particularly Jules Stein, head of MCA, who raised the finances, it was open for business every night until hostilities ended. Big bands, headline performers and an endless stream of stars provided the entertainment, while many of Hollywood's biggest names voluntarily waited tables, washed dishes, peeled potatoes, and danced with the patrons, even after a heavy day of filming. Davis was one of the most regular and popular presences, and was prepared to do anything, from scrubbing floors to making victory speeches from the stage. A film, *Hollywood Canteen*, released in December 1944, was made by Warner Bros. to commemorate a unique West Coast institution.

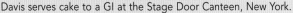

Davis serves cake to a GI at the Stage Door Canteen, New York.

MR. SKEFFINGTON

Davis as Fanny with Claude Rains.

Warner Bros. (1944)

Credits

Director: Vincent Sherman
Producers: Philip and Julius Epstein
Screenplay: Philip and Julius Epstein;
based on the story by "Elizabeth"
(Elizabeth von Arnim)
Cinematographer: Ernest Haller

Cast

Bette Davis, Claude Rains, Walter Abel,
Richard Waring, George Coulouris,
Marjorie Riordan. Robert Shayne, John
Alexander, Jerome Cowan, Johnny Mitchell,
Dorothy Peterson, Peter Whitney, Bill
Kennedy, Tom Stevenson, Halliwell Hobbes,
Bunny Sunshine, Gigi Perreau, Dolores
Gray, Walter Kingsford, Molly Lamont

Running time: 146 minutes

In the beginning, Fanny Trellis (Davis) is the toast of New York, a society belle besieged by suitors, unaware that her feckless brother Trippy (Richard Waring) has run through the family fortune and is now fleecing his Jewish banker employer, Job Skeffington (Claude Rains). Conscious that Skeffington is a kind, adoring man, as well as being excessively rich, Fanny marries him to save Trippy from disgrace and the law. Instead of gratitude Trippy is filled with hatred and storms off to Europe, enlisting in Lafayette Escadrille, the largely American wing of the French air force.

Fanny, meanwhile, is pregnant. Trippy is killed in action. Fanny blames Job, and spends much of the Roaring Twenties in an open marriage that eventually ends in divorce. The child, young Fanny, is sent to school in Switzerland under the careful eye of Job, who has relocated to Europe. By the time World War II looms, young Fanny, now an attractive woman, returns to her mother, an unwelcome reminder of her advancing years and the fact that her admirers are more interested in her wealth than her beauty. Of Job, last known to be in Berlin, there is no word.

Fanny contracts diphtheria, and after a grim battle that nearly kills her, loses her looks completely. Adding to her mortification, her former young admirer marries her daughter and goes off to California. Alone, ugly, and despairing, she is suddenly made aware that Job has returned, broken and penniless, from a Nazi concentration camp. She refuses to see him, conscious of her hideous appearance, but is finally persuaded. He is blind and remembers only her beauty, and she vows to tend and love him for the rest of his life.

"A woman is beautiful only when she is loved" is Job Skeffington's mantra, and it takes two-and-a-quarter hours of running time before the heroine finally appreciates his point. Davis's character is vain, selfish, narcissistic, and utterly shallow. Initially she is meant to be such a knockout that men fall at her feet, eager to make idiotic fools of themselves. Davis was never the sort of ravishing beauty who could command irrational devotion, but she makes a creditable stab at acting like a Gibson Girl, assisted by Orry-Kelly's gowns, Perc Westmore's makeup, and Ernie Haller's lighting. For the most part she succeeds, but her voice is too high and false, making her sound insincere and vacuous.

It helps to know that this was a troubled production. Davis was widowed only three weeks before shooting began, and she had insisted on returning to work too soon, putting others on the film through misery. Both the director, Vincent Sherman, and the writers, Philip and Julius

Epstein, had tried to quit in frustration. Sherman had failed to persuade her to speak more naturally, and eventually had to let her direct herself, so difficult was it to secure proper cooperation. Davis's excessiveness with regard to her "old" makeup was to Westmore's despair, and the result was a grotesque overlay of latex and powder that foreshadowed her look nearly twenty years later in *Whatever Happened to Baby Jane?* Her wig sits on a stand by her bed, and a false curl drops off when the most indigent of her former beaus attempts a gauche marriage proposal.

"A woman is beautiful only when she is loved."

"I find one should never look for admirers while at the same time one is falling to bits."

Fanny Skeffington's comeuppance arrives in a strange way.

As the queen of the Warner Bros. lot Davis was used to having her own way, but on *Mr. Skeffington* she exploited her privileges as on no other film. It was her contention that her followers always expected her to be prepared to do whatever it took to overturn the conventional glamorous image, and other Hollywood figures such as Merle Oberon, Irene Dunne, and Claudette Colbert had declined the role. Davis had no qualms about taking it on, and earned an Academy Award nomination, losing to Ingrid Bergman for *Gaslight*.

Claude Rains once again gave a masterly performance in a difficult role, as a reasonable man attempting to deal with an unreasonable situation. His Jewishness is understated, and apparently Jack Warner wanted it expunged altogether, even though this would have made the plot more difficult. Tripp's animus toward Job is entirely based on his anti-Semitism, although it is implied obliquely.

Other roles are performed well, particularly Walter Abel as Cousin George, a sort of choric voice of reason who, with ever-graying hair, intervenes across the years to nudge Fanny's undeveloped conscience. George Coulouris has a magnificent single scene as a psychiatrist Fanny consults after her illness and, in a riotous reversal of the usual Hollywood portrayal of the sensitive analyst, devastatingly lays into her for her moral shortcomings and lack of self-awareness.

The film is overlong, even after the Epstein brothers had made a number of cuts. It opened to mixed reviews, with some critics suggesting that it bordered on self-parody, but it was a popular success and one of the three top hits produced by Warner Bros. in the year. It went down particularly well with women ("super soap opera" said James Agee) and the saccharin ending, with Franz Waxman's score surging as Fanny guides the blind Job up the grand staircase of her spacious mansion, announcing that she will not be able to keep a lunch date with her unseen woman friend who has been stood up again and again across more than two decades.

Hollywood Canteen

Bette Davis was just one of an ensemble cast.

The Hollywood Canteen on Cahuenga, near Sunset, was an institution co-founded by Bette Davis with John Garfield, and was a servicemen's club where soldiers and sailors passing through Los Angeles could be entertained by top acts and headline bands, dance with and be served meals and drinks by real movie stars, and not have to pay a cent. Following Davis's persuasive lobbying, the movie industry willingly cooperated, raising huge sums of money for the undertaking, and even the craft unions pitched in by supplying labor and materials. It was one of Hollywood's most notable contributions to the war effort.

It was seen as an excellent subject for a portmanteau musical, and a plot was concocted that had Robert Hutton and Dane Clark as a couple of GIs soon to be shipped back to New Guinea who seek solace at the Canteen. Clark faints when he discovers his dance partner is Joan Crawford and Hutton is designated the millionth serviceman to enter the club, and becomes infatuated with Joan Leslie, Warner Bros's young "girl-next-door" star. Davis, as herself, is a sort of emcee, introducing acts and bestowing Hutton's honor. Joan Leslie recalled that she was ill-at-ease having to be herself and not one of the characters created for a screen role.

Warner Bros. (1944)

Credits
Director: Delmer Daves
Producer: Alex Gottlieb
Screenplay and original story: Delmer Daves

Cast
Joan Leslie, Robert Hutton, Janis Paige, Dane Clark, Richard Erdman, James Flavin, Joan Winfield, Jonathan Hale, Rudolf Friml, Jr., Bill Manning, Larry Thompson, Mell Schubert, Walden Boyle, Steve Richards

Guest stars
The Andrews Sisters, Jack Benny, Joe E. Brown, Eddie Cantor, Kitty Carlisle, Jack Carson, Joan Crawford, Helmut Dantine, Bette Davis, Faye Emerson, Victor Francen, John Garfield, Sydney Greenstreet, Alan Hale, Paul Henreid, Andrea King, Peter Lorre, Ida Lupino, Irene Manning, Nora Martin, Joan McCracken, Dolores Moran, Dennis Morgan, Eleanor Parker, William Prince, Joyce Reynolds, John Ridgely, Roy Rogers and Trigger, S. Z. Sakall, Alexis Smith, Zachary Scott, Barbara Stanwyck, Craig Stevens, Joseph Szigeti, Donald Woods, Jane Wyman, Jimmy Dorsey and His Band, Carmen Cavallero and His Orchestra, Rosario and Antonio, Sons of the Pioneers, Virginia Patton, Lynne Baggett, Betty Alexander, Julie Bishop, Robert Shayne, Johnny Mitchell, John Sheridan, Colleen Townsend, Angela Green, Paul Brooke, Marianne O'Brien, Dorothy Malone, Bill Kennedy

Running time: 124 minutes

THE CORN IS GREEN

John Dall as the young Welsh miner coached arduously by Davis's stern teacher.

Warner Bros. (1945)

Credits
Director: Irving Rapper
Producer: Jack Chertok
Screenplay: Casey Robinson, Frank Cavett;
based on the play by Emlyn Williams
Cinematographer: Sol Polito

Cast

Bette Davis, John Dall, Joan Lorring, Nigel Bruce, Rhys Williams, Rosalind Ivan, Mildred Dunnock, Gwyneth Hughes, Billie Roy, Thomas Louden, Arthur Shields, Leslie Vincent, Robert Regent, Tony Ellis, Elliott Dare, Robert Cherry, Gene Ross

Running time: 115 minutes

On Broadway Ethel Barrymore, in her mid-sixties, had played the school-teacher who enabled a young Welsh miner in the 1890s to win a scholarship to Oxford. At thirty-six, Davis took on the role for the film version. The play was a *roman-a-clef*, based on the experience of the British playwright and actor Emlyn Williams, who had been coached from a poor Welsh background into Oxford by a redoubtable Miss Cooke. In the film Richard Waring, who had played the part on Broadway and was Trippy in *Mr. Skeffington*, was due to play the young man, but he was drafted in spite of efforts by the studio to secure his deferment until production had finished. In his stead John Dall was cast in his film debut.

Davis's Miss Moffat is a middle-aged English schoolmistress who attempts to set up a school in a poor mining village. The local landowner (Bruce) is unhelpful, fearing that education in a community where children are expected to start work in the pit at the age of twelve will upset the order of things, so she sets up a schoolroom in her house. Young Morgan (Dall) is the pupil in whom she detects a spark, but he is rebellious and resistant, and has a drunken fling with Bessie (Joan Lorring), the brassy daughter of her housekeeper. On the day Morgan is due to sit his Oxford examination Bessie announces she is pregnant, but Miss Moffat bribes her to leave before he finds out. He passes, but just as he is about to depart for the university Bessie reappears waving a baby at him, and he feels obliged to give up his place and marry her. The indefatigable Miss Moffat even has a way to solve that dilemma.

The film is stage-bound and claustrophobic, even the few exteriors are clearly shot on an indoor stage. Welshness is laid on thickly; for instance, there is never a shot of miners returning from the pit without the soundtrack filled with their voices singing in perfect harmony. The phoniness is forgivable given the strength of Davis's performance, which subdued the suggestion of a sexually frustrated spinster and instead imbued her with a higher concern for betterment through education. It was Dall, however, not Davis who received the Oscar nomination.

Bette Davis in 1945.

PART 4
FREE AT LAST
1946–51

by George Perry

WHEN it came to fighting the plush-lined slavery of the studio system, Bette Davis may have been one of the pioneers but others had waged the same war. James Cagney and Humphrey Bogart were notable rebels at Warner Bros. and Katharine Hepburn assailed RKO. Carole Lombard, who was one of very few film personalities killed during war service, engaged in dispute with Paramount, Eddie Cantor tussled with Samuel Goldwyn, and so it went on. The breakthrough was achieved by Olivia de Havilland, who won a suit against Warner Bros. in 1944, with a ruling that had repercussions throughout the industry by extending greater creative freedom to actors and ending the practice of adding suspension time to contracts. In spite of the gratitude of her fellow performers she was quickly bounced out of Warner Bros., a film about the Brontë sisters, *Devotion*, made in 1943 and ready for release, was put on the shelf for three years, and she was billed in third place.

Had magnanimity entered Jack Warner's soul, or was he merely extending an invitation to Davis to dissolve her long and profitable career at Burbank? For her next film was to be her very own production, a remake of an earlier British picture, released in 1939 and called *Stolen Life*, with Michael Redgrave and Elisabeth Bergner (in a dual role as twin sisters). As director she had selected Curtis Bernhardt who had been responsible for *Devotion*, but on the strength of another film, *My Reputation*, starring Barbara Stanwyck, which had been finished in early 1944 and not put before the public until 1946. Delays in the release of his films seemed to dog Bernhardt.

Franklin D. Roosevelt was re-elected for the fourth time in the November, and Davis was invited to dinner at the White House. She had been one of Roosevelt's most ardent supporters among his many adherents in the film colony. The war was in its closing stages, although he would not see it through to the end, dying in March 1945.

With her daughter B.D. at her christening, San Clemente, California, 1948.

Opposite: Davis in 1950, mature and established.

"I was a person who couldn't make divorce work. For me, there's nothing lonelier than a turned-down toilet seat."

Picnicking with her husband, Norman Grant Sherry, 1947.

Davis's personal contribution to the war effort, apart from the Hollywood Canteen, was slightly strange. It seems she had become involved with a corporal in the Army Signal Corps who was twelve years younger than her, and although there had been many brief and covert one-night flings with servicemen, she was publicly dating him, taking him to dinner at expensive Hollywood restaurants and slipping away in disguise (not effective as her voice was a big giveaway) to a hotel in Santa Barbara. He was then posted to Fort Benning, Georgia, and she decamped to Phenix City, Alabama, just across the state line. This was ostensibly a vacation, but the press soon became aware of her presence and began to surmise.

After his re-election, Roosevelt went to his estate at Warm Springs, Georgia, to recover from the strain, and Davis managed to inveigle the corporal into his Thanksgiving dinner there as her guest. Her sojourn in Alabama lasted three months, and she was joined by her sister, Bobby, recovering from a nervous breakdown and waiting for her divorce to come through. Bobby enthusiastically joined her sister in dating attractive servicemen. Davis was hoping that her muscular, tanned corporal would propose, but she waited in vain. He went overseas without seizing the opportunity, a rebuff that she took in her stride at first, but after months of exchanging letters she decided to terminate the relationship.

In November 1945, after years as a divorced widow, Davis's mother remarried, at the age of sixty. Her groom was a fifty-three-year-old Massachusetts businessman, Robert Palmer, who had previously been married for thirty-two years and had gone through a Reno divorce only ten days before. A few days later Davis herself married for the third time. Her new husband was William Grant Sherry, a boxer-turned-artist and naval man who was awaiting his medical discharge after a shipboard explosion. He was seven years younger than she was, but professed to like older woman. Bizarrely, even though she was the most famous Hollywood actress of the time, he claimed never to have heard of her. Ruthie was not well-disposed toward the union, scornful that Sherry's mother worked as an elevator operator in San Diego. The dislike was mutual, as he perceived Ruthie as a grand-scale sponger who was seeing that her meal ticket provided by Davis was now threatened.

The ceremony took place at the Mission Inn, Riverside on November 30, and was fraught with ill-feeling between the groom and his new mother-in-law. The honeymoon was to be in Mexico and the newlyweds embarked for it in Davis's handsome Buick. The journey, on interminable rugged highways, played havoc with the tires, all of which had to be replaced. During the war and for some time after good tires were hard to find, and inferior rubber substitutes were not up to the job. The couple became marooned far from their destination and had to await the posse of press and police to catch up and rescue them. It was an inauspicious start to a marriage that would be fraught with quarrels and even occasional violence.

Joan Crawford had been brought to Warner Bros. to play the title role in Michael Curtiz's *Mildred Pierce*, a part that Davis had turned down on the grounds that she did not like the implications of the age of the character being old enough to have a sixteen-year-old daughter, as required by the script. The role would win Crawford the Best Actress Oscar. Sherry, unfamiliar with Hollywood's little ways, was surprised to be accosted on the studio lot by Crawford, who offered her congratulations on his marriage to Davis and an invitation to dinner. He learned that he was not expected to bring his new bride.

For *A Stolen Life* Davis had formed a company, B.D. Productions, but soon found that it was a

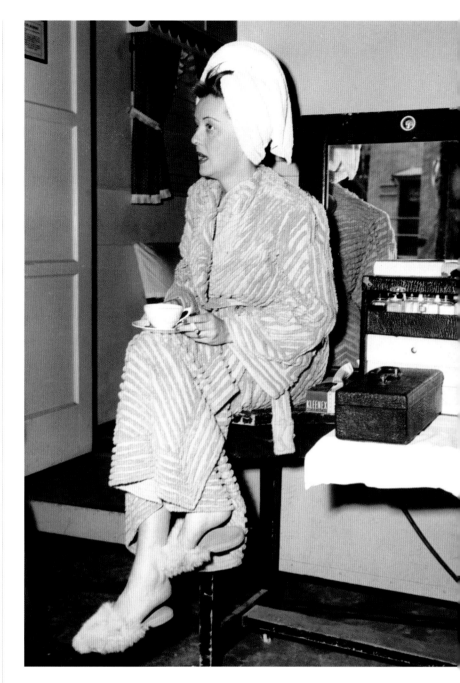

Davis in her dressing room during filming *A Stolen Life*, 1946.

proposition that nobody at the studio took very seriously. Hal Wallis had by that time departed for Paramount, and Curtis Bernhardt later claimed that, as Davis took such little interest in the minutiae, he had to produce as well as direct. She and Bernhardt (another of her bedded directors) had hired Glenn Ford as the male lead, and in her own performance as the twin sisters she attempted to give them color sufficient to discern the good from the bad. Davis was a failure as a

In a script discussion on *Deception*, 1946.

producer, resorting to abuse and peevishness when things went wrong, taking little interest in the mundane aspects of the job, meddling where it was unhelpful to do so, and often not being available when needed to make decisions. The film was unimpressive and received indifferent reviews, but made a healthy profit nonetheless.

Jack Warner had skillfully outpointed Davis, aware that her career had peaked and that the $6,000 a week she was being paid was becoming harder to justify. After just this one film B.D. Productions was closed down. A new acting contract was negotiated with Warner Bros. that would last until 1949. Two of her favorite potential subjects remained unproduced: the first an adaptation of *Ethan Frome,* the gloomy Edith Wharton novel over which Jack Warner had become lukewarm in the harsher postwar climate, and an expensive biography of Mary Lincoln, the wife of the Great Emancipator. The latter would have to be conceived elaborately with Civil War battles, recreations of Lincoln's Washington, especially the fateful evening at the Ford's Theatre, elaborate costumes, hundreds of extras, and a commensurate budget. Such films had no place in the postwar production lineup as far as Warner Bros. was concerned.

Davis's next film was *Deception,* directed by Irving Rapper, with Paul Henreid and Claude Rains completing the *Now, Voyager* reunion. An old property was updated into a triangle set amidst the world of music, with Davis and Henreid respectively playing a pianist and a cellist, Rains played an egotistical composing and conducting genius who becomes her lover after Henreid was thought killed in Europe during the war. It was a troubled production. Tussles with the PCA had imposed a melodramatic climax that made little sense to the plot. Davis had a car crash a week into filming, and lost time to recuperate from a head injury. When she returned, so did the dizzy spells, forcing a further hiatus. Then came a serious cold, exacerbated by her move to an oceanfront house at Laguna Beach to please her new husband. The production slipped further behind schedule to the consternation of the studio. Her behavior alienated the crew, who had become bored and angry at her constant temperamental exhibitions. It was later discovered she was pregnant.

When shooting of *Deception* wrapped it was a month behind schedule, and had cost more than any other Bette Davis movie. The audience reception was indifferent, and it turned out to be the first of her films, after the forty-nine that had gone into profit ,that lost money. Not by a narrow margin, either, but by around half a million dollars, then a substantial deficit. It was the severest warning to an actress who had achieved sustained success for so long, but who was now nearing forty. Her role in *Deception* was meant to be glamorous but in many shots she looked dumpy and dowdy.

After a long leave of absence Davis spent her confinement at Butternut, hoping that the child would, like her, be a New Englander. Severe weather and the possibility of difficulties in a snowbound emergency prompted a return to California. Her baby daughter was born on May 1, 1947, at Santa Ana and given the name Barbara Davis Sherry. It was soon abbreviated to B.D., and she was thereafter known only by her initials.

The next film was *Winter Meeting,* with a new director, Bretaigne Windust, who had scored a hit with a Broadway musical, *Finian's Rainbow.* Davis had a hand in casting the leading man, settling on an actor who bore her own surname, James Davis, and would be earning less than a tenth of her salary. It was an inauspicious pairing that absolutely failed to ignite any onscreen sparks. The plot was also unpromising; a dull, cocooned spinster meets a dashing young naval officer who really wants to be a priest. Davis was not enamored of Windust's directing style either, finding that he required lengthy rehearsals before shooting, as though he had not been able to adapt his theatrical technique to the swifter methods of filmmaking. Again the film was met with indif-

ference, and if *Deception* was a financial disaster, *Winter Meeting* was an apocalyptic tragedy, losing nearly a million dollars. Significantly the film opened just two days after she turned forty.

Inexplicably Windust was assigned to direct her next film, a romantic comedy derived from a Broadway play, *June Bride,* with Davis now reinvented in career-woman mode as a magazine editor, and Robert Montgomery costarring as a former war correspondent adjusting to peacetime by working on a women's magazine. The titular role was played by a young newcomer,

Davis and her husband William Grant Sherry at B.D.'s christening.

The veteran director King Vidor with Davis, *Beyond the Forest.*

Barbara Bates. Again the box-office results were lackluster, although at least it finished in the black. Davis was still sufficiently powerful to negotiate a new four-picture contract that paid her over $10,000 a week and required her to make only one film in a year.

Beyond the Forest, the first under this new arrangement, turned out to be the last. Directed by King Vidor, one of the biggest names in Hollywood since silent days, it proved disastrous. From the outset the material, a screenplay by Lenore Coffee, adapted from a novel by Stuart Engstrand, ran into censorship problems, its plotline involving an industrial-belt housewife yearning for bright lights, and a hookup with a wealthy manufacturer that she thinks she can achieve after a self-induced abortion. Davis hated the script and accepted that she was too old for the part, suggesting that Virginia Mayo, who had

performed well as Cagney's moll in the gangster thriller *White Heat,* would have been more suitable. Davis also found the choice of Joseph Cotten to play her dull doctor husband bizarre. She thought him too attractive for a middle-aged woman to abandon. In any case, she was photographed badly, with thick makeup and unattractive clothes in which even someone twenty years younger would have looked drab. It is one of those films that is so sensationally bad that it has become something of a camp classic, and its notoriety was sealed when the playwright Edward Albee had the leading female character in *Who's Afraid of Virginia Woolf?* in 1962 pick up Davis's line, "What a dump!"

By mutual agreement it was decided that enough was enough. After eighteen years, her tenure at Warner Bros. came to an end. She had reigned long as their top, best-paid star, at the apex of her influence even being described as "the fourth Warner brother." The emotion generated by her departure was somewhat one-sided. There was no farewell party or even any well-wishers to see her pass through the studio gate for the last time. Jack Warner later wrote in his autobiography, "I was relieved to see her go."

Coupled with the dismal experience of leaving the place that had been a spiritual home for such a large part of her life was the collapse of her third marriage. Sherry was neither timid nor subservient, and was often violent. Short-fused and resentful, he would lose his temper and throw things, although he later denied any intention to hurt her and claimed that he aimed to miss. She was unforgiving, and elevated his temperamental outbursts into furious assaults. In the midst of this domestic turmoil their daughter, B.D., cowered uncomprehendingly, not understanding what was going on. When *Beyond the Forest* opened in October 1949 Davis was filing her divorce petition. There was a court attempt to patch things up with counseling, to no avail, and the marriage was formally ended a few months later.

Davis was, as it happened, making her first film after an eight-month hiatus following her departure from Warner Bros. The studio was RKO, which was under the ownership of the multi-millionaire and former Davis lover, Howard Hughes. The director was Curtis Bernhardt and the film, aptly, was called *The Story of a Divorce*. The designation did not stick and by the time of its release it had been changed to *Payment on Demand*, which Davis felt sounded cheap and demeaning. She played a fierce career

"*An affair now and then is good for a marriage. It adds spice, stops it from getting boring. I ought to know.*"

woman who pushes her husband into overachieving and unhappiness until he finds genuine devotion with another woman. When he demands a divorce, the wife of twenty years holds an introspective evaluation; she decides to take everything he has and grind him into the dust. Hughes intervened to reduce the impact of a downbeat ending. In the death throes of his marriage, Sherry was convinced that Davis and her costar, Barry Sullivan, were engaged in a heavy affair. The married Sullivan denied it but the subsequent altercation was reported and Davis took the final steps to end her union, moving out of Laguna Beach to a rented house in Beverly Hills.

Davis with costar Barry Sullivan in *Payment on Demand*.

As the shoot of *Payment on Demand* neared its conclusion Davis received an onset telephone call from Darryl F. Zanuck, her boss in the early days at Warner Bros. and who had been scathing when she quit her presidency of the Academy in 1941. She had not spoken to him since. His call was professional rather than cordial. As the head of Twentieth-Century Fox he was asking her to drop everything to read a script by Joseph L.

Davis with Joseph L. Mankiewicz, director of *All About Eve.*

Mankiewicz, for a film that he would also direct. Mankiewicz was very renowned, and a recent double Oscar winner for writing and directing *A Letter to Three Wives.* Zanuck explained that the part had been intended for Claudette Colbert, but she had sustained a serious back injury on a Swiss skiing holiday and had pulled out. He did not tell her that his preferred substitutes were Ingrid Bergman and Marlene Dietrich, neither of whom were available. Davis was not his favorite person, but he was shrewd enough to appreciate that she could make much of the role, Margo Channing in *All About Eve.*

Such was the brilliance of Mankiewicz's intelligent, satirical screenplay, crackling with sardonic one-liners and sharply observed portraits of the denizens of midtown Manhattan, the actors, producers, directors, writers, critics, agents of the theater world, and even a trenchant seen-it-all personal maid and dresser, that is hard to believe it was not specially written for Davis. It is arguably her most memorable role, and one that she made so personally appropriate that she utterly defined it, as every actress found who later played the part on stage. The critic Alexander Walker noted that Margo is a portrait of what Davis might have become had she stayed on Broadway rather than venturing out to the West Coast. It is the story of a celebrated actress who has become used to being at the top but has run into the one career problem that has no solution. She is getting old.

Almost immediately after the RKO film was finished, Davis began *All About Eve,* travelling by train to San Francisco where the Curran Theatre had been taken over for two weeks to simulate a Broadway counterpart. The titular role of Eve Harrington, brilliantly played by Anne Baxter, is the lesser one because Margo, the victim of Eve's insidious ambition, is center stage. Unwisely Margo succumbs to Eve's flattery, mistaking it for loyal adulation, and allows her into the gilded circle, unaware that she has embraced a ticking time bomb that will eventually blow up and finish her. Such was the cleverness of the screenplay that the film ends with cunning symmetry, with Eve, now at the top, finding she is being shadowed by a young person in her mold.

The cast included George Sanders, languid of voice, epicene in manner, deprecating in tone, as

Opposite: Davis as Margo Channing in *All About Eve.*

A triumphant role, only hers because Claudette Colbert injured her back.

"Margo Channing was not a bitch. She was an actress who was getting older and was not too happy about it. And why should she be? Anyone who says that life begins at forty is full of it. As people get older their bodies begin to decay. They get sick. They forget things. What's good about that?"

the drama critic Addison DeWitt, and in a small role as a vacuous starlet he escorts to a party, Marilyn Monroe, introduced by him as "a graduate of the Copacabana School of Acting." Thelma Ritter was particularly effective as the hardboiled dresser Birdie whom Mankiewicz supplied with caustic and irreverent observations. In the cast as Margo's lover and director was the rugged actor Gary Merrill, a New Englander with lineage back to the *Mayflower,* eight years younger than Davis and who had received glowing notices for his role as an air commander in the war film *Twelve O'Clock High.* Reality imitated art. Not only did they become lovers, but three weeks after her divorce from Sherry came through they were married, on July 28, 1950, in Juarez, Mexico. He was her fourth and last husband. By coincidence, her mother Ruthie had also married again in April that year, to a retired army captain. It would only last a little over eighteen months. Sherry married the twenty-one-year-old nanny of B.D. in August, and unwisely embarked on a custody battle that was thrown out when the judge found he was receiving alimony from Davis.

It was as though her life had taken an abrupt turn for the better. When *All About Eve* opened it was hailed as the greatest triumph of her career. It was deluged with Oscar nominations, fourteen in total, a record that was not surpassed until *Titanic* in 1998. Davis received eight nominations, and it is likely that she would have won her third Best Actress award if Anne Baxter had not also been nominated. It was the first time that two leads in the same film had been selected in the same category; the consequence was that although *All*

About Eve won Best Film of 1950, Davis and Baxter canceled each other out, and the award went instead to Judy Holliday for *Born Yesterday.*

Nevertheless, Davis had made one of the most celebrated comebacks in Hollywood history, comparable with and perhaps surpassing the triumph enjoyed by Joan Crawford five years earlier for *Mildred Pierce.* She had also escaped an unsatisfactory marriage and found a new husband with whom she felt a great rapport in spite of the age difference. But who was it that Gary Merrill had married? Was it Davis, forty-two-year-old Hollywood superstar with her best years behind her? Or was it Margo, in a bizarre extension of the film's plot which has Bill, Merrill's character, leading her into a quiet life in a New England farmhouse, after she accepts that her days in the limelight are at an end?

Davis with *All About Eve* costar Gary Merrill, soon to be husband number four.

A STOLEN LIFE

Warner Bros. (1946)

Credits

Director: Curtis Bernhardt
Producer: Bette Davis
Screenplay: Catherine Turney;
adaptation by Margaret Buell Wilder;
from the novel by Karel J. Benes
Cinematographers: Sol Polito, Ernest Haller

Cast

Bette Davis, Glenn Ford, Dane Clark,
Walter Brennan, Charles Ruggles,
Bruce Bennett, Peggy Knudsen, Esther
Dale, Clara Blandick, Joan Winfield

Running time: 109 minutes

Davis had wanted a chance to produce, choosing to remake a 1939 film starring Elisabeth Bergner and Michael Redgrave. She may have been attracted by the fact that she could play two parts, good and bad twin sisters, with Glenn Ford as the man between. It is an uninspiring work. Kate, a sweet, aspirant artist, falls for marine engineer Bill during a summer at Martha's Vineyard, but he is smitten by her lively twin, Patricia. She studies under a brilliant but difficult artist (Dane Clark), but accepts that she has no talent for painting and returns to Martha's Vineyard. There she is surprised to find Patricia, whom she believed had gone to Chile with Bill. There is a sailing mishap in a storm and Patricia is drowned. When Kate is washed ashore a lighthouse keeper (Walter Brennan) misidentifies her as Patricia, and she tries to deceive Bill on his return in the hope she can keep him. He sees through the ruse, revealing that it was Kate for whom he always really cared.

Trite and melodramatic, with a cliché-ridden screenplay, *A Stolen Life* was the only film Davis produced, and although she had hired Curtis Bernhardt to direct, the result was undistinguished.

Davis cake cuts with Glenn Ford in *A Stolen Life*, flanked by Peggy Knudsen and Rosalie Rey.

Scene still with Glenn Ford. Davis played a dual role as twin sisters.

Warner Bros. (1946)

Credits

Director: Irving Rapper
Producer: Henry Blanke
Screenplay: John Collier, Joseph Than;
based on the play *Jealousy* by Louis Vernuil
Cinematographer: Ernest Haller

Cast

Bette Davis, Paul Henreid, Claude Rains,
John Abbott, Benson Fong, Russell Arms,
Bess Flowers, Gino Corrado, Clifton Young,
Cyril Delevanti, Jane Harker

Running time: 112 minutes

After a run of forty-nine profit-makers, *Deception* proved a box-office failure for Davis. The production had been troubled and the budget over-extended. She was at an insecure juncture in her life, and it projects on the screen. The plot, loosely adapted from a stage play that had been filmed with Jeanne Eagels and Frederic March in 1929, was updated and made melodramatic.

Davis plays a pianist, a refugee who has anglicized her name to Christine Radcliffe and made a home in New York. The war has ended and she finds her former lover, Karel Novak (Paul Henreid), who had been left behind in Europe and presumed dead, is giving cello recitals on the college circuit, under the admiring eyes of gushing coeds. Their old passion is immediately rekindled and they agree to marry. He is whisked off to her loft apartment, a lush penthouse atop a

Davis strums Beethoven's *Appassionata* in *Deception*.

Reunited with
Paul Henreid,
returned from the
wartime dead.

tall, dowdy commercial building accessed by an industrial elevator, and is surprised to find it stuffed with high-end paintings and objets, with a rail of expensive furs in the closet, and a labor-saving kitchen that would have been the dream of 1946 housewives. Mystified, Karel asks how an impoverished musician can afford such luxuries and is told she teaches, but only very prosperous students who bestow her with gifts. She is dissembling, putting up a false appearance. The riches stem from a benefactor, a celebrated composer, Alexander Hollenius (Claude Rains) and she has been his mistress. Karel suppresses his suspicions and a whirlwind wedding takes place.

During the celebratory party Hollenius makes a dramatic entrance, demands champagne and

"Until you're known in my profession as a monster, you're not a star."

With Claude Rains, jealous and enraged by his mistress's desertion.

caviar, deprecates Karel, and during Christine's spirited rendering of Beethoven's *Appassionata*, crushes a wine glass in his hand in rage. He exits as abruptly as he arrives, effectively bringing the party to an end. The next day Christine visits him in his brownstone mansion and is deluged with bogus contrition and a promise to give Karel a chance to play his new cello concerto, which would establish him in the music mainstream. Hollenius insists on entertaining the wedded couple to a restaurant dinner before hearing Karel play, and

engages in an insufferable display of gamesmanship as he vacillates over a ridiculously lavish menu, torturing a man only lately liberated from starvation who is nervous enough already. The audition takes place off-screen but Karel reports that Hollenius humiliated him with interruptions.

Again Christine goes to see her former lover, this time bursting into his bedroom while he is immersed in the Sunday funnies, and is assured that Karel will be allowed his night of glory. Later she learns that he is also hearing a lesser musician called Gribble (John Abbott) and suspects that Hollenius intends to replace her husband. At the dress rehearsal Karel is ordered from the stage after objecting to Hollenius's treatment of a flautist, and is told to go home and prepare for the night's performance. Christine understands from Hollenius that his price for allowing her husband to play is that he will reveal to him and the world that she has been his mistress.

Just before the concert she calls on him again, and as he fails to withdraw his threat she shoots him dead, returning to the hall where Karel is giving a masterly performance and is hailed as a great new discovery. Afterward she confesses to him, and as they both walk out of the concert hall past the applauding onlookers an unknowing woman calls out, "Oh Christine—you must be the happiest woman in the world!"

Revealing the ending is usually regarded as a spoiler, but Warner Bros. saw to it that the principal poster artwork for *Deception* showed Davis firing a gun at Claude Rains, clutching his heart as if mortally wounded, so moviegoers were already aware of his fate. The poster may also have misled them into thinking they had paid to see a thriller rather than an intense, somewhat camp drama. It had been hoped that a reunion of the *Now, Voyager* team would bring similar success, but it was not to be.

The film is not without merit. Outstanding is Ernest Haller's silvery cinematography, with its deep shadows and luminous closeups. Ingenuity was used to make it look as though Henreid was actually playing the cello, and in tight shots the fingering is done by a real musician off-camera immediately behind him. The score is by Erich Wolfgang Korngold, even eliminating the traditional Warner Bros. fanfare, and his own Cello Concerto is used as Hollenius's magnum opus.

Paul Henreid has to play a glum, tormented, and somewhat charmless hero. Davis is not at her best. Her articulation occasionally hints at Central European roots, but not enough to suggest that she has made a deep study. She seems worried and unsure, and although it could be argued it would have been in character, she was undergoing various personal ordeals: a collapsing marriage, absence through illnesses including a car crash that left her with a hairline skull fracture, even a badly bruised finger when she slammed her dressing-room door on it in a tantrum. Her age was beginning to bother her as she approached forty, and she pleaded with Ernest Haller: "Why can't you make me look as I did in *Jezebel*?" Tactfully, he answered, "I was eight years younger then."

It is Claude Rains who steals the picture, in a bravura performance as an egomaniac. His lines are witty and beautifully delivered, even eluding the hawkeyed Production Code enforcers in innuendo.

Davis with Paul Henreid on the set of *Deception*.

"Christine you look ravishing tonight," he says. "Forgive me if I remain seated." The restaurant scene is a *tour-de-force* as he dithers over the ordering while the unctuous staff hover, burying his face in the carcass of raw game to sniff its worthiness, demanding trout from a good stream, abruptly deciding that his choice of wine would suit woodcock rather better than partridge, while his guest can only watch with swelling exasperation.

The plot holes are glaring, such as Karel's refusal to grasp the obvious where Christine's lifestyle is concerned, and why a wealthy unmarried man would want a mistress anyway. The homicide is illogical. It is premeditated since Christine has taken a gun with her, and if it is to conceal the past she might as well not have bothered because at the first opportunity she confesses all to Karel.

Warner Bros. (1948)

Credits

Director: Bretaigne Widust
Producer: Henry Blanke
Screenplay: Catherine Turney;
based on the novel by Ethel Vance
Cinematographer: Ernest Haller

Cast

Bette Davis, Janis Paige, James Davis,
John Hoyt, Florence Bates, Walter Baldwin,
Ransom Sherman, Hugh Charles,
George Taylor, Lois Austin, Robert Riordan,
Mike Lally, Doug Carter, Harry McKee,
Joe Minitello, Paul Maxey, Cedric Stevens

Running time: 104 minutes

Bretaigne Windust was making his film debut, having come from Broadway. A number of actors had been rejected or had turned down the male lead, including Burt Lancaster and Richard Widmark, but the eventual choice, the thirty-three-year-old James Davis, in spite of a number of previous credits, was not up to it. Davis, by now nearing forty, was conscious of Windust's instruction to Ernest Haller to light her softly—the traditional way of dealing with actresses over a certain age—and it did not help her confidence.

The story is a romantic triangle in which a young naval officer (James Davis) meets the spinster daughter of a minister, who fills her life with charity work and writing dull poetry. Smitten, he dumps his glamorous date (Janis Paige) and visits her apartment. The next day they drive to the house in Connecticut where her father killed himself after her mother left him for another man, and she explains why loving has proved so difficult for her. He tells her that he had wanted to be a priest, and she encourages him to follow his faith. It is a bleak, verbose, and unsatisfying work, and the screenplay is anemic, carefully avoiding offending religious susceptibilities, Catholic and non-Catholic.

The public shared the unease, and it was a box-office flop.

With James Davis, her limp costar keen to join the priesthood in *Winter Meeting*.

JUNE BRIDE

Her costar Robert Montgomery was as adept a screen-stealer as Miriam Hopkins.

Warner Bros. (1948)

Credits
Director: Bretaigne Windust
Producer: Henry Blanke
Screenplay: Ranald MacDougall;
based on the play *Feature for June* by
Eileen Tighe and Graeme Lorimer
Cinematographer: Ted McCord

Cast
Bette Davis, Robert Montgomery,
Fay Bainter, Betty Lynn, Tom Tully,
Barbara Bates, Jerome Cowan,
Mary Wickes, James Burke, Raymond Roe,
Marjorie Bennett, Ray Montgomery,
George O'Hanlon, Sandra Gould,
Esther Howard, Jessie Adams,
Raymond Bond, Debbie Reynolds,
Alice Kelley, Patricia Northrop

Running time: 96 minutes

In spite of the tensions of *Winter Meeting*, Bretaigne Windust directed the subsequent film, a sex-conflict comedy in which Davis plays a career woman who must give it all up if she wants her man. She is a high-powered magazine editor who has a former lover (Robert Montgomery), a war correspondent without a war, foisted on her by her publisher (Jerome Cowan). They cover an Indiana wedding together as she hopes that the subject matter will bore him enough to quit, but he relishes interfering with the nuptials to prevent a serious mismatch. Davis fires him for wrecking her article, but then realizes he has generated a far better human-interest story. It ends, rather appallingly for feminists, with her relinquishing her career to become a willingly subservient wife.

She found Montgomery had Miriam Hopkins's propensity for scene-stealing and could handle it more adroitly, particularly as Windust was not experienced enough as a movie director to know when to rein it in. He was also equally at home in comedy or drama. As a change of pace for Davis it merely demonstrated that broad comedy was not her *forte*. The public reaction was not entirely negative, and *June Bride* made a modest profit.

A break during filming of *June Bride*, 1948.

David Brian offers her escape to better things.

Warner Bros. (1949)

Credits

Director: King Vidor
Producer: Henry Blanke
Screenplay: Lenore Coffee; based on the
novel by Stuart Engstrand
Cinematographer: Robert Burks

Cast

Bette Davis, Joseph Cotten, David Brian,
Ruth Roman, Minor Watson, Dona Drake,
Regis Toomey, Sarah Selby, Mary Servoss,
Frances Charles, Harry Tyler,
Ralph Littlefield, Creighton Hale,
Joel Allen, Ann Doran

Running time: 97 minutes

Davis's last film after an almost unbroken eighteen-year reign at Warner Bros. was a severe disappointment. She was apprehensive at playing the lusty wife of a doctor (Joseph Cotten) in a dismal industrial town in Wisconsin who destroys her marriage by her desire to be with a Chicago industrialist (David Brian). Pregnant by him, she kills his lodge-keeper who has threatened to spill the secret, then tries to force her lover into carrying out an illegal abortion. She eventually receives her desserts in a grisly fashion.

Davis knew she was too old for the role. She also questioned the casting of handsome Joseph Cotten as the husband, instead of the loathsome, gross figure in the original novel. In spite of King Vidor as director, it is a bad film, Vidor later confided that he had very little rapport with Davis, but it has nevertheless survived in the memory on account of its famous line, "What a dump!"

Davis as flashy, flawed female lead, possibly too old for the part.

Bette's Husbands

Arthur Farnsworth ("Farney") died mysteriously.

Bette Davis Davis was married four times. Her first husband (1932–38) was Harmon Oscar Nelson, nicknamed "Ham," a college sweetheart when she was at Cushing Academy. He was a musician and they drifted apart, but he re-emerged in 1932 after she had become a movie actress, and they had a rapid marriage in Yuma,

Arizona. They divorced not long after her lawsuit in England when he left her to pursue his career in New York. Next up was Arthur ("Farney") Farnsworth (1940–43), a New Hampshire hotelier and pilot. Davis was at the peak of her career and they were often apart. He died suddenly in 1943, apparently from a head injury. He was thought to be engaged in secret aviation work for the government. William Grant Sherry (1945–50) followed—an artist of alcoholic disposition and violent propensity. They had a daughter, B.D., before divorcing. Finally came Gary Merrill (1950–60), Davis's costar in *All About Eve* and another prodigious drinker. They adopted a girl, Margot, who turned out to be brain-damaged, and a boy, Michael, now a successful lawyer. The marriage collapsed in acrimony and throughout the tour of their stage show, *The World According to Carl Sandburg*, they stayed in separate rooms.

License ceremony with William Grant Sherry.

With fourth husband Gary Merrill and Mike, Margot, and B.D.

Twentieth Century-Fox (1950)

Credits

Director/writer: Joseph L. Mankiewicz,
from the story and play by Mary Orr
Producer: Darryl F. Zanuck
Cinematographer: Milton Krasner

Cast

Bette Davis, Anne Baxter, George Sanders,
Celeste Holm, Gary Merrill, Hugh Marlowe,
Gregory Ratoff, Barbara Bates,
Marilyn Monroe, Thelma Ritter

Running time: 138 minutes

Margo Channing (Davis) is a celebrated Broadway actress, a winner of the fictitious Sarah Siddons award (named after the eighteenth-century British actress), whose dazzling career has peaked. Her fears and insecurities lie only just below the surface, as she becomes all too aware that a young upstart is set to knock her off her perch. She is Eve Harrington (Anne Baxter), who enters Margo's life as a starstruck idolizer, becomes her secretary, personal assistant, and understudy, and by insidious manipulation motivated by her ruthless ambition and steely talent, sets about supplanting her as the toast of Broadway. Narrating the flashback story on the night of the awards ceremony is Addison De Witt (George Sanders), a cynical drama critic.

Mankiewicz's screenplay not only flawlessly captures the brittle insincerities of the New York theater world, but crackles with iridescent wit and biting observation. As was often the case with his films, it is the women who have the best roles, and supporting Davis and Baxter are

With Gary Merrill and Anne Baxter as the titular Eve.

The costars in a studio portrait.

Davis married Merrill and retreated just like Margo.

Joseph Mankiewicz, Davis, assistant director Gaston Glass, and Gregory Ratoff

Celeste Holm as a friend, Thelma Ritter as the dresser who has seen it all, and even Marilyn Monroe in an early role as a vacuous blonde aspirant. But Sanders is languid to the point of narcolepsy, playing an effete role that Clifton Webb could have performed much better, while Hugh Marlowe as playwright and Holm's husband, and Gary Merrill as director and Davis's lover, are colorless and unmemorable.

For Davis, then forty-two, to play a star of that age, on the cusp of the downward slope, was a brave move. It was one of her best performances, and some of Mankiewicz's lines—particularly her loud comment at an edgy party: "Fasten your seatbelts. It's going to be a bumpy night"—became an indelible part of Hollywood folklore. Usually seen wreathed in cigarette smoke, her voice husky and rasping, her eyes betraying her growing terror, Davis is magnificent. Baxter, contrastingly, cleverly projects a false sweetness and bright-eyed guile. The film concludes on a satisfying note of irony after the usurper has become the youngest-ever recipient of the Siddons award.

A myth arose that Davis had modeled Margo on the flamboyant actress Tallulah Bankhead, who was so convinced and flattered that she railed against anyone who suggested otherwise. Margo was, in fact, an original creation, with at most a passing reference to an incident in the career of Elisabeth Bergner.

Joseph L. Mankiewicz won the Screenwriting and Best Director Academy Awards, and it was also Best Picture that year. Davis was nominated for Best Actress, as was Anne Baxter, the second female lead. To have two nominations from the same film was unprecedented, and unsurprisingly the split vote canceled each of them out. The Oscar that year went to Judy Holliday for her performance in the comedy *Born Yesterday,* a fine performance, but nevertheless a surprise, as the expectation was that the duel would be between Davis and Gloria Swanson for her role in *Sunset Boulevard.*

"*Fasten your seatbelts, it's going to be a bumpy night!*"

PAYMENT ON DEMAND

RKO-Radio (1951)

Credits
Director: Curtis Bernhardt
Producers: Jack H. Skirball, Bruce Manning
Screenplay: Bruce Manning,
Curtis Bernhardt
Cinematographer: Leo Tover

Cast
Bette Davis, Barry Sullivan, Jane Cowl,
Kent Taylor, Betty Lynn, John Sutton,
Frances Dee, Peggie Castle, Otto Kruger,
Walter Sande, Brett King,
Richard Anderson, Natalie Schafer,
Katherine Emery, Lisa Golm, Moroni Olsen

Running time: 91 minutes

Made before *All About Eve* but released after it, *Payment on Demand* was originally called *The Story of a Divorce*. Davis plays a wife of twenty years' standing who suddenly finds her husband (Barry Sullivan) wants a divorce. She learns that he has become involved with a schoolteacher (Frances Dee) and threatens to counter-sue unless he lavishes trust funds on their daughters (Betty Lynn and Peggie Castle). On a cruise before the final decree she meets a woman (Jane Cowl) who makes her aware of the plight of a middle-aged divorced wife. One of the daughters decides to marry, and her mother hastens home to warn her not to push her new husband too hard if she wants to keep her marriage from degenerating like her own. Her separated husband and she talk things over and the film ends on a hopeful note, suggesting the possibility of reconciliation.

Bette Davis with Barry Sullivan, the husband who wants a divorce.

An atmospheric example of the stillsman's art, Davis and Sullivan.

Davis's performance is relatively subdued and lacks the flashy bravura of *All About Eve*. On the other hand, it is well-judged for the subject matter, and although she hated the new title, thinking it sounded cheap, *Payment on Demand* was well received by the critics and the public.

The ending was imposed by Howard Hughes, the owner of RKO, who felt that the original, in which the couple went their own ways with finality, was too bleak and uncompromising, and would not be popular. Re-shooting took place at the last moment before the premiere at Radio City Music Hall in New York, giving the projectionist a headache as the film was already rolling when the amended last reel arrived hot from the airport. Fortunately Hughes also owned TWA, the airline, which helped save the situation.

PART 5
BEYOND THE PEAK
1952–89

by George Perry

THE fact that *Payment on Demand,* made before *All About Eve,* was not released until February 1951 was unhelpful in consolidating Davis's position as the comeback queen. Anticipating more of the entertaining bravura of Davis's performance as Margo Channing, the public was to be disappointed. Far from being inundated with attractive job offers Davis found herself mired in another professional hiatus. In addition, her new husband was not exactly making the best career choices for himself. At the instigation of Douglas Fairbanks, Jr., who had settled in London, the Merrills agreed to make a British film, a stagy thriller called *Another Man's Poison,* to be directed by Irving Rapper. They sailed to Britain on the *Queen Elizabeth* together with B.D., their newly adopted daughter Margot, a couple of nannies, and a housekeeper and were received by the British press as though they were Hollywood royalty.

In the early 1950s the gulf between American and British lifestyles was immense. Britain was shabby, rundown, and starved of luxuries. Food rationing still prevailed, severe exchange controls restricted foreign travel (which in any case was beyond the means of most people), and the streets of London still displayed many wartime bomb scars. Davis had insisted in her contract on a regular supply of prime-cut steaks to be flown in, and was not discreet in consuming them, causing ill-feeling while filming, when crew members would watch at lunch breaks as an entire week's meat ration would disappear in a single meal. The couple's extravagances made the newspapers, and Davis was criticized for behaving tactlessly and brashly, characteristics that defined the attitudes of postwar Americans for many Britons, their belts tightened by the demands of austerity.

Davis has lunch on a moor at Malham, Yorkshire.

Opposite: Davis as the matriarchal Alice Gwynne Vanderbilt in Little Gloria... Happy at Last, 1982

Adopting a casual feet-up pose, Davis in 1956.

Negulesco, *Phone Call from a Stranger* is about a man who walks out on his wife, takes a flight, and is delayed by bad weather, during which time he talks to three other travelers who each have a reason for their journeys. Later the plane crashes and as the sole survivor he visits the kin of his dead companions. Davis's character is paralyzed and bedridden, and her part is a catalyst in the tangled plot, devised by Nunnally Johnson in what must have been an off-moment.

She fared better with *The Star,* in which she plays an over-the-hill actress who goes on a drunken night drive through the streets of Hollywood and Beverly Hills, her Oscar wedged above the dashboard, a jaunt that finishes with her being locked up in jail. The screenplay by Katherine Albert and Dale Eunson, makes Margaret Elliot seem very close to a reflection of herself, with leechlike relations demanding a monthly paycheck, producers who wriggle out of encounters, and her own failure to come to terms with the ravages of time. In one scene she goes up for a test, fails to appreciate that it is for a middle-aged part, does herself up to look like Crawford (deliberately), and then vamps her way through the scene, embarrassing even herself when she views the rushes. As a comment on the state of Hollywood it has good moments, and even won Davis a ninth Oscar nomination, but it proved unpopular with the public.

Then, without any films on offer, Davis accepted an improbable invitation to be the lead in a Broadway revue, *Two's Company,* with lyrics by Ogden Nash set to music by Vernon Duke, and the numbers staged by Jerome Robbins. Davis

The film was another poor one, and Davis's performance as a murderess dosed with her own medicine was melodramatic and unconvincing. The locations in North Yorkshire were uncomfortable and the studios, Nettlefold at Walton-on-Thames, upstream from London, were tiny and decrepit, a leftover from silent days. After three months, Davis and Merrill were happy to return to the sunshine and abundance of California.

Gary Merrill was the star of Davis's next film, and she was billed way down the cast list, with only one scene amounting to a mere fifteen minutes of screen-time. Directed by Jean

had not been on the New York stage for twenty-two years and was choosing to appear in a song-and-dance show as the star. Gertrude Lawrence, Mary Martin, and Beatrice Lillie, *grandes dames* more suited to this kind of thing, were unavailable. Davis and Robbins had an edgy association and by his own admission, he was unaware of her talent in musical theater (which he disparaged), but admitted her abundance of personality and the strength of her fan following. The show was drastically revised on its preview tour, and opened in New York in December 1952 to unfriendly reviews but full houses, stimulated by curiosity. Sadly the run ended at ninety performances. Davis had been suffering from energy loss and a painful wisdom tooth, the treatment of which revealed severe osteomyelitis requiring drastic surgery on her jaw. Walter Winchell printed in his newspaper column that she had cancer, an untrue report that brought about legal rebuttal.

She went off to Maine to recuperate, a lengthy process during which she and Merrill were forced to accept that Margot, their adopted daughter, was brain-damaged and would require special residential care for the rest of her life. The Merrills' son Michael, who had been adopted by them in 1952, was mercifully unaffected. It was a strained domestic scene in their clapboarded rural house, Witch-Way. Gary Merrill gave up on his career, but not on the booze. Davis was bored with not working. Confrontations and violence occurred. Davis used B.D. as a weapon against Merrill. He used Michael in retaliation.

It was not until 1955 that she went back to work, to reprise an old role, that of Queen

Elizabeth, in *The Virgin Queen*, directed by Henry Koster in Technicolor and CinemaScope. She was playing the monarch this time at twelve years younger than as she was portrayed in *The Private Lives of Elizabeth and Essex* in 1939, and instead of Errol Flynn romancing her she had the wiry British actor Richard Todd, playing the freebooting, social-climbing Walter Raleigh, with the voluptuous Joan Collins as Elizabeth's young and attractive rival. Davis looked grotesque, her head

The Merrills and their children arrive in New York, 1953.

Revisiting her great role of Elizabeth in *The Virgin Queen*, 1955.

shaved and given a few wisps of white hair under a ludicrous and hideous orange wig. The film lost money for Twentieth Century-Fox.

Next came *Storm Center,* a misfired attempt to tackle the denial of freedom of speech when a town has a library book banned because it expresses communist views. It was released after *The Catered Affair,* which originated as a Paddy Chayefsky teleplay in which Davis played a Bronx housewife urging an expensive wedding on her daughter. Neither made much of an impact, and they were her last leading film roles for five years.

She made her television debut in 1956, in *The 20th Century-Fox Hour's* "Crack-up," but footage from *Phone Call from a Stranger* was recycled, and her true launch was not until the following year, when she appeared in dramas for General Electric Theatre, Ford Theatre, Schlitz Playhouse, and others. She even appeared in a segment of *Alfred Hitchcock Presents* directed by Paul Henreid, and in three episodes of the popular western series *Wagon Train,* playing the madam of a whore-house in one of them. From this point on, her main career income would be derived from television. Films became interludes.

Her role as Catherine the Great in *John Paul Jones,* directed by John Farrow, amounted to little more than a cameo, and in *The Scapegoat* (which starred Alec Guinness in a dual role), she played a bedridden, cigar-smoking, morphine-addicted dowager.

Meanwhile, her marriage had gone sour. There was a separation and a strained reconciliation. Both she and Merrill drank considerably and she became increasingly worried by his disinclination to resume his career. Eventually they moved back to California to be close to the television industry, and he began working again. The quarreling and domestic dramas did not diminish, though. She was obliged to withdraw from a play after falling down a cellar staircase in their rented Brentwood house.

On their return from Europe, she and Merrill took to the stage in 1960 in *The World of Carl Sandburg,* an evening of readings from his poetry and prose. It toured thirty-two different locations nationwide, but they occupied separate hotel rooms throughout. In San Francisco they played in the theater that had been the location for *All About Eve,* and they even stayed in the same hotel where their romance had begun ten years earlier. But Davis served divorce papers, Merrill quit the show, and without a celebrated married couple as a magnet, *The World of Carl Sandburg* fizzled on its brief New York run. As she wrote in *The Lonely Life*: "I am sure I have been uncompromising, peppery, intractable, monomaniacal, tactless, volatile and oftimes disagreeable. I stand accused of it all."

There were fraught court battles for the next four years, mostly involving custody issues, and all suits brought by her. She embarked on *The Lonely Life* with a sympathetic and often exasperated ghostwriter, Sanford Dody, as much out of an acute need for money as a desire to set the record straight. To compound her misfortunes, her mother Ruthie died in 1961, aged seventy-five, from coronary thrombosis. Extravagant to the last, her dying wish had been for a silver coffin, which her daughter, at that time desperately short of ready cash, ordered in plain oak. Even though her mother had sponged mercilessly off her for years, Davis carefully excised every derogatory reference to her from Dody's manuscript, and when *The Lonely Life* was finally published he felt that the account was flawed, compromised, and unreliable.

Davis was offered her first central role in an important film in many years when Frank Capra cast her as Apple Annie in *A Pocketful of Miracles,* a glossy color remake in Panavision of his Depression-era hit *Lady for a Day.* It was a Damon

Bob Hope, with Davis and Oscar winners Marlon Brando and Grace Kelly in 1955.

Runyon story in which a down-and-out apple seller is temporarily transformed into an elegant lady of wealth to impress her daughter visiting from Europe with a rich foreign fiancé, the philanthropist being a bootleg king with all the right underworld connections. Davis found her costar, Glenn Ford, unappealing, especially when he made an attempt to annex her dressing room for his girlfriend Hope Lange, who was playing his moll. The film was overlong, ponderous, and sentimental, and it was a failure.

In 1961 Davis appeared on Broadway in Tennessee Williams' new play, *The Night of the Iguana,* with her name big but the part small (the third lead). She worked hard on the playwright to have the role souped up, and was gratified to find that audiences would give her a show-stopping ovation when she stepped on stage, which she milked shamelessly. Some critics were less admiring, however, and pronounced the play not so much an iguana as a turkey. After 128 perform-ances Davis quit for medical reasons, possibly the onset of chronic boredom from having to sit in her dressing room before she could make her next entrance.

There was a backlog of heavy expenses to cover, so she was happy to accept an offer from Robert Aldrich to make a film with Joan Crawford, her long-term rival, who according to the script she was sent would undergo humiliation and torture from her sadistic sibling, to be played by Davis.

Her part in *Whatever Happened to Baby Jane?* was as showy a role in an upscale horror film as it would be possible to find, a forgotten Hollywood child star who lives in a decaying Norma Desmond-style faded Hollywood mansion with her seriously crippled sister, once the leading romantic actress of her time before she was mys-teriously injured in a car crash. Jane (Davis) becomes so consumed by insane jealousy that instead of looking after Blanche (Joan Crawford) she turns her into her victim, serving her a cooked parakeet and a roasted rat on her meal tray, kicking her senseless, fettering her to her bed with her arms bound over her head and her mouth gagged with duct tape, and starving her to the point of death.

Both women were the same age, although Davis claimed that Crawford was born in 1904, not 1908 and lied because where she came from they had not gotten around to registering births properly. What was undeniable was that Davis had not aged well. She was wrinkled and dumpy, her mouth set in a permanently sour, sneering expression. Crawford on the other hand was glamorous, elegant, and took great care to pre-

Filming the Malibu finale of *Whatever Happened to Baby Jane?* with Joan Crawford.

serve her slender figure. Davis was not worried at having to look grotesque in the film, with thickly applied makeup "like Mary Pickford in ruin" and ridiculously childish ringlets, while Crawford hankered to wear chic peignoirs and show off her well-shaped legs, both desires vetoed by the script, which required her to be bedridden most of the time. When Blanche finally expires on the beach at Malibu, while Jane, in an advanced stage of infantilism, prances around like a little girl concerned with finding ice cream, she was wearing such outrageously erect falsies that when Davis fell on her she was almost winded by the impact.

With a director's canniness, Aldrich used the tensions between his stars to make *Whatever Happened to Baby Jane?* work on film, and the relatively low-budget production turned an excellent profit at the box office. Davis received another Academy Award nomination, but the statuette that year went to Anne Bancroft for *The Miracle Worker*. Davis's triumph over her costar not even being nominated was effectively squelched on Oscar night, when Crawford went up to collect the award for Bancroft who could not be there. Davis later blamed Crawford for campaigning against her, although she had no evidence.

In the immediate aftermath of *Baby Jane*'s opening she puzzled the industry by placing an advertisement in the Hollywood trades that said she was "more affable than rumor would have it" and "wants steady employment in Hollywood (has had Broadway)." Was it a joke, desperation, a mad aberration, an act of career suicide? It was

widely noticed, and brought her considerable publicity, but the success of *Baby Jane* led to her being regarded as only suitable for horror roles, which she resisted.

In 1963 B.D. married a young British film executive, Jeremy Hyman, whom she had met at the Cannes Film Festival. Davis was unexcited and suspicious, especially as B.D. was only sixteen, almost half his age. As the years passed both would be subsumed by mutual loathing, although she would bestow considerable chunks of her declining wealth on the couple.

Davis and Crawford, and their *Baby Jane* flashback selves, Julie Allred and Gina Gillespie.

A makeup artist touches up Davis's nose for *Where Love Has Gone.*

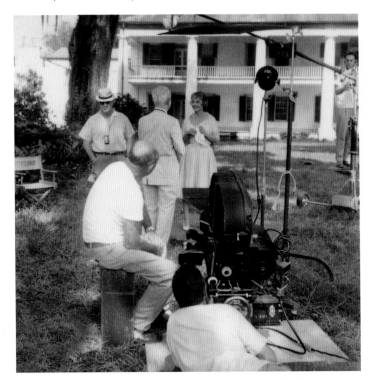

Robert Aldrich and plantation house, *Hush...Hush, Sweet Charlotte.*

Her next film was a tedious and undistinguished dual-identity thriller, *Dead Ringer,* directed by Paul Henreid, using the twin sibling plot device of *A Stolen Life.* It was the last time she worked with her favorite cinematographer, Ernest Haller. This was followed by a film in Italy, *The Empty Canvas,* produced by Sophia Loren's

husband Carlo Ponti, in which she played Horst Buchholz's mother. She was also in a film from a Harold Robbins novel, *Where Love Has Gone,* with echoes of the Lana Turner–Johnny Stompanato case, and found herself in contention with its star, Susan Hayward, who outpointed Davis in the finer ways of divadom. Davis's excuse for appearing at all was that it helped meet the enormous costs of B.D.'s wedding.

The reunion of Crawford and Davis was seen as a magic formula for box-office success, and Robert Aldrich began shooting them in *Hush...Hush, Sweet Charlotte,* a southern gothic melodrama set in a Louisiana plantation house. The strains between them were too much this time, and Crawford, constantly absent through illness, left the production within a month. She was replaced after an anxious shutdown by Olivia de Havilland. Davis was cast once again as an unhinged participant in a mystery from many years earlier, and others in the cast included Joseph Cotten, Agnes Moorehead, and in her last screen appearance, Mary Astor.

It was followed by a trio of films in England, two from the producer-writer Jimmy Sangster. The best was *The Nanny,* a psychodrama directed by Seth Holt, in which a disturbed little boy is unable to convince the adults in his life that his nanny is psychotic and dangerous and has already killed his baby sister. It was followed by *The Anniversary,* with Davis playing a domineering, one-eyed matriarch who insists on gathering her dysfunctional sons and their partners to celebrate her marriage to their deceased father, a hellish evening in which she grinds everyone present to

Davis playing a grandmother in *Where Love Has Gone.*

Davis, two years before her death, with honorees including Sammy Davis, Jr.

paste. She failed to endear herself to the rest of the cast by having the director Alvin Rakoff fired because he used television, not film methods. A more serious film, *Connecting Rooms*, with Michael Redgrave as costar, was little seen. A ludicrous pairing with Ernest Borgnine in *Bunny O'Hare* had them playing a senior-citizen Bonnie and Clyde, robbing banks and making getaways on a motorbike.

In 1974 there was great excitement in theatrical circles at the announcement that Davis was to return to the stage in a musical version of *The Corn Is Green* under the direction of Joshua Logan, with the title *Miss Moffat*. Sadly, stage fright, temperament, a weak score, incompatibility with her director, and many other factors brought about its closure before it had even opened.

Much of her work in later years was in television, occasionally with sparks of the old Davis emerging. On film she was one of the many suspects in *Death on the Nile*, and was seen in a couple of Disney films, *Return from Witch Mountain* and *The Watcher in the Woods*. Her last film was *Wicked Stepmother* as a witch, but she withdrew during the production, forcing a drastic change to the script and her replacement by a young and beautiful Barbara Carrera. As the character was a witch anything was possible.

Her true envoi to cinema was a film made in her beloved Maine by the British director Lindsay Anderson and adapted by David Berry from his play. She costarred with Lillian Gish, many years her senior, in *The Whales of August*. They play two elderly sisters who have spent each summer in the same island cottage overlooking a point where the whales used occasionally to appear. Davis is blind, lame, and cantankerous, and is looked after by Gish with the awareness that their time together is nearly done. The presence of two other great veterans of the screen, the septuagenarians Ann Sothern and Vincent Price, added to the elegiac tone. That two great cinematic icons of different generations should have appeared together in their twilight years makes the film remarkable, and Gish proved far tougher and more impervious to Davis's barbs than many lesser players by simply switching off her hearing aid whenever any nonsense occurred.

Davis's final years were not easy. On the one hand she had received attention earlier when she toured *The Bette Davis Show,* an evening of film clips and a Q and A session, and it was clear that she was still held in high regard for her achieve-

Robert Wagner congratulates Davis as she receives the American Film Institute's Lifetime Achievement Award, 1977.

ments. She appeared in several TV features, some of which were notable, such as *The Disappearance of Aimee,* with Faye Dunaway, and *Little Gloria…Happy at Last,* for which she received an Emmy nomination. She was the first woman to receive the American Film Institute's Lifetime Achievement Award, which meant that she was the center of attention at a glitzy Hollywood ceremony beamed by television to the millions.

Her son Michael, meanwhile, had graduated, married his high-school sweetheart, and embarked on a normal, stable life that he continues to enjoy. Davis's disorganized life came under better control when she hired as her personal assistant a young woman, Kathryn Sermak, who, with astonishing dedication and loyalty, stayed with her until the end.

As Bette Davis progressed through her middle age mostly only character roles came her way

ANOTHER MAN'S POISON

United Artists (1952)

Credits
Director: Irving Rapper
Producers: Douglas Fairbanks Jr.,
Daniel M. Angel
Screenplay: Val Guest; based on the play
Deadlock by Leslie Sands
Cinematographer: Robert Krasker

Cast
Bette Davis, Gary Merrill, Emlyn Williams,
Anthony Steel, Barbara Murray,
Reginald Beckwith, Edna Morris

Running time: 88 minute

Davis and her husband Gary Merrill went to England to make *Another Man's Poison* at the behest of Douglas Fairbanks, Jr., with whom she had appeared in *Parachute Jumper* in 1933. He co-produced the film with Daniel M. Angel, and Irving Rapper directed it at the tiny Nettlefold Studios at Walton-on-Thames to the southwest of London, and on location in North Yorkshire.

She plays a mystery writer having an affair with the young fiancé (Anthony Steel) of her secretary (Barbara Murray), but her husband (Reginald Beckwith) suddenly appears, having escaped prison and robbed a bank, wrecking her devious plans. She kills him when he tries to blackmail her, and his accomplice (Gary Merrill) helps her dispose of the body. A suspicious vet (Emlyn Williams) is misled into believing he is her returned husband, but when the accomplice kills her beloved horse she poisons him, and tells the doctor that he was an imposter. When the doctor tells her he has called the police she faints, and he tries to revive her with the same spiked brandy.

Such indifferent melodrama was scarcely worth the Atlantic crossing, and Rapper allowed Davis too much self-indulgent emphasis in her performance.

With Gary Merrill in her first film made in England.

PHONE CALL FROM A STRANGER

Gary Merrill plays David, a husband who walks out of his marriage, unable to forgive his wife for having deceived him. He boards a plane for Los Angeles and makes the acquaintance of three other passengers: Binky (Shelley Winters), a failed showgirl returning to a husband dominated by a fierce mother; Dr. Fortness (Michael Rennie) who is on his way to confess to a district attorney his part in an automobile crash that killed three people; and Eddie, a loudmouthed traveling salesman (Keenan Wynn) who is determined to be the life and soul of the party with his inane jokes, pranks, and noisy laughter, and who flashes a photograph of the lovely wife who awaits him. The aircraft crashes in a heavy storm over the Rockies and David is the only survivor of the group.

In Los Angeles he makes it his business to seek out the spouses of his companions, and in so doing is able to effect closure on their bereavement, in two of the three cases by being imaginative with the truth. Davis does not make her entrance until nearly the end of the film and is only on screen for about fifteen minutes. She is Eddie's widow, and far from the leggy bathing belle in his photograph, she is bedridden and paralyzed. She explains how she had run away with another man, been seriously injured in an accident, and had been abandoned by her fickle lover, and how her husband came for her at the hospital, said "Hello, beautiful," and spent the rest of his life tending and loving her with unquestioning devotion. David is so moved by her story that he calls his wife long-distance for a joyful reconciliation.

Nunnally Johnson's story follows the pattern of *A Letter to Three Wives* in weaving together a number of stories with an intriguing theme, but it seems rather more contrived than the former film. The look is also cheap, with basic sets, crude miniatures (on a good print the wires holding the model airliner aloft are visible), and flashbacks bookended by a negative freeze frame. Davis appears in little more than a cameo role, but even playing most of it in bed she is in total control, and brings distinction to what would otherwise be a mundane work.

Swimming accident with runaway lover Warren Stevens.

Twentieth Century-Fox (1952)

Credits

Director: Jean Negulesco
Producer: Nunnally Johnson
Screenplay: Nunnally Johnson; based on a story by I. A. R. Wylie.
Cinematographer: Milton Krasner

Cast

Shelley Winters, Gary Merrill, Michael Rennie, Keenan Wynn, Evelyn Varden, Warren Stevens, Beatrice Straight, Ted Donaldson, Craig Stevens, Helen Westcott, Bette Davis, Sydney Perkins, Hugh Beaumont, Thomas Jackson, Harry Cheshire, Tom Powers, Freeman Lusk, George Eldredge, Nestor Paiva, Perdita Chandler, Genevieve Bell

Running time: 96 minutes

Twentieth Century-Fox (1952)

Credits

Director: Stuart Heisler
Producer: Bert E. Friedlob
Screenplay: Dale Eunson, Katherine Albert
Cinematographer: Ernest Laszlo

Cast

Bette Davis, Sterling Hayden,
Natalie Wood, Warner Anderson,
Minor Watson, June Travis, Paul Frees,
Robert Warrick, Barbara Lawrence,
Fay Baker, Katherine Warren, Herb Vigran

Running time: 90 minutes

Margaret Elliott (Davis) is an actress on the Hollywood scrap heap, in her forties and unemployable in the romantic roles that made her name. A messy divorce, bad investments, a fire-sale auction of her possessions, and leechlike relatives have reduced her to bankruptcy. A nocturnal drunk-driving spree, her Oscar propped on the dashboard, lands her in jail. Bailed out by Jim Johannsson (Sterling Hayden), a decent boat repairer with a years-long crush on her, she follows his advice and gets a job selling lingerie at the May Co. department store. It ends disastrously when she is recognized. She is auditioned for a character part in a film that has long been on her wish list, but alters her costume and makeup, twists the script, and ignores the director in the belief that she can usurp the up-and-coming Barbara Lawrence for the lead. When she watches the test even she realizes what a horrible mistake she has made. Later she is offered the role of a declining Hollywood star who has forgotten to be a woman, and in her moment of epiphany, decides to rush back to the ever-hopeful Jim, and in Congreve's words "dwindle into a wife."

The washed-up star theme had been much more satisfactorily explored in Billy Wilder's *Sunset Boulevard* two years earlier, and

Jailed for drunk driving, Davis as the washed-up star Margaret Elliott.

Natalie Wood, 13, plays Elliott's daughter who lives with the divorced husband, a successful cowboy star.

Heisler's direction plods its way to Davis's next histrionic outburst. The final sequences are rushed and unconvincing, and the conclusion reinforces the stereotypical view of American womanhood before women's lib became a factor. Hayden, with his blond hair, tanned torso, and sweet, forgiving nature is a little too good to be true. As is Natalie Wood, playing her fourteen-year-old daughter Gretchen, who lives in a sumptuous Beverly Hills property with her movie-star father and his second wife. She is utterly wholesome and totally loyal to her mother, believing all her lies about her career.

The writers Eunson and Albert had been associated with Joan Crawford, and when she reworked her appearance in the screen-test sequence Davis most certainly had her in mind, applying Crawfordesque eyebrows and lipstick, and saying, "Bless you" to the crew at the end of the take in the manner of her rival. There would have been resonances for Davis, too, in Margaret Elliott's plights of advancing age, marital problems, and disillusionment with Hollywood, and even the constancy of dependent relatives.

THE VIRGIN QUEEN

Twentieth Century-Fox (1955)

Credits
Director: Henry Koster
Producer: Charles Brackett
Screenplay: Harry Brown, Mindret Lord
Cinematographer: Charles C. Clarke

Cast
Bette Davis, Richard Todd, Joan Collins,
Jay Robinson, Herbert Marshall, Dan
O'Herlihy, Robert Douglas, Romney Brent,
Marjorie Hellen, Lisa Daniels, Lisa Davis,
Barry Bernard, Robert Adler, Noel Drayton,
Ian Murray, Margery Weston, Rod Taylor,
David Thursby, Arthur Gould-Porter

CinemaScope
DeLuxe Color

Running time: 92 minutes

Good Queen Bess is revisited, sixteen years after Davis made *The Private Lives of Elizabeth and Essex*. Oddly the action predates the earlier film by twelve years or so, yet the monarch at forty-eight, roughly corresponding to the star's own age, looks rather older, for the most part wearing a grotesque carrot-colored wig that traverses her scull at the middle point, making it appear as though her forehead is extending halfway across her head.

The action is centered on her meeting and sponsoring the dashing privateer Walter Raleigh, while conceiving an impossible passion for him. In the earlier film Raleigh was a minor role, played by Vincent Price, and the enemy of its hero, Essex (Errol Flynn). This Raleigh is small and agile, portrayed by Richard Todd as something of an opportunist who uses the queen as a means of voyaging to the New World and securing his fortune. These two leading men do not compare well. Flynn was lithe, graceful, and heroically handsome. Todd's Raleigh is chippier, bumptious, and not particularly likeable, and lacks Flynn's presence. It is like comparing an elegant golden retriever with a yapping terrier.

He is first seen in a sixteenth-century rural inn, populated by gallants quaffing ale from pewter tankards and where comely wenches frolic with customers in the alcoves. The *faux* Elizabethanism is compounded by antique dialogue that approximates to the language of Shakespeare's time without a shred of the poetry. Having engaged in an over-choreographed sword fight with a rival, Raleigh, newly returned from the Irish wars, wins the task of detaching the Earl Marshal of England's coach from a muddy pothole, securing a visit to the royal court. As his lordship, Herbert Marshall is unrecognizable behind a bushy gray beard, but his silver voice identifies him, and he genially remains a stalwart supporter of Raleigh who inveigles himself into the queen's favor, most notably by spreading his expensive (rented) cloak across a puddle in her path.

He is immediately appointed captain of the guard, displacing others in patronage, notably Chadwick (Robert Douglas), who becomes a sworn enemy. He also attracts Beth Throgmorton (Joan Collins), a forward lady-in-waiting well aware of the risks associated with incurring the queen's displeasure. Sure enough, when Beth and Raleigh marry clandestinely, both are carted off as prisoners, and her neck is only spared because she is pregnant.

Elizabeth visits Raleigh in the Tower on the eve of his execution, reminisces about how she was kept there as a little girl when her mother Anne Boleyn was beheaded, and spectacularly relents, giving him a ship to seek riches for her court. With her extraordinarily powerful telescope she watches the couple leaning over the rail as it makes its way down the Thames. Her vantage point would suggest that her palace had been relocated to Rotherhithe on the south bank, otherwise Raleigh would be sailing the wrong way, but this is, after all, Hollywood history where anything can happen.

Essentially, though, that is what is wrong with the film. It is Hollywood bunkum, absurdly over-lit, so that the interiors, particularly when it is dark outside, suggest that Elizabethans conducted their indoor life under powerful floodlights. The ladies-in-waiting, led by Joan Collins, are young, glamorous, and Max Factorized to an absurd degree, so that when the red-wigged queen is in their midst she looks like Danny Kaye in drag attended by the Goldwyn Girls. The ultra-wide CinemaScope compositions are clumsy, and over the years television viewers have been frustrated

Davis as Elizabeth carries off an unflattering marmalade hairpiece.

when even "pan and scan" adjustment has been defeated by two-shots where each performer is at opposite ends of the frame.

Nevertheless, Davis gives a strong, courageous performance as a queen who must suppress her womanliness in the face of the unyielding call of monarchical duty. She allows herself to be made up to look like an old bat, even at one point snatching off her nightcap to reveal a head almost bald from the effects of disease. In many ways it is a sounder portrayal than her 1939 version, as though the toil of the intervening years have given her greater insight to discern more of the complexities of Elizabeth.

The Catered Affair

Metro-Goldwyn-Mayer (1956)

Credits

Director: Richard Brooks
Producer: Sam Zimbalist
Screenplay: Gore Vidal; based on the
teleplay by Paddy Chayefsky
Cinematographer: John Alton

Cast

Bette Davis, Ernest Borgnine,
Debbie Reynolds, Barry Fitzgerald,
Rod Taylor, Robert Simon, Madge Kennedy,
Dorothy Stickney, Carol Veazie,
Joan Camden, Ray Stricklyn, Jay Adler,
Dan Tobin, Paul Denton, Augusta Merighi,
Sammy Shack, Jack Kenny,
Robert Stephenson, Mae Clarke

Running time: 92 minutes

Made before *Storm Center* but released after it, *The Catered Affair* (released as *Wedding Breakfast* in the UK) was originally a television drama. Davis plays Agnes, the wife of a Bronx cab driver (Ernest Borgnine). Their daughter, Jane (Debbie Reynolds), is anxious to marry and drive to Los Angeles with her fiancé (Rod Taylor) before honeymooning in Mexico. Davis has other ideas, and in an attempt to move into the same league as the prospective in-laws, decides to blow the family savings dedicated for a new taxicab on an extravagant hotel reception, which leads to familial ructions and near disaster. It comes right in the end.

Davis allowed herself to be turned into a dumpy, ageing housewife with an Irish-American accent, but she is at the center of the plot as a formidable matriarch. According to Debbie Reynolds, Richard Brooks, the director, was not happy with either her or Davis, and would have preferred both actresses to have come from the New York theater rather than Hollywood. There is small-scale look to the film that indicates its television origins.

"You're going to have a big wedding whether you like it or not! And if you don't like it, you don't have to come!"

Davis as a Bronx housewife with Debbie Reynolds as her soon-to-be married daughter.

STORM CENTER

Playing a beleaguered librarian, Davis with Paul Kelly, the judge who supports her.

Columbia (1956)

Credits
Director: Daniel Taradash
Producer: Jukian Blaustein
Screenplay: Daniel Taradash, Elick Moll
Cinematographer: Burnett Guffey

Cast
Bette Davis, Brian Keith, Kim Hunter,
Paul Kelly, Kevin Coughlin, Joe Mantell,
Sallie Brophy, Howard Wierum,
Curtis Cooksey, Michael Raffetto,
Edward Platt, Kathryn Grant,
Howard Wendell, Burt Mustin,
Edith Evanson

Running time: 86 minutes

Storm Center was an issue film, highlighting Cold War paranoia. Davis is a librarian who defies her municipal bosses by refusing to suppress a book that supports Communism, citing the Constitution and free speech. She is nevertheless dismissed, and investigations suggest that she has harbored pro-Communist sympathies in the past. A misguided boy (Kevin Coughlin) who has been inspired by her burns the library down, an act that causes the townspeople to rethink. They accept that political censorship has no place in America and ask her to lead the reconstruction. The poor script resonates with implausibility, and the idea, which had some validity in the Eisenhower years, goes entirely to waste.

Warner Bros. (1959)

Credits

Director: John Farrow
Producer: Samuel Bronston
Screenplay: John Farrow, Jesse Lasky, Sr.
Cinematographer: Michel Kelber

Cast

Robert Stack, Marisa Pavan, Charles Coburn, Erin O'Brien, Tom Brannum, Bruce Cabot, Basil Sydney, Archie Duncan, Thomas Gomez, Judson Laure, Bob Cunningham, John Charles Farrow, Eric Pohlmann, José Nieto, Jack Crawford, Patrick Villiers, Franl Latimore, Ford Rainey, Bruce Seton; Guest Stars: Macdonald Carey, Jean-Pierre Aumont, David Farrar, Peter Cushing, Susanna Canales, Georges Rivière, Bette Davis

Technicolor
Technirama

Running time 126 minutes

As Catherine the Great, with Robert Stack as the American seadog.

Made in Spain, *John Paul Jones* was a biography of the founder of the US Navy, with Robert Stack playing the seafarer of the early days of Independence, who had to fight political battles to gain recognition for the US as a sea power. Davis spent four days on the film playing Catherine the Great of Russia, who offers Jones a command but with conditions of a personal nature that he feels disinclined to accept. The film was filled with stiffly clichéd historical figures, and her Catherine was no exception.

THE SCAPEGOAT

Better things might have been expected from the director, producer, and star of Ealing Studios' sublime *Kind Hearts and Coronets*, especially as Alec Guinness this time attempts only two parts rather than eight. He plays an English professor on holiday in France who meets his doppelganger, an aristocrat who uses their similarity to kill his wife (Irene Worth), and then plots to have the Englishman who has convincingly masqueraded as him murdered as well. In a duel to the death, one of them will emerge to marry the mistress (Nicole Maurey).

Bette Davis plays the aristo's bedridden, drugaddicted mother, a relatively small part made smaller by the inroads Guinness made on her part of the script. The film failed, and was not even one she enjoyed making, finding Guinness too self-absorbed to offer much to other actors. In turn, he considered her aloof, and felt she ignored all overtures of friendship. To compound the disaster the once-brilliant Robert Hamer was consumed by the alcoholism that would eventually kill him, and he had little rapport with Davis.

Metro-Goldwyn-Mayer (1959)

Credits

Director: Robert Hamer
Producer: Michael Balcon
Screenplay: Gore Vidal, Robert Hamer;
based on the novel by Daphne du Maurier
Cinematographer: Paul Beeson

Cast

Alec Guinness, Bette Davis,
Nicole Maurey, Irene Worth,
Pamela Brown, Annabel Bartlett,
Geoffrey Keen, Noel Howlett, Peter Bull,
Leslie French, Alan Webb, Maria Britneva,
Eddie Byrne, Alexander Archdale,
Peter Sallis

Running time: 92 minutes

Left: Davis appears as a fuddled, ailing countess in a rare Guinness failure.

Apple Annie offers fruit to Dave the Dude.

United Artists (1961)

Credits

Director and Producer: Frank Capra
Screenplay: Hal Kanter, Harry Tugend;
based on *Madame La Gimp* by Damon
Runyon and a screenplay by Robert Riskin
Cinematographer: Robert Bronner

Cast

Glenn Ford, Bette Davis, Hope Lange,
Arthur O'Connell, Peter Falk, Thomas
Mitchell, Edward Everett Horton, Mickey
Shaughnessy, David Brian, Sheldon
Leonard, Ann-Margret, Peter Mann, Barton
MacLane, John Litel, Jerome Cowan, Jay
Novello, Frank Ferguson, Willis Bouchey,
Fritz Feld, Ellen Corby, Gavin Gordon,
Benny Rubin, Jack Elam, Mike Mazurki,
Hayden Rorke, Doodles Weaver, Paul E.
Burns, George E. Stone, Snub Pollard

Eastmancolor
Panavision

Running time: 137 minutes

Damon Runyon's story had originally been filmed rather more economically by Frank Capra in 1933 as *Lady for a Day*, with May Robson in the principal role of Apple Annie. Dressed in rags, she peddles apples on the streets around Times Square. She has a long-lost daughter who has been raised in Europe and intends to come to New York on a visit with her fiancé, a young Spanish nobleman. Annie has been writing to her on stationery filched from a deluxe hotel and is horrified that her daughter will find that she is little more than a bag lady. An underworld leader and ace bootlegger Dave the Dude (Glenn Ford) rides to the rescue, using a vacated penthouse complete with an attentive butler (Edward Everett Horton) and engaging the services of crimpers, manicurists, couturiers, beauty consultants, and sundry other specialists. To cap it they also have to lay on a party to which the *crème de la crème* are invited. Can they pull it off? In Runyonland anything is possible.

Capra's second version of the yarn is far too long for a comedy with a predictable ending, and Glenn Ford is not an obvious comic lead as the crook with a heart of gold. Hope Lange as his fiancée tends to be too shrill and abrasive, but Horton, his famous prune-like features even more wizened and wrinkled in his later years, shamelessly scene steals, even from Davis. She handles the transformation well enough, emerging from her Apple Annie castoffs as a rather regal figure, a dignified dowager who

has acquired the bearing and manner of the high-born. It is, after all, sheer fantasy, so should not be judged too harshly for its plausibility.

There are two auspicious debut perform-ances. Ann-Margret, playing the daughter, looks young and bubbling but is given no opportunity to dance, although she does manage part of a song. Peter Falk excels as Glenn Ford's top aide, and delivers his witty lines with an immac-ulate touch.

Hope Lange salutes the transformed street seller, now lady for a day.

Baby Jane, losing her mind, bent on cruel revenge.

Bette Davis and Joan Crawford play Hollywood sisters whose glory days expired a quarter of a century earlier. Baby Jane (Davis) had been a child star in vaudeville whose brief film career fizzled after the early 1930s. Her sister Blanche (Joan Crawford) has been a wheelchair recluse since being paralyzed in an automobile accident at the height of a successful film career. Baby Jane looks after her sister, who cannot venture downstairs in the big old Hollywood mansion where they live on the investments Blanche made in her glory days. Jane goes around in a blonde wig of cascading ringlets and plasters her face with more makeup than a circus clown, while Blanche, in her chair or in bed, merely looks like an older, more sedate version of

Crawford herself (emphasized while she is seen tearfully watching one of her own movies, and complaining that the director should have held her close-up for longer).

Baby Jane is fast sliding into dementia and is tormenting her sister to the point where she dare not remove the cover from her dinner plate lest

Seven Arts and Warner Bros. (1961)

Credits
**Director and associate producer:
Robert Aldrich
Executive producer: Kenneth Hyman
Screenplay: Lukas Heller; based on the novel by Henry Farrell
Cinematographer: Ernest Haller**

Cast
Bette Davis, Joan Crawford, Victor Buono, Marjorie Bennett, Maidie Norman, Anna Lee, Barbara Merrill, Julie Allred, Gina Gillespie, Dave Willock, Ann Barton

Running time: 133 minutes

Left: Taunting her crippled sister (Joan Crawford) in her role as guardian.

"Blanche, you aren't ever gonna sell this house ... and you aren't ever gonna leave it either."

The jailer preparing slow death by starvation for her helpless victim.

there be a cooked cage bird or a roasted rat with all the trimmings beneath. Harboring insane notions of a comeback, Jane orders replicas of her little-girl costumes and advertises for a music arranger. A bloated, epicene Victor Bueno arrives, eager more for the money than the job, and picks his way at the piano through her excruciating rendering of "I've Written a Letter to Daddy," while she is starving her sister and has chained

her to the bed with duct tape over her mouth. Their cleaner (Maidie Norman) discovers the prisoner on an unexpected return to the house when she thinks Baby Jane is out. She is hammered to death before she can reveal the goings-on.

In the final stages Jane drives her dying sister to Malibu, where eventually the police find her on the beach, waving ice creams and performing her Baby Jane routine to a bemused crowd. Before dying, Blanche has finally told her the truth about the accident for which Jane was always to blame.

The pairing of two ageing and legendary divas renowned for their icy disposition to each other was enormously appealing to the public, who saw some elements of real-life conflict in their portrayals. Davis designed her own makeup and was undismayed by her grotesque appearance. Crawford demanded she maintain a normal appearance, and underplayed her part in a carefully measured voice no matter how great was her suffering. At one point Davis gives an excellent impersonation of the Crawford tones when she poses as her on the telephone to a doctor to cancel a demand for an immediate house call.

Davis emotes manically throughout the film, in what was probably her greatest feat in an impressive career of scenery chewing, but remains rooted in character as the crazy Baby Jane, while Crawford is much more passive, sometimes because she is bound and gagged. There is a remarkable overhead shot in which she rotates vigorously in her wheelchair as the desperation of her situation sinks in, and another where she makes a painful attempt to ease herself downstairs, clutching the banister in order to reach a telephone to summon help.

Robert Aldrich, who had a talent for the horrific thriller, builds what begins as a satirical comment on Hollywood's fickle abandonment of its former moneymaking stars—a topic for which both actresses would have a regard. He develops it into black comedy, particularly with the early scenes involving Victor Buono and his diminutive, pushy Australian mom (Bennett), then escalates it into a Grand Cuignol horror story, as though *Psycho* had imposed itself on *Sunset Boulevard*.

At the beginning of the film are two pre-title flashback sequences, the first set in 1917 with the precocious child in her nauseating stage act tap-dancing, simpering, shaking her curls, and singing nasally, with her beaming father hawking Baby Jane dolls to the patrons, while her sister Blanche watches with silent envy in the wings. After the show Baby Jane has a nasty tantrum at the stage door in front of the fans. The other flashback is in the mid-1930s, with Baby Jane's dud acting on screen viewed by a jaded executive who brings a halt to her career. He has actually been watching an amalgam of clips from a couple of real Bette Davis films from the period, *Ex-Lady* and *Parachute Jumper*, the latter starring Crawford's husband of the time, Douglas Fairbanks, Jr. Davis was self-deprecating enough to have them used to show Baby Jane was no good as a film actress, unlike her successful sister Blanche who has become a leading romantic star. The sequence that ends with the "accident" shows that it was the deliberate act of one sister to gun the accelerator

and run down the other while she is opening the gate of their driveway after a Hollywood party.

Legend has it that during the sequence where Baby Jane viciously beats and kicks Blanche as she lies helpless on the floor, Davis did not restrain herself and Crawford ended up needing twelve stitches to her head. Examination of the film itself shows that there is no shot of Davis actually making contact with Crawford, although her frenzy and loss of control is so bloodcurdlingly realistic that it is perfectly possible to be deluded into thinking that Crawford was sustaining a real beating.

Blanche slowly expires on the beach at Malibu, while Jane re-enters childhood.

Joan Crawford

Davis and Crawford: a prickly teaming, but magnificent box-office.

Lucille LeSueur (there was some Huguenot blood in her ancestry) was born in San Antonio, Texas, in 1905 or possibly 1904, but certainly not 1908 as she later claimed. Births were not registered there then. She had a difficult childhood, with broken homes, early lost virginity, and menial drudgery. A talent for dancing got her into chorus work, and by 1925 she had reached Hollywood. She became Joan Crawford with her second film and a star with *Our Dancing Daughters* in 1928.

By the time Davis arrived in Hollywood Crawford was well-established. Later she upset Davis by stealing and marrying her romantic interest and *Dangerous* costar, Franchot Tone. Crawford's contract with MGM was terminated in 1943, but Warner Bros. signed her and she won the Oscar for *Mildred Pierce*, a role Davis had declined because

she did not want to be encumbered with a sixteen-year-old daughter. Crawford was a lesser actress, but outclassed Davis in glamour and grooming, and constantly strived to project a starry façade to the public. Their only film together, *Whatever Happened to Baby Jane?*, was riddled with tension and acrimony but was an enormous box-office hit. A follow-up, *Hush ... Hush, Sweet Charlotte* was completed with Olivia de Havilland replacing Crawford, who withdrew because of illness.

Animosity between them persisted until death, and even beyond it. Davis was reminded once when she was in full rant that Crawford had been dead for two years, and snarled back: "Just because a person's dead doesn't mean they've changed."

Reunited with two of his greatest stars, a pleased Jack L. Warner.

The two great divas strived to stay professional for the film's sake.

"She has slept with every male star at MGM except Lassie."

LA NOIA
(THE EMPTY CANVAS)

Davis with Horst Buchholz and Catherine Spaak. Below: Games with Buchholz.

Embassy (1964)

Credits

Director: Damiano Damiani
Producer: Carlo Ponti
Screenplay: Tonino Guerra, Ugo Liberatore,
Damiano Damiani; based on a novel
by Alberto Moravia
Cinematographer: Roberto Gerardi

Cast

Bette Davis, Horst Buchholz, Catherine
Spaak, Daniela Rocca, Lea Padovani,
Isa Miranda, Leonida Repaci, Georges
Wilson, Marcella Rovena, Daniela Calvino,
Renato Moretti, Edoardo Nevola, Jole
Mauro, Mario Lanfranchi

Running time: 118 minutes

Davis went to Rome to film this dismal work, which had Horst Buchholz playing a painter whose deficient artistic muse is led astray by a model (Catherine Spaak). Davis plays his mother, who sports a bizarrely incongruous southern accent and who picks up the pieces for him after he has shredded his career out of frustrated love. The direction varies from mere incompetence to criminal neglect.

DEAD RINGER

Once again Davis played twin sisters, and was photographed for the last time by Ernest Haller, who died shortly afterward, their collaboration having begun with *The Rich Are Always With Us* in 1932. Like *A Stolen Life* the plot hinges on one sibling taking the place of the other after disguising murder as suicide. In assuming the new identity she finds that her lover, a police sergeant (Karl Malden) believes her dead, but her sister's slimy boyfriend (Peter Lawford) is not deceived and blackmails her. After he is killed by her late brother-in-law's dog she is accused and sentenced to death for poisoning her sister's husband, and nobody believes that she has switched identities. On the whole the film is a trashy melodrama of no distinction, in spite of being directed by Paul Henreid, her *Now, Voyager* costar.

Paul Henreid shooting *Dead Ringer* with Peter Lawford and Davis.

Warner Bros. (1964)

Credits
Director: Paul Henreid
Producer: William H. Wright
Screenplay: Albert Beich, Oscar Millard;
based on a story by Rian James
Cinematographer: Ernest Haller

Cast
Bette Davis, Karl Malden, Peter Lawford,
Philip Carey, Jean Hagen,
George Macready, Estelle Winwood,
George Chandler, Mario Alcalde,
Cyril Delevanti, Monika Henreid,
Bert Remsen, Charles Watts, Ken Lynch

Running time: 115 minutes

Davis in the second role of her career in which she played twin sisters.

WHERE LOVE HAS GONE

Paramount (1964)

Credits

Director: Edward Dmytryk
Producer: Joseph E. Levine
Screenplay: John Michael Hayes; from
the novel by Harold Robbins

Cast

Susan Hayward, Bette Davis, Michael
Connors, Joey Heatherton, Jane Greer,
DeForest Kelley, George Macready, Anne
Seymour, Willis Bouchey, Walter Reed,
Ann Doran, Bartlett Robinson, Whit Bissell,
Anthony Caruso, Jack Greening, Olga
Sutcliffe, Howard Wendell, Colin Kenny

Running time: 114 minutes

Harold Robbins seems to have taken his inspiration for an element of his steamy novel from the Lana Turner–Johnny Stompanato case, in which the star's teenage daughter stabbed and killed her mother's shady lover. Susan Hayward takes the principal role, with Joey Heatherton as her daughter and Davis as grandmother, a role played with as much commanding dignity as could be mustered in such trashy surroundings. It appears that she only took the role to meet the inflated costs of her daughter's wedding. She and Hayward clashed, with the younger actress having the edge. In spite of a screenplay by John Michael Hayes, screenwriter of Hitchcock's *Rear Window*, it was a meretricious work, mercifully soon forgotten. As Davis's character so remarks: "Somewhere along the line the world has lost all its standards and all its tastes."

Davis with Susan Hayward and Michael Connors.

HUSH...HUSH, SWEET CHARLOTTE

An aborted attempt to make a second film with Crawford.

Twentieth Century Fox (1964)

Credits

Director and producer: Robert Aldrich
Screenplay: Henry Farrell, Lukas Heller;
based on a story by Henry Farrell
Cinematographer: Joseph Biroc

Cast

Bette Davis, Olivia de Havilland,
Joseph Cotten, Agnes Moorehead,
Cecil Kellaway, Victor Buono, Mary Astor,
William Campbell, Wesley Addy,
Bruce Dern, George Kennedy,
Dave Willock, John Megna, Ellen Corby,
Helen Kleeb, Marianne Stewart,
Frank Ferguson, Mary Henderson,
Lillian Randolph, Geraldine West,
William Walker, Idell James,
Terry Buckner and His All-Stars

Running time: 134 minutes

Before any hint of opening titles other than it is 1927, a handsome Louisiana plantation house is seen, in which a vigorous argument is taking place between a young Bruce Dern as John Mayhew and Victor Buono as Big Sam, the bellicose owner who is in a thunderous mood. Mayhew is a married womanizer who has been dallying with Big Sam's daughter. He buys him off, forcing him to tell her that evening at a big party that he is rejecting her. That night, while the bright young things are jigging to the All Stars, John has his difficult moment with Charlotte (Davis) who is badly upset. A little while later a missing chopper is used to hack his hand and head off, and Charlotte appears among the dancers with her dress covered in blood, in one of the greatest party-pooping moments in film history.

After the opening titles the action moves to the present (1964) and Charlotte is living in the old house as a recluse, with only a bizarre house-keeper (Agnes Moorehead), as manic as her mistress, for company.

Davis with housekeeper Agnes Moorehead. Who was the crazier?

The case against her in the 1920s collapsed for lack of witnesses, and ever since she has lived like a southern Miss Havisham, not quite always in her wedding dress, but haunted by the memories of the past and the irrational notion that her lover is still somehow present.

The house is about to be torn down to allow a new bridge to be built across the Mississippi, but she has refused to move out, and her cousin Miriam (Olivia de Havilland), a successful New York career woman, visits, ostensibly to help. Miriam had left many years earlier when Drew (Joseph Cotten), now Charlotte's doctor, had broken their engagement, but they are now on friendly terms. Charlotte believes that all her problems are the consequence of a vendetta conducted by Jewel (Mary Astor), John Mayhew's widow.

An insurance investigator and amateur criminologist (Cecil Kellaway) has long been fascinated by the case and turns up to try to work out what really happened. He is puzzled why Jewel had not claimed John's life assurance, finding her excuse that there was too much paperwork feeble and implausible. Strange things begin to happen in the old mansion—the piano playing in the night when nobody is there, relics of the tragedy suddenly appearing, including the severed head rolling down the staircase, a ghostly voice calling Charlotte's name. Death will revisit the doomed house and the mystery will be resolved.

Originally Joan Crawford was to have costarred with Davis in the hope of repeating the success of *Whatever Happened to Baby Jane?* (the original title was *Whatever Happened to Cousin Charlotte?*) but after a month of shooting in which she was repeatedly absent through illness, she abruptly quit. Her health was cited as the cause, and she checked into the Cedars of Lebanon hospital, but the atmosphere on set between the two divas had been poisonous. Production was suspended for several weeks until a substitute could be found. Olivia de Havilland, who took over at short notice, was an admirable choice, albeit in a role that was not as sympathetic as she would have liked. In fact, with Davis, de Havilland, Moorehead, Cotten, and Astor, Aldrich had assembled a formidable cast.

The result was an elegant, if lengthy, exercise in Grand Guignol horror, and the tone becomes increasingly macabre. Olivia de Havilland represents unusual casting, and embraces the role in a completely different way from Joan Crawford. The plot twists are many, and while some are flagged well in advance, there are still some unsettling surprises.

Olivia de Havilland came to the rescue when Crawford quit.

Davis went to England and to Hammer, responsible for a broad range of horror films that had established a viable niche. *The Nanny* turned out to be at the top end of their output. The director, Seth Holt, was capable but died after only three films so his talent went largely unfulfilled. Wendy Craig and James Villiers are dysfunctional parents in London whose ten-year-old child Joey (William Dix) is returning home after a two-year spell in a special school, where he had been sent after being thought to have drowned his two-year-old sister in the bathtub. He is

Davis in her Norland nanny uniform.

Seven Arts–Hammer, Twentieth Century-Fox (1965)

Credits

Director: Seth Holt
Producer: Jimmy Sangster
Screenplay: Jimmy Sangster; based on the novel by Evelyn Piper
Cinematographer: Harry Waxman

Cast

Bette Davis, Wendy Craig, Jill Bennett, James Villiers, William Dix, Pamela Franklin, Jack Watling, Maurice Denham. Alfred Burke, Nora Gordon, Sandra Power, Harry Fowler, Angharad Aubrey

Running time: 93 minutes

With William Dix as her ten-year-old charge.

Whatever is Nanny doing with that cushion?

convinced that Nanny (Davis) was responsible, but nobody heeds him. He tells his aunt (Jill Bennett) that Nanny has since tried to drown him. She tries to check out his story, but suffers a heart attack which Nanny ignores while describing how she had come home to find the little girl dead in the bath.

It is somehow typical of a certain class of British parents who leave their children in the charge of people who are clearly unbalanced, and then ignore every warning sign that anything is amiss. The tension builds well, and Davis plays her role admirably. It is more a psychological thriller than a horror story. Pamela Franklin is effective as a young teenager who is more sinisterly knowing than she appears.

BETTE DAVIS'S CHILDREN

The Merrills at home with their daughters, B.D. and Margot.

Barbara Davis Sherry was born May 1, 1947 when her parents were living in Laguna Beach, California. Her mother was then thirty-nine. The child was given the nick-name "B.D." by her father and henceforth was generally known by these initials. After the marriage break-up Bette Davis married the actor Gary Merrill who formally adopted B.D. in 1950. She appears as a child in *Payment on Demand,* and as the teenage daughter of the next-door neighbour in *Whatever Happened to Baby Jane?* but she had no high aspirations to pursue an acting career. In Cannes with her mother for the latter film's premiere she met and quickly married a British movie executive, Jeremy

Above: B.D. visits her mom at work on a soundstage.

Right: Bette greets Michael while filming *The Nanny* in London.

Hyman, in the face of parental misgivings as she was only sixteen. Nevertheless, her mother, who doted on B.D., lavished a fortune on the wedding, and subsequently gave them much financial support as well as bailing the couple out of risky ventures. The shock Bette Davis endured in 1985 after her stroke, when B.D. published a scathing denunciation of her upbringing, *My Mother's Keeper,* was brutal, and caused a permanent rift. B.D. expressed public indifference on national television on her mother's death in 1989, and was cut out of the will. She became a born-again Christian and now lives in Virginia.

The Merrills adopted a baby girl in 1950 and named her Margot, after Margo Channing, her most recent screen portrait. Sadly the child was severely retarded and had to spend her life in

With B.D. before her book and irreparable rift.

professional care. They were luckier when they adopted a boy, Michael, in 1952. In spite of his stormy infancy in which the Merrills outdid each other in alcoholic abuse as the marriage disintegrated, he grew up to be remarkably well-adjusted and became a respected lawyer. After the publication of B.D.'s book (followed by another which had less success) Michael ceased to have any dealings with her. A few years after Davis died he and her loyal assistant Kathryn Sermak established the Bette Davis Foundation to award college scholarships to promising young acting talents. The Foundation's first lifetime achievement award was given at Boston University in 1998 to Meryl Streep.

Davis at home with Margot, Bel Air, 1964.

THE ANNIVERSARY

Seven Arts–Hammer (1968)

Credits

Director: Roy Ward Baker
Producer: Jimmy Sangster
Screenplay: Jimmy Sangster; based on the play by Bill McIlwraith
Cinematographer: Harry Waxman

Cast

Bette Davis, Sheila Hancock, Jack Hedley, James Cossins, Christian Roberts, Elaine Taylor, Timothy Bateson, Sally-Jane Spencer, Arnold Diamond, Albert Shepherd, Ralph Watson

Color

Running time: 95 minutes

The second film Davis made in England for Jimmy Sangster was a lightweight Shaftesbury Avenue comedy that gave her the opportunity to play one of her most monstrous females. Mrs. Taggart is the widow of a wealthy house builder who has carried on the family business with the help of her three sons, who she bullies mercilessly. The eldest, Henry (James Cossins), is a closet gay who steals women's underwear from laundry lines. His brother Terry (Jack Hedley) has four children and another on the way, borne stoically by the wife (Sheila Hancock) Mrs. Taggart openly despises. The youngest, Tom (Christian Roberts) is having another try at introducing a girlfriend (Elaine Taylor) to his mother. They are all gathered to celebrate her wedding anniversary, a ritual she insists on carrying out in spite of her spouse's deceased state, and which gives her an opportunity to inflict her barbs on everybody present. The startled girl is told, "My dear, would you mind sitting somewhere else. I cannot stand body odor."

Davis relished the role of the fearsome termagant, who has only one eye (the reason emerges in the course of the grisly evening) and a wardrobe of color-coordinated patches. The stage origins of the piece are somewhat obvious in spite of attempts to open it up, such as having the anniversary dinner take place at a pretentious restaurant where most of the items on the menu are served flambé. By the end of the evening each son will have his plans for the future crushed or eviscerated, and the old harpy will revel in her fiendish triumphs of manipulation, with her single eye set on further humilia-

Family gathering: the matriarch flanked by Elaine Taylor, Christian Roberts, Jack Hedley, and Sheila Hancock.

tions to be bestowed on the next occasion. Alvin Rakoff was originally intended to direct, but after a week Davis had him fired because she found that he blocked his scenes as if it was television.

CONNECTING ROOMS

Davis was proud to play opposite Michael Redgrave.

Hemdale (1972)

Credits

Director: Franklin Gollings
Producers: Harry Field, Arthur Cooper
Screenplay: Franklin Gollings; based on
the play by Marion Hart
Cinematographer: John Wilcox

Cast

Bette Davis, Michael Redgrave,
Alexis Kanner, Kay Walsh, Gabrielle Drake,
Olga Georges-Picot, Leo Genn,
Richard Wyler, Brian Wilde, John
Woodnutt, Tony Hughes

Running time: 103 minutes

Eking a living as a cellist playing to a theater line.

Connecting Rooms was another film made in England, but its release was so limited that it was hardly seen, and although shot in 1969 it was not shown in the US until 1972. Davis plays a cellist who barely makes a living. Alexis Kanner is a young songwriter who flirts with her, and is put out when a newly unemployed teacher (Michael Redgrave) comes to stay in the same London boarding house and becomes amiable. The younger man discovers that he lost his job because of a suspected homosexual relationship with a pupil, and reveals the fact. However, she remains true to her new friend, who has been unjustly accused.

Davis made the film largely for the opportunity to work with Sir Michael Redgrave, one of Britain's most distinguished theatrical knights. The result was one of the least known of her films, a fate that seems inexplicable. It is a long way from being one of her worst.

BUNNY O'HARE

American International (1971)

Credits

Director: Gerd Oswald
Producer: Norman T. Herman
Screenplay: Stanley Z. Cherry,
Coslough Johnson
Cinematographers: Loyal Griggs,
John M. Stephens

Cast

Bette Davis, Ernest Borgnine, Jack Cassidy,
Joan Delaney, Jay Robinson, Reva Rose,
John Astin, Robert Foulk, Brayden Linden,
Karen Mae Johnson, Francis R. Cody, Darra
Lyn Tobin. Hank Whickam, David Cargo

Color

Running time: 91 minutes

Above: Too old to be hippies, Ernest Borgnine and Davis.
Left: Evicted, Davis samples the outdoor life in New Mexico.

In this embarrassingly unfunny caper comedy, Davis plays an Albuquerque widow, thrown out of her home by a heartless bank, and watches it destroyed in front of her. She hits the road, and ties up with Ernest Borgnine, who makes a living selling used toilet equipment to Mexicans. After finding out that he is a retired bank robber she persuades him to teach her the business. Dressed as geriatric hippies they ride around on a motorbike sticking up banks, pursued by an inept policeman played by Jack Cassidy. The director is way out of his depth, or was totally squelched by a Davis in a belligerent mood.

MADAME SIN

A pilot for a projected television series, *Madame Sin* was made in England and released theatrically in Europe. It is a James Bond-style thriller, with Robert Wagner as the action hero and Davis a grand-scale Asiatic villainess with a Scottish castle and a plot to seize a nuclear submarine skippered by Gordon Jackson. The series never transpired and in the US, *Madame Sin* played as TV Movie of the Week.

Davis with Robert Wagner, action hero.

Davis: villainess in a TV pilot released theatrically outside the US.

ITC (1972)

Credits

Director: David Greene
Producers: Lou Morheim, Julian Wintle
Screenplay: David Green, Barry Oringer
Cinematographer: Anthony B. Richmond

Cast

Bette Davis, Robert Wagner, Denholm Elliott, Gordon Jackson, Dudley Sutton, Catherine Schell, Pik Sen Lim, Paul Maxwell, David Healy, Alan Dobie, Al Mancini, Roy Kinnear, Charles Lloyd Pack, Frank Middlemass, Arnold Diamond

Color

Running time: 90 minutes

LO SCOPONE SCIENTIFICO

(THE SCIENTIFIC CARDPLAYER)

Davis deals with Alberto Sordi, Silvana Mangano, and Joseph Cotten.

C.I.C. (1972)

Credits
Director: Luigi Comencini
Producer: Dino de Laurentiis
Screenplay: Rodolfo Sonego
Cinematographer: Giuseppi Ruzzolini

Cast
Alberto Sordi, Silvana Mangano, Joseph Cotten, Bette Davis, Domenico Modugno, Mario Carotenuto

Running time: 113 minutes

Davis plays a wealthy card addict who has a perverse pleasure in pitting her skills against people who are in a position to lose. She gambles a million lire with a poor couple (Alberto Sordi and Silvana Mangano), who are determined to outsmart her but are nevertheless trounced. So they plot a revenge.

Burnt Offerings

Oliver Reed and Karen Black play a couple with a young son (Lee Montgomery) who rent an old house for the summer, unaware that it is malevolently haunted and will try to destroy them. Davis plays an old aunt who battles against the malignancy and is killed. As old, dark house films go it is the minor league, stuffed with the clichés of the genre without any panache. Although Davis strived hard to give a memorable performance, particularly effective when she is engulfed by evil, she was miserable throughout the filming, and later described making it as "amateur night in Dixie." Critics and public did not disagree.

Davis with Karen Black, unwitting renter of a haunted house.

United Artists (1976)

Credits
Director: Dan Curtis
Screenplay: William F. Nolan, Dan Curtis.
Based on a novel by Robert Marasco
Cinematographer: Jacques Marquette

Cast
Karen Black, Oliver Reed, Burgess Meredith, Eileen Heckart, Lee Montgomery, Dub Taylor, Bette Davis, Joseph Riley, Todd Turquand, Orin Cannon, Jim Myers, Anthony James

Color

Running time: 116 minutes

Davis cradles a frightened boy (Lee Montgomery).

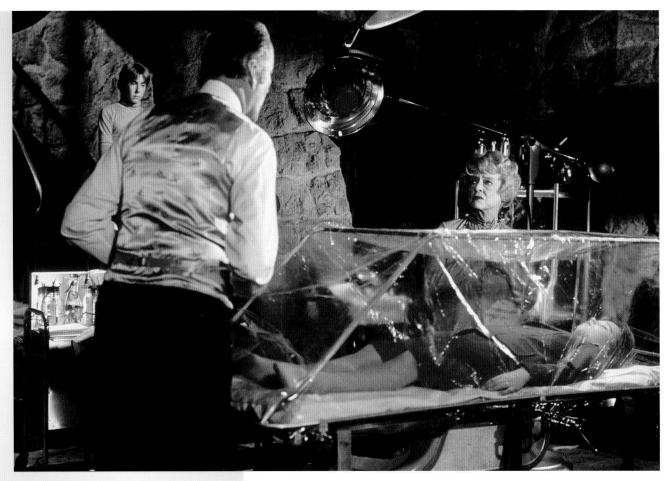

Christopher Lee faces inert Kim Richards, watched by Ike Eisenmann and Davis.

Disney (1978)

Credits

Director: John Hough
Producers: Ron Miller, Jerome Courtland
Screenplay: Malcolm Marmorstein; based
on characters created by Alexander Key
Cinematographer: Frank V. Phillips

Cast

Bette Davis, Christopher Lee, Kim Richards,
Ike Eisenmann, Jack Soo, Anthony James,
Richard Bakalyan, Ward Costello,
Christian Juttner, Brad Savage,
Poindexter Yothers, Jeffrey Jacquet

Color

Running time: 95 minutes

In the sequel to the 1975 Disney success *Escape to Witch Mountain*, Kim Richards and Ike Eisenmann again play the extraterrestrial siblings, this time taking an earthly vacation. They are hijacked by a villainous scientist (Christopher Lee) and his colleague in avarice (Davis) for some nasty-mind experimentation, but are eventually rescued by a posse of imaginative street kids. See Davis levitate. Or not. An undignified milepost in her late career, it was inevitably not a patch on its predecessor although it attracted reasonable box-office attention. Why did Davis appear? She argued that she wanted to be in a film that her grandchildren could actually go and see, which was difficult when so many were in the horror category. Having Lee as a co-villain would have been another incentive, and John Hough was an amiable, understanding director.

DEATH ON THE NILE

A lavish Agatha Christie whodunit, *Death on the Nile* has Peter Ustinov as Hercule Poirot unmasking the killer of a female guest (Lois Chiles) aboard a private steamer cruising on the Nile. Only in the final drawing-room scene, where the suspects are all gathered, does he deftly reach a surprising conclusion. The cast is impressive, the cinematography of Egypt shimmering in the heat impeccable, and the suspense holds. Anthony Shaffer handles the standard Christie plot framework with deftness, as though he is toying with an art form. Davis's role is that of a haughty Washingtonian, with Maggie Smith as her traveling companion. Both are suspects, of course, in this superbly mounted exercise in nostalgia.

EMI (1978)

Credits

Director: John Guillermin
Producers: John Brabourne,
Richard Goodwin
Screenplay: Anthony Shaffer; based on
the novel by Agatha Christie
Cinematographer: Jack Cardiff

Cast

Peter Ustinov, Jane Birkin, Lois Chiles,
Bette Davis, Mia Farrow, Jon Finch,
Olivia Hussey, George Kennedy,
Angela Lansbury, Simon MacCorkingdale,
David Niven, Maggie Smith, Jack Warden,
Harry Andrews, I. S. Johar,
Sam Wanamaker

Color

Running time: 140 minutes

An upper-class murder suspect in a Christie whodunit.

THE WATCHER IN THE WOODS

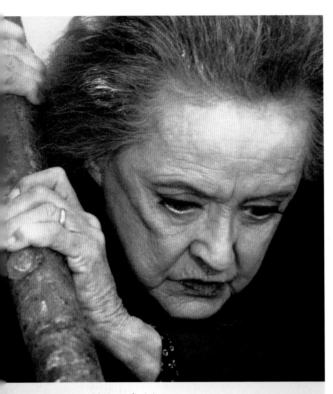

An aged, sinister presence.

Disney (1980)

Credits

Director: John Hough
Producer: Ron Miller
Screenplay: Brian Clemens, Rosemary Ann
Sisson, Harry Spalding;
based on the novel *A Watcher in the Woods*
by Florence Engel Randall
Cinematographer: Alan Hume

Cast

Bette Davis, Lynn-Holly Johnson, Kyle
Richards, Carroll Baker, David McCallum,
Benedict Taylor, Frances Cuka,
Richard Pasco, Ian Bannen, Katharine Levy,
Eleanor Summerfield, Georgina Hale

Color

Running time: 84 minutes

David McCallum playing a composer and Carroll Baker his wife, accompanied by their teenage daughters (Lynn-Holly Johnson and Kyle Richards), rent a big English country house for the summer from an old woman, Davis, who lives in a cottage in the grounds. The girls feel a presence, as though they are being watched, and it is as though they are channeling a spirit from the woods surrounding the place of a girl who disappeared thirty years earlier. Davis's role is not large but it is memorably sinister. It is actually a ghost yarn for older children, and there was some indecision over how it should have ended, with an alternative version released later.

IT WAS JUST AN INNOCENT GAME
UNTIL A YOUNG GIRL VANISHED...
FOR THIRTY YEARS.

the watcher in the woods

WALT DISNEY PRODUCTIONS PRESENTS "THE WATCHER IN THE WOODS"
Starring BETTE DAVIS · CARROLL BAKER · DAVID McCALLUM
LYNN-HOLLY JOHNSON · KYLE RICHARDS · IAN BANNEN as "Keller"
RICHARD PASCO as "Colley" Music Composed and Conducted by STANLEY MYERS Associate Producer HUGH ATTWOOLL
Screenplay by BRIAN CLEMENS, HARRY SPALDING and ROSEMARY ANNE SISSON From the novel "A Watcher in the Woods" by FLORENCE ENGEL RANDALL
Co-produced by TOM LEETCH Produced by RON MILLER Directed by JOHN HOUGH TECHNICOLOR ®
Released by BUENA VISTA DISTRIBUTION CO., INC. © 1981 Walt Disney Productions

Davis in creepy form in a children's ghost story.

Two generations of great screen icons: Lillian Gish and Bette Davis.

Nelson Entertainment (1987)

Credits
Director: Lindsay Anderson
Producers: Carolyn Pfeifer, Mike Kaplan
Screenplay: David Berry, based on his play
Cinematographer: Mike Fash

Cast
Lillian Gish, Bette Davis, Vincent Price,
Ann Sothern, Harry Carey Jr.,
Frank Grimes, Frank Pitkin, Mike Bush,
Margaret Ladd, Tisha Sterling,
Mary Steenburgen

Color

Running time: 90 minutes

Davis's penultimate film is really her valedictory. Remarkably she is teamed with Lillian Gish, who at ninety-three remains the oldest actress to have appeared in a starring role. The era is the early 1950s and they play a pair of old sisters, both widows, who have stayed in the same Maine summer cottage for fifty years. Gish is in better health and remains lively and optimistic. "Busy, busy, always busy," mutters Davis. She is blind, demanding, and cantankerous, and quickly vetoes the handyman's suggestion that a picture window looking out to sea might be a good idea. She is also much more aware than her sister that the Grim Reaper is soon to call. The other characters in what is essentially a four-hander are Ann Sothern, a slightly younger neighbor and a friend for half a century, and Vincent Price, an elderly Russian aristocrat down to his mother's last piece of jewelry, who survives by visiting friends.

Not much happens in David Berry's adaptation of his own play beyond a realization and an acceptance of the little of life's joys that are still left. The sisters end as they began, in flashback to a much earlier time on the point looking out to watch the whales that customarily used to visit each summer, but which have now stopped coming. Almost certainly this will be the last summer that they share.

That two such great icons should be on screen together in their twilight years was a matter of considerable interest, particularly as Lillian Gish represented the film generation before Davis, the era of D. W. Griffith and silent cinema. She found Davis oddly aloof and not easy to know. Perhaps it was simply awe. Lindsay Anderson directed it in a muted, restrained manner, quite unlike the rest of his oeuvre, which tended to be satirical and polemical in tone. When he praised Gish for delivering a particularly fine closeup, Davis allegedly said, "So she should—she invented them."

The sisters wait on the point for the whales to return, in vain.

WICKED STEPMOTHER

It is best not to dwell on Davis's last film, in which she played a witch who has married a widowed father, much to the alarm of the young folk. She was by then an octogenarian and ill, and left the production after a week. In order to save the film the director Larry Cohen had the character morph into Barbara Carrera, the same witch in a more presentable guise. The film was still a disaster, and a sad final note for one of Hollywood's greatest stars.

The sad last film appearance. After a week's shooting she retired.

MGM (1989)

Credits

Writer and Director: Larry Cohen
Producer: Robert Littman
Cinematographer: Bryan England

Cast

Bette Davis, Barbara Carrera, Colleen Camp, Lionel Stander, David Rasche, Shawn Donahue, Tom Bosley, Richard Moll, Evelyn Keyes, James Dixon, Seymour Cassel, Susie Garrett, Laurene Landon

Running time: 90 minutes

"Acting should be bigger than life. Scripts should be bigger than life. It should all be bigger than life."

TELEVISION FILMS

Davis on *The Andy Williams Show*, 1962.

The Judge and Jake Wyler

Universal Television

Director: David Lowell Rich
Producers: Richard Levinson, William Link
Teleplay writers: David Shaw, Richard Levinson, William Link

Cast: Bette Davis, Doug McClure, Eric Braeden, Joan Van Ark, Gary Conway, Lou Jacobi, James McEachin, Lisabeth Hush, Kent Smith, Barbara Rhoades, John Randolph, Milt Kamen, John Lupton, Rosanna Huffman, Eddie Quillan, Virginia Capers

NBC *Movie of the Week* December 2, 1972

Scream, Pretty Peggy

Universal Television

Director: Gordon Hessler
Producer: Lou Morheim
Teleplay writers: Jimmy Sangster, Arthur Hoffe

Cast: Bette Davis, Ted Bessell, Sian Barbara Allen, Charles Drake, Allan Arbus, Tovah Feldschuh, Johnnie Collins III, Jessica Rains, Christiane Schmidtmer

NBC *Movie of the Week* November 22, 1973

In the *The Dark Secret of Harvest Home*.

The Disappearance of Aimee

Tomorrow Entertainment

Director: Anthony Harvey
Executive producer: Thomas W. Moore
Producer: Paul Leaf
Teleplay writer: John McGreevey

Cast: Faye Dunaway, Bette Davis, James Sloyan, James Woods, John Lehne, Lelia Goldoni, Severn Darden, William Jordan, Sandy Ward, Barry Brown, Irby Smith

November 17, 1976

The Dark Secret of Harvest Home

Universal Television

Director: Leo Penn
Producer: Jack Laird
Teleplay writers: Jack Guss, Charles E. Israel. Adapted by James M. Miller and Jennifer Miller from novel *Harvest Home* by Thomas Tryon

Cast: Bette Davis, David Ackroyd, Rosanna Arquette, René Auberjonois, John Calvin, Norman Lloyd, Linda Marsh, Michael O'Keefe, Laurie Prange, Lina Raymond, Tracey Gold, Micahel Durrell, Donald Pleasence (voice over)

Five hour miniseries premiering January 23, 1978

With Suzy Gilstrap in *Skyward*.

Strangers: The Story of a Mother and Daughter

Chris-Rose Productions

Director: Milton Katselas
Producers: Robert W. Christiansen, Rick Rosenberg
Teleplay writer: Michael DeGuzman

Cast: Bette Davis, Gena Rowlands, Ford Rainey, Donald Moffat, Whit Bissell, Royal Dano, Kate Riehl, Krishan Timberlake, Renee McDonell, Sally Kemp

May 13,1979 (Bette Davis awarded Emmy as Outstanding Lead Actress in a Limited Series or Special)

White Mama

Tomorrow Entertainment

Director: Jackie Cooper
Executive producer: Thomas W. Moore
Producer: Jean Moore Edwards
Teleplay writer: Robert C.S. Downs

Cast: Bette Davis, Ernest Harden Jr., Eileen Heckart, Virginia Capers, Anne Ramsey, Lurene Tuttle, Peg Shirley, Ernie Hudson, Dan Mason, Vincent Schiavelli, Cheryl Harvey, John Hancock, Eddie Quinlan

March 5, 1980

Skyward

Major H/Anson Productions

Director: Ron Howard
Executive producers: Ron Howard, Anson Williams
Producer: John A. Kuri
Teleplay writer: Nancy Sackett from story by Anson Williams

Cast: Bette Davis, Howard Hesseman, Marion Ross, Clu Galager, Ben Marley, Lisa Whelchel, Suzy Gilstrap, Jana Hill, Mark Wheeler, Jessie Lee Fulton, Rance Howard, Clint Howard, Cheryl Howard, Kate Finlayson

November 20, 1980

Family Reunion

Columbia Pictures Television

Director: Fielder Cook
Producer: Lucy Jarvis
Teleplay writer: Allan Sloane based on story by Allan Sloane and Joe Spartan from article *How America Lives* by Joe Spartan in *Ladies' Home Journal*

Cast: Bette Davis, J. Ashley Hyman, David Huddleston, John Shea, Roy Dotrice, David Rounds, Kathryn Walker, Roberts Blossom, Roberta Wallach, Jeff McCracken, Ann Lange, Beth Ehlers, Paul Rudd, Paul Hecht, Charles Brown

Four-hour miniseries premiering October 11, 1981

A Piano for Mrs. Cimino

Roger Gimbel Production for EMI Television

Director: George Schaefer
Executive producers: Roger Gimbel, Tony Converse
Producers: George Schaefer, Christopher N. Seitz
Teleplay writer: John Gay based on book by Robert Oliphant

Cast: Bette Davis, Keenan Wynn, Penny Fuller, Alexa Kenin, George Hearn, Christopher Guest, Graham Jarvis, Paul Roebling, LeRoy Schulz, Walter Marsh

February 3, 1982

Little Gloria...Happy at Last

Scherick Associates/London Film Productions

Director: Waris Hussein
Executive producers: Edgar J. Scherick, Scott Rudin
Producers: David Nicksay, Justine Héroux

Teleplay writer: William Hanley based on book by
Barbara Goldsmith

Cast: Martin Balsam, Bette Davis, Michael Gross, Lucy
Gutteridge, John Hillerman, Barnard Hughes, Glynis Johns,
Angela Lansbury, Rosalyn Landor, Joseph Maher, Christopher
Plummer, Maureen Stapleton, Leueen Willoughby, Jennifer
Dundas

October 24, 1982

Right of Way

Schaefer-Karpf Productions

Director: George Schaefer
Producers: George Schaefer, Philip Parslow
Teleplay writer: Richard Lees from his 1978 play at Guthrie
Theatre, Minneapolis

Cast: Bette Davis, James Stewart, Melinda Dillon, Priscilla
Morrill, John Harkins, Louis Schaefer, Jacque Lynn Colton,
Charles Murphy, Edith Fields

HBO November 21, 1983

Murder with Mirrors

Hajeno Productions for Warner Bros. Television

Director: Dick Lowry
Executive producer: George Eckstein
Producer: Neil Hartley

Davis teamed with James Stewart in *Right of Way*.

Guesting as Laura Trent in the *Hotel* series, 1983.

Teleplay writer: George Eckstein based on novel by
Agatha Christie

Cast: Helen Hayes, Bette Davis, John Mills, Leo McKern,
Liane Langland, John Laughlin, Dorothy Tutin, Anton Rodgers,
Frances de la Tour, John Woodvine, James Coombes

February 20, 1985

As Summers Die

Chris/Rose Productions and Baldwin/Aldrich Productions

Director: Jean-Claude Tramont
Executive producers: Frank Konigsberg, Larry Sanitsky
Producers: Robert W. Christiansen, Rick Rosenberg
Teleplay writers: Jeff Andrus, Ed Namzug based on novel by
Winston Groom

Cast: Scott Glenn, Jamie Lee Curtis, Bette Davis,
John Randolph, Ron O'Neal, Beah Richards, Richard Venture,
Paul Roebling, Penny Fuller, Bruce McGill, C.C.H. Pounder,
John McIntire, Tammy Baldwin, Nadia Gay Brown

May 18, 1986

ENVOI

In 1980 Davis's sister Bobby died from breast cancer, and in 1983 Davis was diagnosed with the same affliction and endured a mastectomy. She then suffered a debilitating stroke. In 1985 she was greatly shocked by the publication of a book by her daughter B.D. called *My Mother's Keeper,* which appeared to have cashed in on the huge success of *Mommy Dearest,* a notorious account of Joan Crawford's deficiencies as a mother. At least Crawford had been dead when it was published. In spite of a strained relationship, Davis had kept her son-in-law's business afloat and had drained her own financial resources as a result. B.D. had become a born-again Christian of considerable fervor, but her book signaled both betrayal and a final, permanent estrangement.

Davis's cancer returned and required painful treatment. Her face twisted and distorted, her frame skeletal, and her stamina maintained by massive intakes of various pills, she managed to travel in her last months, making appearances at festivals where crowds, mesmerized by seeing her onscreen, poured uncritical adulation on her. At San Sebastian, having flown thousands of miles sedated by tranquillizers to receive a lifetime achievement award, it became clear that she was in the closing stages of her life. She was immediately flown to Paris in an ambulance Learjet and taken to the American hospital at Neuilly, which had a high reputation for cancer treatment. By this point she was beyond anything other than morphine. Her cancer had spread and was ineradicable. Shortly after 11 p.m. on October 6, 1989, she died, with Kathryn Sermak at her bedside. She was eighty-one years old.

Her death attracted world headlines and the realization that the keystone of Hollywood's Golden Age had gone. The *New York Times* led its announcement: "Bette Davis, who won two Academy Awards and cut a swath through Hollywood trailing cigarette smoke and delivering drop-dead barbs, died of breast cancer Friday night at the American Hospital in Neuilly-sur-Seine, France." Said the *London Times,* "The resolution and capriciousness Bette Davis displayed on screen was very much part of her private character and during her career she had inevitable battles with studios who tried to curb her independence of spirit. It was a spirit that enabled her to survive an unhappy childhood and three broken marriages and long before feminism became a rallying cry, she was the epitome of the liberated woman."

Davis was buried at Forest Lawn Memorial Park, Glendale, on October 12 after a small private service, with B.D. and her family notably absent. She was interred alongside her mother Ruthie and her sister Bobby in the Davis crypt on a hillside from which the Warner Bros. studios at Burbank could be seen.

Her estate was mainly divided between Michael Merrill and Kathryn Sermak. B.D. had been disinherited, but claimed to feel total indifference. In a television interview she said: "I won't shed a single tear. Her death was only a technicality. For me she died years ago."

Steven Spielberg managed to buy Davis's two Oscars, one of which had been acquired by Planet Hollywood, for a total of $785,000. He donated them to the Academy. Davis's epitaph is etched on her tomb in accordance with her wishes.

It says: "She did it the hard way."

In the last year of her life, with her younger self.

BIBLIOGRAPHY

Bret, David, *Joan Crawford: Hollywood Martyr,*
Carroll & Graf, 2006

Carey, Gary, *More About All About Eve,* Random
House, 1972

Carr, Larry, *More Fabulous Faces: The Evolution and
Metamorphosis of Bette Davis, Katharine Hepburn,
Dolores del Rio, Carole Lombard and Myrna Loy,*
Doubleday and Company, 1979

Chandler, Charlotte, *The Girl Who Walked Home
Alone: Bette Davis, A Personal Biography,* Simon
and Schuster, 2006

Collins, Bill, *Bill Collins Presents "The Golden Years of
Hollywood,"* The MacMillan Company of Australia, 1987

Considine, Shaun, *Bette and Joan: The Divine Feud,*
Sphere, 2007

Davis, Bette, *The Lonely Life: An Autobiography,*
G. P. Putnam's Sons, 1962

Davis, Bette, Michael Herskowitz, *This 'N That.*
G. P. Putnam's Sons, 1987

Guiles, Fred Lawrence, *Joan Crawford, The Last Word,*
Conrad Goulden Books, 1995

Haver, Ronald, *David O. Selznick's Hollywood,*
Bonanza Books, 1980

Kael, Pauline, *5001 Nights at the Movies,* Zenith Books,
1982

Higham, Charles, *The Life of Bette Davis,* Macmillan,
1981

Hyman, B.D., *My Mother's Keeper,* Morrow, 1985

Leaming, Barbara, *Bette Davis,* Simon and Schuster, 1991

Merrill, Gary, *Bette, Rita and the Rest of My Life,*
Tapley, 1988

Moseley, Roy, *Bette Davis: An Intimate Memoir,*
Donald I. Fine, 1990

Nickens, Christopher, *Bette Davis: a Biography in
Photographs,* Doubleday, 1985

Robinson, Jeffrey, *Bette Davis,* Proteus, 1982

Ringgold, Gene, *The Films of Bette Davis,* Citadel, 1970

Schickel, Richard, George Perry, *You Must Remember
This,* Running Press, 2008

Shipman, David, *Movie Talk,* St. Martin's Press, 1988

Sikov, Ed, *Dark Victory: The Life of Bette Davis,* Henry
Holt and Company, 2007

Spada, James, *More Than a Woman,* Little, Brown and
Company, Sperling, 1993

Springer, John, Jack Hamilton, *They Had Faces Then,*
Citadel Press, 1978

Staggs, Sam, *All About "All About Eve,"* St. Martin's Press,
2000

Stine, Whitney, *I'd Love to Kiss You: Conversations with
Bette Davis,* Pocket Books/Simon & Schuster, 1990

Stine, Whitney, Bette Davis, *Mother Goddam: The Story
of the Career of Bette Davis,* 1974

Walker, Alexander, *Bette Davis: A Celebration,*
Pavilion Books, 1986

Warner, Cass, Cork Milner and Jack Warner Jr.,
Hollywood Be Thy Name: The Warner Brothers Story,
Prima Publishing, 1998

Index

Acknowledgments

It's the lady herself I should thank most. I remember seeing her splendidly dressed lunching in the Pinewood restaurant during the making of Death on the Nile but only ever managed to talk to her over tea at the Savoy, London a few years later. Although the famous mouth was by then grotesquely twisted by her stroke, she conversed on all manner of things with astonishing candor, unafraid to dismiss minor talents, refusing to regret her setbacks, pleased that a younger generation perceived her as a great icon of a vanished Hollywood. To spend time in such company was a privilege, as was working on this book, with the superb professional hand of Colin Webb on the tiller, the careful touch of Sonya Newland ensuring the smooth flow of text with layout, the disciplined eye of Bernard Higton creating an imaginative layout from thousands of pictures, and the unwavering encouragement of Cindy De La Hoz of Running Press, a true believer in the power and beauty of film. Mention should be made of hours spent at the extraordinary Howard Gotlieb Archival Research Center at Boston University where so much of Bette Davis's life is preserved, and my thanks to fine friends and loved ones, Marion Rosenberg in Los Angeles, Chrissy White in New York, my wife Frances and son Matthew, both of whom offered unwavering support, and my old friend and colleague Richard Schickel whose cinematic wisdom is unsurpassed (although we may never agree on *Beyond the Forest*).

George Perry

★

Picture Credits

Corbis/Bettman
13, 30, 46r, 109, 166, 167t, 195br, 205, 231.

Dreampinups/Tom Maroudas
2, 6, 14, 22, 51, 55, 77, 99, 111, 125, 174.

Getty Images
24t (Time & Life Pictures), 24b (Time & Life Pictures), 25, 33 (Popperfoto), 39l, 41, 50, 52r, 100 (Popperfoto), 103t, 103b (Time & Life Pictures), 105t (Time & Life Pictures), 149t (Popperfoto), 167b, 176, 203 (Popperfoto), 204, 210t, 238t (Popperfoto), 238br.

The Kobal Collection
10, 11, 17, 31, 32tr, 32bl, 34, 35, 36, 37, 39r, 43, 44, 45, 46l, 49, 107, 179, 207; **A.I.P.:** 244t, 244b; **Alive Films:** 252, 253 (Jonathan Levine); **Capital Films:** 61l, 61r; **Columbia:** 221l, 221r; **Cosmopolitan/Warner Bros.:** 91; **Tony Costa:** 259; **Embassy:** 232t, 232b; **Ference:** 47; **First National:** 96t, 96b; **First National/Vitaphone:** 69l, 69r, 74; **First National/Warner Bros.:** 54 (Elmer Fryer), 66, 67, 68r, 73t, 73b; **Elmer Fryer:** 15, 53, 60; **EMI:** 249r; **Hammer:** 242; **Hammer/Assoc British:** 238bl, 238r, 239; **George Hurrell:** 8, 98; **ITC/Cecil Films:** 245l, 245r; **Dino de Laurentiis:** 246t, 246b; **Bert Longworth:** 16; **MGM:** 220, 223t, 223b, 254l, 254r; **NBC-TV:** 256; **Paramount:** 211, 234; **Radio Pictures:** 59; **RKO:** 18 (Samuel Goldwyn), 48, 81, 82, 83, 106 (Samuel Goldwyn), 150 (Samuel Goldwyn), 151r (Samuel Goldwyn), 181, 200, 201; **Telstar/Gollings:** 243t, 243b; **20th Century Fox:** 28, 183, 184 , 185, 196t, 196b, 197, 198t, 199, 210b, 215, 216t, 216b, 218, 219, 235l, 235r, 236, 237; **United Artists:** 5, 7, 214t, 214b, 224t, 224b, 225, 247l, 247r; **Universal:** 42 (Ray Jones), 56l, 56r, 57, 58t, 58b; **Universal TV:** 255b; **Warner Bros.:** 9 (Elmer Fryer), 12, 20, 23b, 27, 52l, 62, 63, 64l , 64r, 70b, 71, 72, 75l, 75r, 78t, 78b, 79t, 79bl, 79br, 80, 84, 85, 86, 87, 88, 89, 90l, 90r, 93 (Ernest Bachrach), 94r, 95, 97l, 97r, 102, 113bl, 114r, 115l, 115r (Bert Longworth), 117t, 117b, 118t, 118b, 119, 124l, 124r, 126t, 126b, 127, 130t, 130b, 131r, 132, 141, 142t, 142b, 143, 144, 145, 147, 154, 156l , 157, 158, 160, 161 (Bert Six), 162, 164, 165, 168, 169r, 170, 186, 187, 188t, 188b, 189, 190, 192t, 192b, 194r, 195t, 208, 209, 212, 222l, 222r, 226, 227t, 227b, 228, 229, 230t, 230b, 233l, 264; **Walt Disney:** 248, 250l, 250r, 251t; **Warner Bros./First National:** 21 (Schuyler Crail), 23t, 76 (Schuyler Crail), 104, 120t, 120b (Schuyler Crail), 121 (George Hurrell), 122, 123 (Schuyler Crail), 136, 137 (Bert Six), 139, 140b (Schuyler Crail), 148t (Bert Six), 148b, 172 , 193t.

mptvimages.com
1, 32tl, 32br, 38 (Bert Longworth), 65 (John Ellis), 92, 94l (Homer von Pelt), 101, 105b, 114l (Scotty Welbourne), 116, 128 (Bert Six), 129, 131l, 134 (Bert Six), 138, 140t, 146 (Bert Six), 149b, 151l, 153 (George Hurrell), 155, 156r (Scotty Welbourne), 159 (Bert Six), 163, 169l, 171, 175, 177, 178 (Pat Clark), 180, 182, 191 (Frank Bjerring), 193b (Morgan), 194l (Morgan), 195bl, 198b, 202, 213t, 217, 233r, 241b, 255t (© 1978 David Sutton), 257t (© 1983 Mario Cassill), 257b (© 1982 Gene Trindl).

Rex Features
108 (SNAP), 112tl (SNAP).

Courtesy the Lou Valentino Collection
19, 68l, 70t, 112tr, 112bl, 112br, 113tl, 113tr, 113br, 133, 135, 173, 206, 213b, 241t, 249l, 251b.